I0113151

England Hull

Municipal and urban sanitary enactments

1854 to 1897

England Hull

Municipal and urban sanitary enactments
1854 to 1897

ISBN/EAN: 9783337268886

Printed in Europe, USA, Canada, Australia, Japan

Cover: Foto ©Andreas Hilbeck / pixelio.de

More available books at **www.hansebooks.com**

MUNICIPAL

AND

URBAN SANITARY

ENACTMENTS

1854 TO 1897

INCLUDING

ELECTRIC LIGHTING PROVISIONAL ORDER 1890

AND

TRAMWAYS PROVISIONAL ORDER 1896

IN FORCE WITHIN THE

CITY AND COUNTY OF KINGSTON UPON HULL.

PREFACE.

The Statutes, and Provisional Orders relating to the Municipality, and Urban Sanitary Authority of Kingston upon Hull, so far as they are now in force, are printed in chronological order.

The Index will, it is hoped, facilitate reference to the text, and, at the same time, give a general idea of the nature of its provisions.

The enactments, which have been repealed, or, which though unrepealed conferred powers that have been exercised, and all recitals are omitted.

The statutes relating to the Railway and Dock undertakings of the City are also omitted, as they are printed in separate volumes.

The Corporation have adopted the provisions of

(a) THE BATHS AND WASH HOUSES ACTS, 1846 to 1882.

(b) THE INFECTIOUS DISEASE (NOTIFICATION) ACT, 1889.

(c) THE INFECTIOUS DISEASE (PREVENTION) ACT, 1890.

(d) Parts II. III. and IV. of the PUBLIC HEALTH ACTS AMENDMENT ACT, 1890.

These Acts will be found amongst the Public General Statutes.

This volume will not be admissible as evidence in Courts of Law; and in some cases, in order to arrive at the proper construction of its contents, it will be necessary to refer to the Queen's Printer's Copy of the Statutes.

E. LAVERACK,

Town Hall, Hull,   TOWN CLERK.

February, 1899.

CONTENTS.

The following Table of Contents consists, so far as Acts of Parliament are concerned, of the side notes printed in the Acts. Provisional Orders have no side notes, but in the following table their place is supplied by notes which indicate the purport of the respective articles to which they refer.

THE KINGSTON-UPON-HULL IMPROVEMENT ACT, 1854.

17 and 18 Vict., Ch. CI.

PROVISIONAL ORDER, 1862.

PROVISIONAL ORDER, 1871.

PROVISIONAL ORDER, 1871.

HULL EXTENSION AND IMPROVEMENT ACT. 1882.

45 and 46 Vict., Ch. CXV.

PART I. PRELIMINARY.

PROVISIONAL ORDER, 1853.

HULL (DRYPOOL) BRIDGE AND IMPROVEMENTS ACT, 1885.
48 and 49 Vict., Ch. CLXXI.

PROVISIONAL ORDER, 1886.

PROVISIONAL ORDER, 1888.

PROVISIONAL ORDER, 1889.

PROVISIONAL ORDER, 1890.

THE KINGSTON-UPON-HULL IMPROVEMENT ACT, 1854.

17 AND 18 VICT., CH. CI.

Royal Assent, 3rd July, 1854.

XXII.   That the Local Board, from Time to Time, for rendering the Streets in the Borough more commodious, by special Order may enter upon, purchase, take, and use any Building, Bulks, Steps, or any other Encroachment projecting into or obstructing the Passage of any Street, and remove the same, and throw the Site thereof into the Street, and may enter upon, purchase, and take in any Piece of Ground for widening, altering, or improving any Street or the Entrances thereto, and throw the same into the Street.

Power to purchase Premises : render Streets, & more commodious.

XXXI.   That it shall be lawful for the said Local Board to cause the several Streets, Squares, Lanes, and other Passages and Places within the said Borough, or such of them as they shall think proper, to be lighted either by means of Oil Lamps or by means of Gas, or partly by one Means and partly by another, or otherwise, at such Times and Seasons as the said Local Board shall think fit, and to direct what Part of the same shall be lighted with Oil, and what Part by means of Gas or otherwise ; and it shall be lawful for the said Local Board from Time to Time to contract and agree with any Company or other Person to light the said Streets, Lanes, and other Passages and Places, or any of them, or any Part thereof respectively, by means of Oil or Gas or otherwise, in such Manner, and upon and subject to such Terms and Conditions, Stipulations, and Agreements, as the said Local Board shall think proper, and to provide, and set up, fix, or place, all necessary Lamps, Lamp Posts, Lamp Irons, and Iron or other Pipes for the Conveyance of Gas or otherwise, and other Works necessary for lighting the same Places, upon or against any House, Tenement, Building, or Enclosure (doing as little Damage or Injury thereto as possible), or in such other Manner as they shall think proper : Provided nevertheless, that no such Lamp, Lamp Post, Lamp Iron, and Iron or other Pipe, shall be set up, fixed, or placed upon any House or Building, or shall be continued so set up, fixed, or placed, without the Consent of the Owner and Occupier of the same Dwelling House or Building.

Power for the Local Board to cause the Streets to lighted.

XXXIII.   That the Local Board shall from Time to Time, upon the Request of the Occupiers of Ten or more Houses, each of the yearly Rent of Six Pounds at the least, in any Street, cause the Street to be lighted as the Local Board think proper.

Local Boa on Reque Occupiers light Stre

Walls, &c. over Sewers

LXIX. That it shall not be lawful, without the previous Consent in Writing of the Local Board, to make or keep up any Wall, Palisade, Fence, or other Erection, over any Sewer of the Local Board ; and the Local Board may cause any such Erection made without their Consent, after the Seventh Day of August One thousand eight hundred and fifty-one, over any such Sewer, to be altered, pulled down, or otherwise dealt with as they think fit ; and the Expenses incurred by them in so doing shall be repaid to them by the Person to whom the Erection belongs, and be recoverable from him as Damages ; and for every Offence against this Enactment the Offender shall forfeit to the Local Board Five Pounds, and a Further Penalty of Forty Shillings for every Day during which the Offence continues after Notice in Writing from them in this Behalf.

Penalty on others than Scavengers, &c. removing Refuse.

LXXIV. That if any Person other than a Person authorised by the Local Board collect or carry away any Dust, Dirt, Soil, Ashes, Filth, or Rubbish from any Street, Footway, House, or Land, except Land used for a Garden or Agricultural Purposes, in the Borough, every Person so offending shall forfeit a Sum not exceeding Forty Shillings for the First Offence, not exceeding Five Pounds for the Second Offence, and not exceeding Ten Pounds for the Third and every subsequent Offence : Provided always, that nothing herein contained shall prevent the Occupier of any Garden or Agricultural Land within the Borough from keeping upon such Premises, or from sending his own Servant with his own Cart or Vehicle to receive, any Manure to be used for the Benefit of the same Garden or Land, and not for the Purpose of Sale.

Permission of Local Board for Removal of Soil for Sale, &c.

LXXV. Provided always, That the Local Board from Time to Time may permit any Persons, without being liable to any Penalty, to collect or remove, for Sale or Shipment, such Dust, Dirt, Soil, Manure, Dung, Ashes, Filth, or Rubbish, and at or within such Times as the Local Board think fit.

Power to throw Land into Streets by Agreement with Owners, &c.

LXXX. That the Local Board from Time to Time may, by Agreement with the Owners of any Lands which the Local Board require for the Purpose of making, altering, or diverting any Street, and by way either of absolute Purchase or Exchange of any Lands vested in the Local Board which may not be required by them for any Part of any such Street which becomes needless, lay such Lands into the Street, or otherwise appropriate them for such Purposes as the Local Board think fit ; and all Parts of such Streets, when so made, altered, or diverted, shall be public Streets.

LXXXIII.   That the Owner of any present or future Court or Passage, or any Part of any Court or Passage, shall flag or pave such Court or Passage, or the Part thereof whereof he is the Owner, and make a Drain through or along the same or such Part thereof as the Local Board require, and keep such Flagging or Pavement and Drain in good Repair, and shall also cause the Houses belonging to him to be sufficiently drained and so to be kept, and shall comply with this Enactment to the Satisfaction of the Local Board; and if any such Owner for One Month after Notice in Writing from the Local Board given to or left at his Dwelling House for him, or if he or his Dewlling House be unknown, or he be out of *England*, affixed to the Premises in respect of which the same is given, fail in any respect to comply with this Enactment, then and in every such Case such Owner shall for every such Default forfeit any Sum not exceeding Five Pounds, and any further Sum not exceeding Ten Shillings for every Week during which such Default continues, and the Local Board may do the Works required by them, and the Expenses incurred by them in that Behalf shall be Private Improvement Expenses, and recoverable accordingly.

LXXXIV.   That no Person shall (without the Consent of the Local Board) have or make in or upon the Footway or flagged or other Pavement of any present or future Street, any Cellar Window, Cellar Steps, Cellar Door, Cellar Hole, Cellar Grate, Stepway, or Hatchway leading or giving Light into any Cellar, Kitchen, or other Place under ground, of any House or other Building adjoining or near to or in the Street, save and except any such Window, Steps, Door, Hole, Grate, Stepway, or Hatchway as shall have been made, formed, or be in existence immediately before the Commencement of this Act.

LXXXVII.   That the Surveyor of the Local Board from Time to Time may inspect any Drain, Privy, Cesspool, or Ashpit, and for that purpose at all reasonable Times in the Daytime, after Twenty-four Hours Notice in Writing to the Occupier of the Premises to which such Drain, Privy, Cesspool, or Ashpit is attached, may enter upon any Lands and Buildings, with such Assistants and Workmen as are necessary, and cause the Ground to be opened where he thinks fit, doing as little Damage as may be ; and if such Drain, Privy, Cesspool, or Ashpit be found to be in proper Condition, he shall cause the Ground to be closed and made good as soon as may be, and the Expenses of opening, closing, and making good such Drain, Privy, Cesspool, or Ashpit shall in that Case be defrayed by the Local Board.

LXXXVIII. That all Sewers and Drains, whether public or private, shall be provided by the Local Board or other Persons to whom they respectively belong, with proper Traps or other Coverings or Means of Ventilation, so as to prevent Stench; and if the Owner of any private Drain fail for Fourteen Days after Notice from the Local Board so to provide against Stench therefrom, the Local Board may do the requisite Works; and the Expense thereof, as certified by their Surveyor, shall be Private Improvement Expenses, and recoverable accordingly.

[NOTE.—*This section is repealed so far as it relates to drains to new buildings by the Provisional Order of 1893, Art. II., page 132.*]

XC. That all Vaults, Arches, Cellars, and Drains now or hereafter made in or under any Street shall be kept in substantial Repair by the Owners thereof to the Satisfaction of the Local Board; and in case any such Vault, Arch, Cellar, or Drain be at any Time not in such substantial Repair, the Local Board may put the same into substantial Repair, and recover the Expenses incurred thereby from the Owner or Occupier thereof, or the Owner or Occupier of any Tenement to which such Vault, Arch, Cellar, or Drain belongs, or with which it is connected and used; and such Owner or Occupier shall also forfeit a Sum not exceeding Twenty Shillings for every Day such Vault, Arch, Cellar, or Drain continues out of substantial Repair after Notice in Writing from the Local Board to repair the same, and a reasonable Time for completing such Repair has elapsed after the Service thereof.

XCII. That the Owner or Occupier of any House or Building in any Street shall cause the Water to be conveyed from such House or Building, either by Drains or Tunnels below the Surface of the Pavement or Flagging of the Footpath, or by Iron Drain Gutters fixed in the Flagging or Pavement; and for that Purpose such Owner or Occupier may take up so much of the Pavement or Flagging of any Street as is requisite, and lay down such Drains or Tunnels, or fix such Iron Drain Gutters, under the Direction of the Local Board or their Surveyor; and all Damage hereby occasioned to the Pavement or Flagging of the Footpath or Carriageway shall be made good by or at the Expense of such Owner or Occupier.

XCIII. That the Local Board, by Agreement with the Owner of any Tenement, or in case of his Default, may make any Drain required for such Tenement at his Expense; and the Expense thereof, as certified by the Surveyor of the Local Board, shall be Private Improvement Expenses, and recoverable accordingly.

XCIV. That the Local Board may turn, tunnel, cover, or *Gutters.* alter, in such Manner as they think proper, the Course of any Gutter or Channel running in, upon, or through any Street.

XCVII. That any Building after the Commencement of this *Front Yards* Act built, or any Building after the Commencement of this Act rebuilt, *to Houses.* except on the Site of a Building used immediately before the pulling down thereof as a Dwelling House, or any Part thereof respectively, or any Building before the Commencement of this Act built and not then used as a Dwelling House, or any Part thereof, shall not without the previous Consent of the Local Board, be used as a Dwelling House, except only during such Time as there is adjoining or belonging thereto, or occupied therewith, either a Street or a clear open Space in and to the full Extent of the Front thereof, and of not less than Twenty Feet in Width; and no Building not at present occupied as a Dwelling House shall be converted into a Dwelling House without previous Notice and Plan being deposited and approved by the Local Board, precisely as required for the Construction of new Houses and Buildings. .

XCVIII. *That every Court, Alley, Square, or Inclosure for* *Size of areas* *Houses to be hereafter rebuilt shall have an open Area or be of* *of Courts,* *Alleys. &c.* *such Width as the Local Board shall determine in each Case; and* *every Court, Alley, Square, or Inclosure for Houses to be hereafter* *built or constructed on vacant Ground (not being the Site of any* *Court or Square theretofore formed or built immediately previously* *to such Construction) shall have an open Area or be of the Width* *of Twenty Feet at the least, measuring from Front to Front of the* *Houses therein; and the same Area and Width shall extend* *from the Street throughout such Court, Alley, Square, or Inclosure,* *and be open from the Ground upwards;* and no Tunnel or covered entrance shall be allowed in any such Court, Alley, Square, or Inclosure last mentioned.

[NOTE.—*The words in italics are repealed by the Provisional Order of 1893, Art. II., page 132. See also Provisional Order of 1877, page 26.*]

XCIX. That every House to be hereafter rebuilt, and every *Back Yards* House to be hereafter built, at the Corner of any Street or Place, *and Areas to* *Houses to be* shall have a Back Yard or Back Area thereto, if the Local Board *provided.* shall in such Case deem it right that any such Back Yard or Back

Area should be made; and in that Case such Back Yard or Back Area shall be of such Dimensions as the Local Board shall determine .

. . . .

As to Buildings not now used as Dwellings.
C. That no Building not at present occupied as a Dwelling shall be converted into a Dwelling House without previous Notice and a Plan being deposited and approved by the Local Board, precisely as is required for Construction of new Houses and Buildings.

Plan of proposed Buildings to be furnished.
CI. That, in addition to the Particulars required to be stated for the Approval of the Local Board by the Fifty-third Section of the "Public Health Act, 1848," there shall be furnished to such Board, by the Person intending to build or rebuild any House or construct any Building, a correct Plan or Plans of the proposed Building, drawn to a Scale of not less than One Inch to every Eight Feet of the Work, showing the Particulars required by the said Act and this Act, and which Plan shall not be carried into execution, nor the Building commenced, until the same Plan shall have been approved by the Local Board.

[NOTE.—*This section is amended by the Provisional Order of 1893, Art. IV. and V., pages 133, 134, as follows*:

Art. IV. Section 101 of the Local Act shall be amended by the addition thereto of the following provisions :—

(1.) It shall not be necessary to furnish to the Corporation any plan of a building which is exempt from the provisions of the Acts or of the byelaws for the time being in force in the Borough.

(2.) In the case of any building erected after the commencement of this Order, and exempt at the time of its erection from the provisions of the Local Acts or of any byelaws for the time being in force in the Borough, with respect to new buildings, by reason of its being intended to be used for any particular purpose, no person shall use such building, or cause or suffer the same to be used, for any purpose not within the exemption, unless and until the same shall conform to such of the requirements of those Acts and byelaws as are applicable to a building used for the intended purpose.

(3.) Where any person shall have erected any building which is exempt from the operation of any byelaw by reason of such building not being within a prescribed distance from any other building, he shall not, without the consent in writing of the Corporation, erect any other building within such distance from the first-mentioned building.

Art. V.   Section 101 of the Local Act shall be further amended so as to include a provision that nothing in the said section contained, or in this Order, shall be deemed to restrict or in any manner interfere with the powers of the Corporation to make byelaws under any other Act with respect to the deposit of plans of buildings.]

CII.   That there shall not be more than One Story in any Part of the Roof of any House hereafter built. *Only One Story in the Roof.*

CIV.   That whenever the Local Board think it requisite, they may require the Owner or Occupier of any Licensed Victualler's House or Beershop to provide and maintain at his Expense, in such a proper and convenient Situation on his own Premises as the Local Board approve, and to keep, at the like Expense, duly cleansed, a proper and convenient Urinal for the Use of Persons frequenting his Premises; and every such Owner or Occupier who, after being thereunto required by the Local Board, wilfully fails to provide to the Satisfaction of the Local Board, and within such Time as they in that Behalf appoint, or to maintain to their Satisfaction, such a Urinal as required by them, shall for every such Offence forfeit a Sum not exceeding Ten Pounds, and for every Day during which the Offence continues a further Sum not exceeding Forty Shillings; and every such Owner or Occupier who does not once in every Day, to the Satisfaction of the Local Board, cleanse such Urinal, shall for every such Offence forfeit a Sum not exceeding Forty Shillings. *Owners of Licensed Victualling Houses, &c. to provide Urinals.* *Penalty on Neglect.*

CV.   That if any Person shall have or use any Candle-house, Melting-house, Melting-place, or Soap-house, or any Slaughter-house, or any Building or Place for boiling Offal or Blood, or for boiling or crushing Bones, or any Pigsty, Necessary-house, Dunghill, Manure Heap, or any Manufactory, Building, or Place of Business, or any Trade or Business, which shall at any Time be certified to the Local Board by the Inspector of Nuisances or Officer of Health, or by any Two Surgeons or Physicians, or One Surgeon and One Physician, to be a Nuisance or injurious to the Health of the Inhabitants, or if any Person shall carry on any Trade or Business or do anything which shall occasion any noxious or offensive *Local Board may order Nuisance to be abated.*

Effluvia, or otherwise annoy the Neighbourhood or Inhabitants, the Local Board shall direct Complaint to be made before Two Justices, and any Justice may summon before any Two Justices such Person, and such Justices shall inquire into such Complaint, and they may, by an Order in Writing under their Hands, order such Person to discontinue or remedy the Nuisance within such Time as they think expedient.

Penalties for Disobedience of Orders of Justices.

CVI. That if any such Nuisance or Annoyance, or the Cause of any such injurious Effects, be not discontinued or remedied within such Time as is ordered by the Justices, the Person by or on whose Behalf the Business causing such Nuisance is carried on shall be liable to a Penalty not exceeding Five Pounds for every Day during which such Nuisance or Annoyance is continued or unremedied after the Expiration of such Time : Provided always, that when any Person who thinks himself aggrieved by any such Order appeals against any such Order, such Person shall not be liable to discontinue or remedy the Nuisance or Cause of the injurious Effects mentioned therein, or to pay any Penalty, until after the Expiration of Five Days after the Determination of such Appeal, and the Confirmation of such Order, unless such Appeal cease to be prosecuted.

Unoccupied or unproductive Property may be let to defray Expenses.

CVII. That if any House, Building, or Land abutting on the Side of any Street or Part of any Street not being a Highway, which or any Part whereof was levelled, made, paved, or flagged by the Commissioners acting under the recited Acts, or before or after the Commencement of this Act by the Local Board, or if any House or Building or Land in respect of which any Drain or other Work was made or re-made by any of those Commissioners, or before or after the Commencement of this Act by the Local Board, be unoccupied or unproductive, and the whole or any Part of the Expense of such Works ought to be repaid to the Local Board by the Owner thereof, and the Owner thereof for Twelve Months fail to pay such Expense, or, as the Case may be, his Proportion thereof, and the same be not recovered by the Local Board from the Occupier, if any, thereof, the Local Board, after the Expiration of Fourteen Days' Notice to that Effect served on the Owner or his Agent, or if such Owner be unknown to the Clerk or Surveyor of the Local Board, or cannot be found by them, affixed to or placed on such House, Building, or Land, may take possession thereof, and fence off and from Time to Time let the same or any Part thereof by the Year or from Year to Year, at the best yearly Rent, until with the clear Rents thereof the Local Board reimburse themselves, and may appoint some Person to deliver the Possession of such House, Building, or Land to the Tenant ; and such letting shall effectually vest the legal Estate in Possession of the House, Building, or Land comprised therein in the Tenant for the Term agreed on, and give him a good Title thereto against the Owner thereof and all other Persons whomsoever, and the Rent reserved shall be paid to the Local Board, who shall thereout, in the first place, pay the Expenses of such fencing and letting, and in the next place retain the Amount so due from such Owner, and shall on Demand pay the Surplus (if any) to such Owner or his legal Representative.

CIX. That any Constable may destroy any Dog or other Animal reasonably suspected to be in a rabid State, or to have been bitten by any Dog or other Animal reasonably suspected to be in a rabid State.

Dogs suspected to be mad, may be destroyed.

CXI. That every Person who causes any Cart, Waggon, Truck, or other Wheel Carriage, with or without Horses, or other Cattle, to stand in any Street longer than is necessary for loading or unloading the same, shall for every such Offence be liable to such Penalty or Punishment as by the Twenty-eighth Section of "The Town Police Clauses Act, 1847," is provided with respect to Offences therein specified.

Penalty on obstructing Streets with Carts, &c.

CXIV. That the Local Board from Time to Time may contract with any Persons for the supplying and keeping in order of such Water Carts or Engines for watering the Streets, and such Fire Engines, with sufficient Hose, Apparatus, and other Things relating thereto, as the Local Board think proper.

Local Board may contract for Water Carts and Fire Engines, &c.

CXV. That the Local Board from Time to Time may make, alter, and repeal such Byelaws, Rules, and Orders for the following Purposes, as they think fit :

Byelaws for regulating Porters, &c.

First, for licensing a sufficient Number of Porters, Porters' Carts, Coal Carriers, Coal Carts, Water Carriers' Trucks, Water Carts, and all other Carts and Carriages to be let or ply for Hire within the Borough :

Secondly, for regulating such Porters, Porters' Carts, Coal Carriers, Coal Carts, Trucks, Water Carts, and other Carts and Carriages, and in what Manner the same shall be provided :

Thirdly, touching the Letters, Messages, Goods, Parcels, and Things to be carried and conveyed by such Porters, or any of them :

Fourthly, touching the Quality and Measure of Coals to be carried by such Coal Carriers, and the weighing and measuring thereof on Delivery :

Fifthly, for preventing Frauds in the Sale of Coals and Water :

Sixthly, for ascertaining and fixing, altering, and removing from Time to Time the Stands for such Porters, Porters' Carts, Coal Carriers, Coal Carts, Water Carriers' Trucks, Water Carts, and other Carts and Carriages respectively :

Seventhly, for trying and punishing the Misconduct and Misbehaviour of Porters, Coal Carriers, Water Carriers, Carmen, Truckmen, and Labourers plying for Hire within the Borough :

Eighthly, for ascertaining and fixing what Rates, Fares, and Prices for Time, Quantity, and Distance shall be taken by such Porters, Coal Carriers and Water Carriers, Carmen, Truckmen, and Labourers respectively :

Ninthly, for ascertaining and fixing to what Distances such Porters, Coal Carriers, Water Carriers, Carmen, Truckmen, and Labourers respectively shall be obliged to drive, carry, go, and come within the Borough.

As to lighting Quays surrounding the Victoria and Railway Dock.

CXX. That the Quays surrounding the *Victoria* Dock and the Railway Dock, and the Basins and Entrances thereof respectively belonging to the Dock Company, shall, for the Purposes of lighting, be deemed public Streets, and shall be lighted by the Local Board accordingly, and the Expense thereof shall be defrayed out of the Rates applicable to lighting, in the same Manner as the Expenses of lighting other public Streets within the Borough are defrayed by the Local Board : Provided always, that, except as to lighting, such Quays shall not further or otherwise than previously to the passing of this Act be constituted public Streets.

Continuing Exemption of Dock Company from Rates.

CXXI. That the Dock Company at *Kingston-upon-Hull* may from Time to Time claim and shall be entitled to any Exemption from Liability to Rates and Assessments which, if the recited Provisional Order had not been made, and this Act were not passed, they might claim and be entitled to under the Provisions of the repealed Acts or any of them.

CXXII. That the Dock Company at *Kingston-upon-Hull*, and their Tenants and Occupiers, shall, in respect of such Part of their Property as shall consist of Land covered with Water, be assessed in respect of the same to Special District Rates and General District Rates respectively, in the Proportion of One Fourth Part only of the net yearly Value thereof, but subject and without Prejudice to any other Exemptions from Liability to Rates and Assessments which under this Act they may claim.

Assessment of Docks.

CXXIII. Provided always, that so long as the Dock Company at *Kingston-upon-Hull* at their own Expense effectually light and cleanse the legal Quay in the Parishes of the *Holy Trinity* and *Saint Mary*, in the Borough, and the Ground lying between the same and the Dwelling Houses, Warehouses, Lands, and Hereditaments of that Company, situate on the Southern Side of or contiguous to that Quay, and which immediately before the Commencement of this Act that Company are bound to light and cleanse, neither that Company, nor any of the Tenants or Occupiers of those Dwelling Houses, Warehouses, Lands, and Hereditaments, shall be liable to the Payment of any Rate or Assessment under this Act for lighting or cleansing Streets ; and so long as that Company at their own Expense effectually light and cleanse all such other Places in the Liberty of *Trippett*, in the Borough, as they are immediately before the Commencement of this Act bound to light and cleanse, neither that Company, nor any of the Tenants or Occupiers of the Dwelling Houses, Warehouses, Lands, and Hereditaments adjoining on those Places, shall be liable to the Payment of any Rate or Assessment under this Act for lighting or cleansing Streets ; and so long as that Company at their own Expense effectually light all such Places in the Borough as they are immediately before the Commencement of this Act bound to light, neither that Company, nor any of the Tenants or Occupiers of the Dwelling Houses, Warehouses, Lands, and Hereditaments adjoining on those Places, shall be liable to the Payment of any Rate or Assessment under this Act for lighting Streets.

Exemption of Dock Company and their Tenants from Rates for lighting and cleansing Streets.

CXXVI. That for the Purpose of defraying all or any Part of the Expenditure of the Local Board in or about the repairing and cleansing respectively of any Highways, the Local Board from Time to Time, if they think fit, may levy and raise such Sums as they think requisite, by One or more Highway Rate or Rates, or

" Highway Rates,"&c., for Highways.

by One or more Special District Rate or Rates, or by One or more General District Rate or Rates, or partly by One or more of such Rates, and partly by another or others of such Rates : Provided always, that all Highway Rates shall be assessed only upon Property chargeable to Highway Rates by virtue of the Laws now in force or hereafter to be passed relating to Highways.

CXXXV. That the Special District Rates and the General District Rates respectively from Time to Time made by the Local Board shall be assessed on the full net yearly Value of the rateable Property as ascertained by the Rate (if any) for the Relief of the Poor made next before the making of such Rates respectively : Provided always, that the Occupier of any Land used as Arable, Meadow, or Pasture Ground only, or as Woodland, Market Gardens or Nursery Grounds, and the Occupier of any Land covered with Water, or used only as a Canal or Towing-path for the same, or as a Railway constructed under the Powers of any Act of Parliament for public Conveyance, shall be assessed in respect of the same in the Proportion of One Fourth Part only of such net annual Value thereof.

CLI. That if any Person commit any of the following Offences within the Borough, every Person so offending shall for every such Offence forfeit a Sum not exceeding Five Pounds over and above all Damages which any Person aggrieved by the Offence may recover for the same ; that is to say,

First, knowingly selling or offering for Sale, or delivering or offering to deliver, any Coal of one Sort as being Coal of any other Sort :

Second, knowingly selling or offering for Sale, or delivering or offering to deliver, Coals of several Sorts mixed together as being Coal of only One Sort :

Third, knowingly selling or offering for Sale, or delivering or offering to deliver, any Coal as being of a given Weight which is of a less Weight :

Fourth, knowingly selling or offering for Sale or Delivery, or offering to deliver, any Coal as being of a given Quantity which is of a less Quantity :

Fifth, knowingly doing any other Thing with Intent to deceive any Person being or proposing to be the Buyer of any Coal, with respect to its Quality, Weight, or Quantity :

Assessments to General and Special District Rates.

Penalties for Frauds in sale of Coals.

Sixth, knowingly authorizing or permitting any such Offence to be committed.

CLIV. That within Fourteen Days after every Vacancy in the Office of Inspector, or so soon thereafter as conveniently may be, the Local Board shall supply the Vacancy : Provided always, that whenever a Vacancy happens, the Mayor may appoint some fit and proper Person to be the Inspector until the Vacancy be supplied by the Local Board.

Vacancies in Office of Inspector to be supplied.

CLV. That before any Person shall act as an Inspector in the Execution of this Act, he shall take and subscribe before the Mayor, or any One or more of the Aldermen, a solemn Declaration, as follows ; (to wit,)

Inspector to make Declaration for due Performance of his Duty.

'I A. B. do solemnly and sincerely declare, That I will
' honestly, truly, faithfully, and impartially, according to the
' best of my Skill and Judgment, execute the Office of Inspector
' of Coals for the Borough of Kingston-upon-Hull, pursuant
' to the Provisions of " The Kingston-upon-Hull Improvement
' Act, 1854." '

CLVI. That the Inspector shall permit the Books in which Entries are by this Act required to be made by him, and also the original Bills or Tickets, and the Accounts and solemn Declarations by this Act directed to be filed by him, to be inspected or examined by any Person requiring the same without Fee or Reward.

Inspector's Books, &c. to be open for Examination.

CLVII. That the Local Board, or any Committee thereof, from Time to Time at their own Will and Pleasure, without previous Notice or Declaration of their Intention so to do, may call for, inspect, and examine the Books, Accounts, Papers, and Vouchers of or belonging to the Inspector in the Matters appertaining to his Office, and the Inspector shall produce the same accordingly ; and if on any such Inspection and Examination it appear to the Local Board or such Committee that there is any wilful and erroneous Entry, Omission, Concealment, Fraud or Misrepresentation in any of such Books, Accounts, Papers, or Vouchers, or that the Inspector has negligently or fraudulently conducted himself in the Execution of his Office, the Local Board may and shall thereupon dismiss, or such Committee may and shall thereupon suspend, the Inspector ; and in every Case of such Suspension the Committee shall forthwith give Notice in Writing thereof to the Clerk of the Local Board, assigning the Cause of such Suspension, and the Local Board may

Examination of Inspector's Accounts.

dismiss the Inspector or remove the Suspension, and any Person so dismissed shall not be capable of being re-appointed to the Office, or of being appointed to any other Office or Place under this Act.

Penalties on Inspector for Neglect or Fraud.

CLVIII.   That if any Inspector, upon Payment or Tender to him of the Sum to be paid in respect thereof, refuse or neglect to receive and register any Bill or Ticket, Accounts or solemn Declaration, made and given to him of or concerning any Coals, or do not truly and faithfully register the same, and make and deliver such Certificate thereof in the Form and Manner required by the Local Board, or do not make and keep such Books, Accounts, Papers, Registers, Vouchers, Notes, and Entries as are by this Act required, or are by the Local Board from Time to Time thought fit and required, or do not produce the same when thereunto required as by this Act provided, or destroy, alter, deface, or mutilate the same or any of them, or in any Manner act in collusion with any Person whomsoever, to assist or enable him fraudulently to evade the Provisions of this Act in reference to the Importation, Sale, or Delivery of Coals, every such Offender shall for every such Offence forfeit a Sum not exceeding Fifty Pounds.

Inspector to file Bills, &c.

CLXI.   That the Inspector shall receive and register, file and keep, all such Bills or Tickets, Accounts, and solemn Declarations, from Time to Time delivered to him.

Penalty for using under-sized Coal Sacks.

CLXV.   That if any Vendor of, or Dealer in, or Carrier of Coals use or cause to be used any Sack for delivering or carrying Coals within the Borough which is not at the Time of using the same capable of containing One hundred and forty Pounds Weight of Coals, then and in every such Case every such Person so offending shall for every such Sack so deficient forfeit and pay any Sum not exceeding Five Shillings, and the Mayor or other Justice before whom the Conviction takes place shall cause every such Sack found so deficient to be destroyed.

Measure of Ton of Coals.

CLXVI.   That the Measure of every Ton of Coals sold and delivered to any Purchaser thereof in the Borough shall contain Sixteen of such Sacks of Coals filled to the Top; and if any Vendor of, or Dealer in, or Carrier of Coals deliver or cause to be delivered to any such Purchaser a less Number of such Sacks for a Ton, and so in proportion for a greater or less Quantity than a Ton, or do not fill the same to the Top, every Person so offending shall for every such Offence forfeit and pay any Sum not exceeding Forty Shillings.

CLXVII.   That every Porter or Carrier of Coals within the Borough shall cause his Name to be registered by the Inspector in a Book to be kept for that Purpose, and the Inspector shall thereupon give and deliver to every such Porter or Carrier an engraved and numbered Ticket of Brass or other durable Material, denoting his Occupation and Order of Entry in such Book, which Ticket shall be worn and carried by the Porter or Carrier in front of his Hat or Cap, and every Owner of any Cart employed in the Carriage and Delivery of Coals shall give an Account to the Inspector of the Number of Carts to be employed by him, and which shall also be registered by the Inspector in such Book.

Coal Porters to be registered.

CLXVIII.   That if any such Porter or Carrier carry any Coals without wearing or carrying such Ticket, or if any such Porter or Carrier, or the Owner of any such Cart, carry or convey any Coals without having caused such Entry to be made, and without having paid the Fees or Charges to which he is by this Act made liable in that Behalf, every Person so offending shall for every such Offence forfeit any Sum not exceeding Twenty Shillings.

Penalty on Coal Porters acting without being registered.

CLXXVI.   That if the Inspector or any such Meter or Weigher be, at any Time during his respective Continuance in Office, directly or indirectly interested or concerned in the Sale of any Coals whatsoever, otherwise than in the Discharge of his respective Office, every such Inspector or Meter or Weigher so offending shall for every such Offence forfeit and pay any Sum not exceeding Ten Pounds, and shall be dismissed from his Office, and be for ever disabled from holding or executing the same, or any other Office or Employment under this Act.

Inspector and Meters and Weighers not to be interested in Sale of Coals.

BOROUGH OF KINGSTON-UPON-HULL.
PROVISIONAL ORDER.

Dated 3rd July, 1862.

Confirmed by the Local Government Supplemental Act, 1863,
26 and 27 Vict., Ch. XXXII.

Royal Assent, 29th June, 1863.

5. The provisions of sections 151 to 158 (both inclusive), 161, 165 to 173 (both inclusive), 176 and 177 of the Improvement Act,* for the purpose of punishing and preventing frauds and impositions with respect to coal, and all other provisions of that Act applicable in that behalf, and this provision and the following provisions respectively, shall be in force in all places within the district for the time being of the Local Board, and with respect to all coal brought to or sent from or passing through such district.

6. The provisions of sections 151 to 158 (both inclusive), 161, 165 to 173 (both inclusive), 176 and 177 of the Improvement Act, and all other provisions of that Act applicable in that behalf, shall be so in force for the purposes of the following provisions, and shall extend and be read and have effect accordingly; that is to say,

Where in these provisions the owner of any coal, or the master of any vessel carrying coal, or the vendor of or dealer in coal is mentioned, his respective agent shall be included; and the inspector or inspectors of coals from time to time appointed under the Improvement Act shall be the inspector or inspectors of all coals which shall be brought for sale to, or sent from, or shall pass through such district of the Local Board, or any part thereof.

7. The owner of any coal brought within such district, or if carried by water the master of the vessel carrying it, shall, before such coal or any part thereof is sold or delivered or otherwise dealt with within the said district, deliver to the inspector or inspectors as aforesaid the original pit note denoting the quantity and quality thereof which was delivered to such owner or master with the coal when it was obtained, and the inspector or inspectors shall register and file the same, and keep it in his or their office, and after the Local Board have by advertisement in the London Gazette, and once in each of six successive weeks in each of four London daily morning papers, and

* *Kingston-upon-Hull Improvement Act, 1854.*

two newspapers published in the county of York, and by placards posted in conspicuous places within such district, and by hand-bills distributed there, giving public notice of this provision, a duplicate of such original pit note shall be sent to the said inspector or inspectors by the clerk or agent of the colliery whence the coal was obtained, by the post next after the delivery of the original pit note to the said owner or master as aforesaid, and the said inspector or inspectors shall thereupon register, file, and keep such duplicate in his or their office. If, however, the pit note do not sufficiently specify the quantity or quality of the coal, or there be not any such pit note delivered with the coal at the colliery or pit whence the coal was obtained, or if the pit note be lost, or if the vessel carrying the coal shall have been originally loaded for any other place and afterwards changed her destination without the proper pit note being accordingly delivered, or if the inspector or inspectors see other good and sufficient cause, then and in every such case the owner of the coal, or if carried by water the master of the vessel carrying it, shall deliver to the inspector or inspectors an account of the quality and quantity of the coal, setting forth when it was obtained and at what place, and from what colliery, and shall verify the same by solemn statutory declaration in lieu of oath, and such inspector or inspectors shall receive, and register, file, and keep in his or their office, every declaration so made.

8. The owner of any coal brought within the said district, or if carried by water the master of the vessel carrying it, or the vendor of or dealer in the coal, shall, before he sells, delivers, or deals with the coal, pay to the inspector or inspectors a tonnage rate at the rate of one halfpenny for every ton of the coals.

9. On payment to the inspector or inspectors of the tonnage rate for coal, he or they shall make out, and give to the owner, master, or agent paying it, a certificate in writing, in such form as the Local Board may from time to time think proper and direct, and to be signed by such inspector or inspectors, setting forth the quantity, quality, and date of arrival within the said district of such coal.

10. If the coal be carried by water the certificate of the inspector or inspectors shall be affixed by the master of the vessel carrying it to the mast of the vessel, and be continued so affixed until the cargo be sold or delivered, or if the coal be delivered into any yard or place within the said district for sale, then the certificate shall be placed by the vendor of or dealer in the coal upon a board or pole in front of the heap of coal, and be continued so placed until such heap be sold or disposed of; and the certificate shall be so affixed or placed immediately after the delivery thereof, or placed and continued in such other place and in such manner as the inspector or inspectors from time to time shall direct.

11. No sack shall be made use of in the delivery of coal within the said district unless it be first marked by the inspector or inspectors with such distinctive mark as the Local Board from time to time may direct, and no sack shall be marked which is not at the time of the marking thereof capable of containing 140 lbs. weight of coal, and all sacks taken before the Mayor or other Justice within the said district, and found by him to be deficient in size or not properly marked, shall under his order be destroyed.

12. The ticket of any porter or carrier of coals within the said district may, if and when the Local Board so order, be worn and carried in such conspicuous manner as they may order instead of in front of his hat or cap.

13. Every owner of any cart employed for the carriage or delivery of coals within the said district shall paint on it on each side in plain figures of not less than three inches in height and proportionate width such distinctive number as shall be assigned to it by the inspector or inspectors.

14. Every porter or carrier of coal within the said district shall on being registered pay one shilling, and shall yearly thereafter while on the register on the first day of January pay one other shilling, and the owner of every cart employed in carrying coal within the said district shall on the cart being registered pay one shilling, and shall yearly thereafter while the cart is on the register on the first day of January pay one shilling, and those payments shall be made to the inspector or inspectors.

15. The Local Board whenever they see occasion may reduce or raise (but not above the specified sums) the sums to be from time to time paid under those provisions to the inspector or inspectors as the tonnage rate for coal, and by porters, carriers, and owners of carts.

16. The monies from time to time paid under these provisions to the inspector or inspectors as the tonnage rate for coal, and by porters, carriers, and owners of carts, shall be accounted for and paid over by such inspector or inspectors, in the month of January in every year, to the treasurer of the Local Board, to the credit of their General District Fund Account.

17. If any owner of coal, or the master of any vessel carrying coal, knowingly commit any of the following offences; that is to say,

First.—Do not within 24 hours after the arrival of the coal within such district, or within such earlier period than 24 hours if he shall earlier deal with any coal within the said district, deliver to the inspector or inspectors the requisite pit note, account or declaration relating thereto ;

Secondly.—Make or deliver a false, feigned, or forged pit note ;

Thirdly.—Alter, deface, erase, or mutilate any pit note ;

Fourthly.—Do not affix or place, or continue the certificate of the inspector or inspectors, as he or they direct ;

Fifthly.—Make or affix or place or continue any false, feigned, or forged certificate ;

Sixthly.—Alter, deface, erase, or mutilate, any certificate of the inspector or inspectors ;

Seventhly.—Make or deliver a false or inaccurate account of the quantity or quality of the coal ;

Eighthly.—Bring within the said district coal of one quality or sort for and as coal of a different quality or sort ; or

Ninthly.—Make or deliver a false declaration of any matter with respect to which he is by the Improvement Act, or these provisions, required to make a declaration ;

Every person so offending shall forfeit and pay any sum not exceeding one hundred pounds.

18. If the owner of any cart carry therein within the said district any coal without having the requisite figures painted thereon, every person so offending shall for every such offence forfeit any sum not exceeding twenty shillings.

19. If any person commit any offence against any of the provisions with respect to coal of the Improvement Act, or of these provisions, and for which no penalty is prescribed, he shall forfeit a sum not exceeding ten pounds.

20. All prosecutions and other proceedings under the Improvement Act, or these provisions, with respect to offences connected with coal, shall be instituted by the Local Board or their officers.

21. The Local Board from time to time may direct any prosecution or other proceedings to be taken for the recovery of any penalties under and for the punishment of any persons offending against any of these provisions, and may defray the expenses thereof as part of their general expenditure.

22. All penalties under the Improvement Act or these provisions shall be recoverable in accordance with the provisions of the Act of the Session of the eleventh and twelfth years of the reign of Her present Majesty, chapter 43, with respect to the administration of justice.

BOROUGH OF KINGSTON-UPON-HULL.
PROVISIONAL ORDER.
Dated 30th March, 1871.
Confirmed by the Local Government Supplemental Act, 1871
(No. 2), 34 and 35 Vict., Ch. LIX.
Royal Assent, 29th June, 1871.

5. If any highway, street, road, or way, or any part or parts thereof, situate within the area of jurisdiction of the said Local Board, which has not heretofore been declared by resolution of the said board a public highway repairable by the board, be not entirely and wholly sewered, levelled (which shall include lowering or raising the level of the same), paved, flagged, and channelled, or otherwise made good to the satisfaction of the Local Board, the Local Board may, by notice in writing under the hand of their clerk for the time being, addressed to the respective owners or occupiers of the lands, houses, hereditaments, and premises fronting, adjoining, or abutting upon such parts thereof as may require to be sewered, levelled, paved, and flagged, or channelled, respectively, require such owners or occupiers, within one calendar month from the date of such notice, to sewer, level (as aforesaid), pave, flag, and channel, or otherwise make good, and to their satisfaction, as aforesaid, the highway, street, road, or way, or part or parts thereof, accordingly, and if the same be not so sewered, levelled as aforesaid, paved, flagged, or channelled, or otherwise made good, in accordance with the terms of such notice, to the satisfaction of the board, within the time aforesaid, then, and upon the expiration of the said one calendar month from the date of such notice, the said Local Board may, if they shall think fit, thereupon cause the works mentioned or referred to in such notice to be executed, done, and performed, at such places or place specified in such notice, in such manner as they may see fit; and the expenses incurred by the said Local Board in respect thereof shall be repaid to them, their successors and assigns, by the owners of such said lands or houses, buildings and premises respectively, in default, according to the frontage of their respective premises, and in such proportion as shall be fixed by the board's surveyor for the time being, and be recoverable, with interest thereon respectively, at the rate of five per cent. per annum, from such said owners or occupiers respectively, by the said Local Board, their successors and assigns, in manner herein-after mentioned. Provided always, that upon payment to the said Local Board, their successors and assigns, of such expenses, the Local Board shall accept and declare such turnpike road, highway, street, or way, or parts or part thereof, to be a public highway thenceforth ; and thereafter, such said highway, street, road, or way, or such part or parts thereof as aforesaid, shall from thenceforth be repairable by the said Local Board out of the rates levied by them for the repairs of public highways under the said *Improvement Act.

6. The 82nd section of the said Improvement Act shall be repealed, and in lieu thereof be it enacted :—That if any causeway, footway, or sideway of any highway, street, or way, whether the same highway, street, or way has been declared a highway or not, before or since the passing of the said Improvement Act, which has not heretofore been flagged or formed with materials of such width or otherwise to the satisfaction of the Local Board, then the said Local Board may, by notice in writing under the hand of their clerk for the time being, addressed to the respective owners or occupiers of the lands, houses, buildings, and premises adjoining or abutting upon the said causeway, footway, or sideway, require such owners or occupiers, within one calendar month from the date of such notice, to flag or form the same to the extent of their respective frontages thereto, of such materials and of such width as the said Local Board may think fit. And the said Local Board shall have the like power and authority with respect to any such causeway, footway, or sides, as to the materials or width of which they may disapprove, as is contained in section 5 herein-before mentioned, and if the same causeway, footway, or sides be not so flagged or formed or otherwise made good, in accordance with the conditions of such notice, then, and upon the expiration of the said one calendar month, the said Local Board may cause such causeway, footway, or sideway to be so flagged or formed or otherwise made good, in such manner as they shall see fit ; and the expenses incurred by the Local Board in respect thereof shall be repaid to them by the owners or occupiers of the lands, houses, buildings, and premises adjoining or abutting upon such said causeway, footway, or sideway respectively, according to and to the extent of their respective frontages thereto, and in such pro-

* *Kingston-upon-Hull Improvement Act, 1854.*

portion as may be settled by the surveyor of the board for the time being, with interest thereon respectively after the rate of 5*l.* per cent. per annum, in the manner and under the provisions herein-after mentioned.

7. For the purposes of the provisions herein contained, all the expenses incurred or to be incurred by the Local Board under the same respectively shall be deemed to be so respectively incurred, and shall be due and payable to the said Local Board, so soon as the said Local Board by resolution shall determine to proceed with the several works referred to in such several provisions respectively, or in any or either of them, as the case may be, and shall give such notice as aforesaid, and such expenses, and interest thereon after the rate of 5*l.* per cent. per annum from the date of such notice, shall be immediately thereupon recoverable by the Local Board, their successors or assigns, as liquidated damages, from the said owners or occupiers in a summary manner, before any justice of the peace of and for the borough of Kingston-upon-Hull, within six years from the date of such notice by the said Local Board, their successors and assigns.

11. The 103rd section of the Improvement Act shall be repealed, and in lieu thereof be it enacted :—Any person who, without the consent of the Local Board, shall build, rebuild, make, clear out, unstop, or in any wise alter any building, messuage, tenement or dwelling house, sewer, drain, privy, cesspool or ashpit respectively, or do any other work therein or thereupon, in contravention of any Act administered by the Local Board, or in alteration of plans which have been approved of by the said board, or contrary to the orders of the said board made under any of the powers vested in them by law, shall for every such offence forfeit a sum not exceeding 5*l.*, and for every day after the first during which the offence continues a sum not exceeding 10*s.* And the Local Board may further in such case at once alter and amend any such work, tenement, or other work, as they think fit, and the expense attending any such amendment or alteration shall be recoverable as liquidated damages in the mode and manner hereinbefore provided.

BOROUGH OF KINGSTON-UPON-HULL.

PROVISIONAL ORDER,

Dated 19th May, 1871.

Confirmed by the Local Government Supplement Act, 1872,
35 and 36 Vict., Ch. XLV.

Royal Assent, 27th June, 1872.

6. The said Local Board shall not, in pursuance of the
*powers conferred upon them by this Order, construct any work on
any part of the shore or bed of the sea where and so far up the
same as the tide flows and reflows without the previous consent of
the Board of Trade, to be signified in writing under the hand of one
of the Secretaries or Assistant Secretaries of the Board of Trade,
and then only according to such plan and under such restrictions
and regulations as the said Board of Trade approve of, such
approval being signified as last aforesaid; and where any such
work shall have been constructed with such consent as aforesaid,
the said Local Board shall not at any time alter or extend the
same without obtaining previously to making any such alteration
or extension the like consent or approval, and if any such work
shall be commenced or completed without such consent or approval
the said Board of Trade may abate and remove the same, and
restore the site thereof to its former condition, at the cost of the
said Local Board, and the amount of such costs shall be a debt
due to the Crown, and recoverable against the said Local Board
accordingly.

9. The municipal corporation may appoint from time to
time, and at pleasure suspend or remove, a person to be the
superintendent of the said landing place or places, who shall have
full power and authority to direct the mooring, unmooring, moving,
or removing of any ship, boat, or other vessel lying at or being
moored at or near any such landing place or places, and also to
appoint and direct the times and manner of any such ship, boat, or
other vessel coming to, lying at, or being moored as aforesaid, and
also to appoint the berth for any such ship, boat, or other vessel
to land or deliver, or to land or take in passengers' luggage or
cargo.

* *The powers conferred by the repealed Articles relate to the Ferry Boat
Dock and Landing Place.*

10. No master or other person having charge or direction of any such ship, boat, or other vessel shall disobey the orders and directions of the said superintendent as to any matter within the scope of his authority hereby given.

11. No master or other person having charge or direction of any ship, boat, or other vessel shall (except with the sanction of such superintendent) permit or suffer such ship, boat, or other vessel to lie across or in any way obstruct the free and convenient use of any such landing-place.

12. No person shall throw, cast, or place any ballast, earth, dust, ashes, stones, or any other article or thing whatsoever upon any such landing-place which may create annoyance to any person using the same, or which may prevent the free and convenient public use of the same.

13. Any person guilty of any of the offences aforesaid shall for each and every offence forfeit and pay any sum not exceeding five pounds.

14. All penalties under these provisions shall be recoverable in accordance with the provisions of the Act of the session of the eleventh and twelfth years of the reign of Her present Majesty, chapter forty-three, with respect to the administration of justice, and shall be applied in the same manner as penalties imposed under the Kingston-upon-Hull Improvement Act, 1854.

15. Nothing contained in this Order or in the Act confirming the same shall authorise the said Local Board to take, use, or in any manner interfere with any portion of the shore or bed of the sea, or of any river, channel, creek, bay, or estuary, or any right in respect thereof, belonging to the Queen's most Excellent Majesty in right of her Crown, and under the management of the Board of Trade, without the previous consent in writing of the Board of Trade on behalf of Her Majesty (which consent the Board of Trade may give) ; neither shall anything in the said Order or Act contained extend to take away, prejudice, diminish, or alter any of the estates, rights, privileges, powers, or authorities vested in or enjoyed or exerciscable by the Queen's Majesty, her heirs or successors.

BOROUGH OF KINGSTON-UPON-HULL.
PROVISIONAL ORDER.

Dated 29th May, 1877.

Confirmed by the Local Government Board's Provisional Orders Confirmation (Belper Union, &c.) Act, 1877.

40 & 41 Vict., Ch. CXXXII.

Royal Assent, 23rd July, 1877.

III.   Section 98 of the Local Act shall be altered so as to provide that *in every case where the average height of the houses in any court, alley, square, or inclosure for houses to be hereafter built or constructed on vacant ground (not being the site of any court or square theretofore formed or built immediately previously to such construction) exceeds twenty feet, such court, alley, square, or inclosure shall have an open area or be of a width, measuring from front to front, of not less than the average height of such houses, unless such height is more than thirty feet, in which case the width of the open area shall be at least thirty feet, and that* every court, alley, square, and inclosure referred to therein shall be properly drained and paved prior to the houses fronting thereto being occupied as dwelling-houses, and that no such court, alley, square, or inclosure shall at any time be used as a carriageway, except with the consent in writing of the said Urban Sanitary Authority first had and obtained.

[NOTE.—*The words in italics are repealed by the Provisional Order of 1893, Art. II., page 132.*]

BOROUGH OF KINGSTON-UPON-HULL.
PROVISIONAL ORDER,

Dated 27th May, 1880.

Confirmed by the Local Government Board's Provisional Orders Confirmation (Kingston-upon-Hull, &c.) Act, 1880.

43 & 44 Vic., Ch. LXXXIV.

Royal Assent, 2nd August, 1880.

Art. II. The Corporation may repair, alter, improve, or reconstruct, wholly or in part, the Victoria Pier, and the gangway or approaches thereto, so as to provide a covered way from Nelson Street to the Victoria Pier, with a flat roof available as a promenade, to be approached by flights of steps from Nelson Street, and may provide and maintain railings, shelters, seats, steps, and all other things appropriate for the use or enjoyment of the Victoria Pier and the approaches thereto. The Corporation may also reconstruct on the same site the whole or part of the existing jetty opposite the Victoria Hotel at the east end of the dock, so however that no part of the new jetty shall extend beyond the site of such existing jetty.

Art. III. The Corporation may, by filling in a portion of the area of the Ferry Boat Dock, and facing the filled-in portion with a wall or otherwise, in a line parallel or nearly parallel to the Victoria Pier, increase the width of Nelson Street, but so as to leave a water space at high water of not less than eighty feet between the Victoria Pier and the newly formed portion of Nelson Street, which said newly formed portion of Nelson Street shall be paved, lighted, and maintained as one of the streets of the Borough.

Art. IV. The Corporation may make and maintain a new sewer under Nelson Street, Queen Street, and Humber Street, commencing at a point in Nelson Street opposite the outfall of the present sewer, and terminating on the south side of the Graving Dock Yard of the Corporation; and may by means of such sewer divert, convey, and discharge, at a place near the gates of the said graving dock, the sewage and other matters which now pass or might pass into the Ferry Boat Dock; and may make and maintain in connection with such sewer all proper culverts, penstocks, tidal gates, and other works. So soon as such sewer is open, the Corporation may close the existing sewer by which sewage now passes into the Ferry Boat Dock, and may cut off any drains communicating therewith : and may provide drains communicating with the new sewer for the drainage of premises which now drain into the existing sewer.

Art. V. For the purpose of flushing and cleansing the Ferry Boat Dock as may be from time to time required, the Corporation may fix sluices in the proposed new front of Nelson Street, and may charge the cost of obtaining water for flushing and cleansing the same to the general district rate of the Borough.

Art. VI. Articles 6 and 15 of the Order of 1871 shall apply to all works below high-water mark, authorised by this Order.

Art. VII. The Corporation may, on any number of days in each year not exceeding fifty-two, exclude the public from free admission to the roof of the proposed covered way from Nelson Street to the Victoria Pier, and may for every person admitted on any such day charge a sum not exceeding twopence. Notice shall be given by the Corporation of all such days by advertisement in at least two local newspapers circulating in the Borough ; and any person who on any such day obtains admission without payment may be summarily removed by any constable.

Art. VIII. For the purposes of this Order the Corporation may, with the sanction of the Local Government Board, borrow such sums as they may require, not exceeding in the aggregate twenty thousand pounds, and may charge the property of the Corporation and the borough fund, and all or any of the rates leviable by the Corporation, with repayment of the sums borrowed and interest thereon.

Art. IX. In order to secure such repayment the Corporation may issue debentures, subject to such conditions and regulations, not inconsistent with this Order, as the Corporation may, with the sanction of the Local Government Board, determine.

Art. X. All moneys borrowed under this Order shall be repaid within such period, not exceeding sixty years from the date at which they were respectively borrowed, as the Corporation, with the sanction of the Local Government Board, may in each case determine, by the creation and application of a sinking fund in manner following ; that is to say,—

(1.) Such equal yearly or half yearly sums shall be paid by the Corporation into the sinking fund as, being accumulated at compound interest at a rate not exceeding four pounds per centum per annum, would be sufficient to pay off the moneys borrowed within such period, not exceeding sixty years from the date of borrowing the same, as the Corporation, with the sanction of the Local Government Board, may in each case determine;

(2.) The first of such payments shall be made within twelve months from the date of the first loan contracted by the Corporation under this Order;

(3.) All sums paid into the sinking fund shall, as soon as may be, be invested by the Corporation in securities in which trustees are for the time being authorised to invest, or in the mortgages, bonds, debentures, debenture stock, or other securities duly created and issued by any local authority as defined by the Local Loans Act, 1875, other than the Corporation, and any such investments may be from time to time varied or transposed; and all dividends and other sums received in respect of such investments shall, as soon as may be after they are received, be paid into the sinking fund and invested by the Corporation in like manner;

(4.) The Corporation may at any time apply the whole or any part of any sinking fund created under this Order in or towards the discharge of the moneys or any part of the moneys for the discharge of which the fund was created;

(5.) Whenever any of such principal moneys have been so paid off, the Corporation shall thenceforward, until the whole of such principal moneys have been paid off, pay into the sinking fund every year, in addition to the other sums hereinbefore required to be paid into the fund, a sum equivalent to the interest which would have been produced by the sinking fund or part of the sinking fund so applied;

(6.) Whenever and so long as the yearly income arising from the sinking fund shall be equal to the annual interest of the principal moneys then due and outstanding, the Corporation may, in lieu of investing the said yearly income, apply the same in payment of such interest, and may during such periods discontinue the payment to the sinking fund of the yearly sums herein-before required to be paid thereto.

[Note.—*This article is amended by the Provisional Order of 1883, Art. III. page 99, so as to provide as follows :—*

The Corporation may from time to time apply or invest temporarily in the purchase for redemption, within the meaning of Section 38 of the Act of 1881, of Corporation Stock issued or to be issued under that Act, the whole or any part of any Sinking Fund which they have set apart or may from time to time set apart, in pursuance of the provisions of Article I. of the Order of 1879, and of Section 13 of the Local Loans Act, 1875, and the whole or any part of any sinking fund created under Article X. of the Order of 1880.

(2.) Where the Corporation in pursuance of the provisions of this Article apply or invest temporarily the whole or any part of any sinking fund in the purchase for redemption of Corporation Stock, the amount so applied or invested shall be deemed to be a debt due to such sinking fund from the Hull Corporation Loans Fund established under Section 32 of the Act of 1881.

In respect of the said debt, interest shall be payable at the rate of four pounds per centum per annum from the date of the cancellation of the Corporation Stock so purchased for redemption until repayment of the same ; and the amount of such debt, together with the interest thereon until repayment thereof at the rate aforesaid, shall be paid, as soon as may be out of the Hull Corporation Loans Fund, to the credit of the said sinking fund, for the purpose of being applied in discharge of the borrowed moneys in respect of which such sinking fund has been created.]

Art. XI. The Corporation may at any time, by the issue of fresh debentures, subject to the provisions of Art. IX. of this Order, re-borrow any moneys borrowed under this Order. Provided that any moneys so re-borrowed shall be repaid within the period within which the moneys in lieu of which they were borrowed would have been required under this Order to be repaid, but no such re-borrowing shall affect the obligations of the Corporation with respect to any sinking fund required to be created under Art. X of this Order.

Art. XII. All sums payable in respect of principal or interest of moneys borrowed by the Corporation under this Order shall be payable in the first instance out of the district fund and general district rate, and all other expenses incurred by the Corporation in the execution of this Order shall be defrayed as if they were expenses incurred by them in the execution of the Public Health Act, 1875.

Art. XIII. The Town Clerk shall, within twenty-one days after the expiration of each year during which any sum is required by this Order to be set apart for a sinking fund in respect of moneys borrowed by the Corporation under this Order, transmit to the Local Government Board a return, in such form as may be prescribed by that Board, and verified by statutory declaration, if so required by them, showing the amount which has been invested or applied for the purpose of such sinking fund during the year next preceding the making of such return, and the description of the securities on which any investment has been made, and the purposes to which any portion of the sinking fund or investment, or of the sums accumulated by way of interest, has been applied during the same period, and the total amount (if any) remaining invested at the end of the year.

Art. XIV. If it appears to the Local Government Board by that return or otherwise, that the Corporation have failed to set apart any sum required for any sinking fund, or have applied any portion of the money so set apart, or of the sums accumulated by way of interest, to any purposes other than those authorised, they may by Order direct that a sum not exceeding double the amount in respect of which default has been made shall be set apart and invested or applied as part of the sinking fund ; and any such Order shall be enforceable by writ of Mandamus, to be obtained by the Local Government Board out of Her Majesty's High Court of Justice.

Art. XV. All mortgages or debentures granted by the Corporation before the commencement of this Order shall, during their continuance, have priority of charge on the security therein comprised over all debentures issued in exercise of the borrowing powers conferred by this Order.

Art. XVI.   A person advancing any money to the Corporation, and receiving in consideration of such advance any security under this Order, shall not be bound to inquire into the application of the money advanced, or be in any way responsible for the non-application or misapplication thereof.

Art. XVII.   A trustee, executor, or other person empowered to invest money in the debentures or debenture stock of any railway or other company may, unless forbidden by the will or instrument under which he acts, whether prior to the commencement of this Order or not, invest the same in debentures issued under this Order : Provided that nothing in this Order shall authorise a trustee to invest in any debenture transferable by delivery.

Art. XVIII.   Section 11 of the Local Loans Act, 1875 (Remedy by Mandamus for non-payment of money), and Section 12 of the same Act (Remedy by appointment of receiver for non-payment of money), shall apply to the Corporation and to debentures issued and the recovery of moneys raised by them under this Order, as if those sections were herein with any necessary modifications enacted.

Art. XIX.   Nothing contained in this Order shall authorise any interference with or in any way affect the rights, powers, or authorities of the guild or brotherhood of masters and pilots, seamen of the Trinity House in Kingston-upon-Hull, or of the haven master appointed by them.

THE HULL CORPORATION LOANS ACT, 1881.
44 AND 45 VICT., CH. XCIV.
Royal Assent 27th June, 1881.

1. This Act may be cited as the Hull Corporation Loans Act 1881. Short title.

2. In this Act unless the context otherwise requires— Interpretation of terms.

" The borough " means the municipal borough of Kingston-upon-Hull ;

" The Council " means the Council of the borough ;

" The borough fund " and " the borough rate " mean respectively the borough fund and the borough rate of the borough ;

" The Municipal Corporation Acts " means the Municipal Corporation Act 1835 and all Acts for the time being in force amending the same or otherwise relating to municipal corporations in England ; 5 & 6 Will. 4
c. 76.

" Person " includes a corporation ;

" Rate " includes water rents and charges for the supply of water and gas or other means of lighting by the Corporation.

3. This Act shall be carried into execution by the Corporation acting by the Council. Act to be executed by Council.

4. Subject to the provisions of this Act the Corporation may from time to time by resolution determine to create capital stock to be called " Hull Corporation Stock " (in this Act referred to as " Corporation stock ") and to be issued in such amounts and manner as they may think fit and as shall be specified in such resolution and at such prices and times and on such terms and subject to such conditions (not being inconsistent with the provisions of this Act) as they may think fit for all or any of the purposes following (that is to say) : Corporation may create stock.

For raising any sum (to be specified in such resolution) on account of any moneys which they have authority to raise by borrowing under any of the borough Acts * and which they have not then raised ; or

For raising instead of re-borrowing any sum (to be specified in such resolution) required by them for the purpose of paying off when due any portion of their debt then subsisting on

* *See Schedule I., p. 55.*

the security of outstanding securities granted by them under any of the borough Acts and which they are authorised to re-borrow or for repaying any moneys temporarily borrowed by them in order to enable them to pay off any portion of such debt ; or

For the conversion into Corporation stock by agreement but not otherwise of any portion (to be specified in such resolution) of their debt then subsisting on the security of outstanding securities granted by them under any of the borough Acts :

Provided that nothing in this Act shall be construed to abridge or interfere with the powers of the Corporation for raising in manner provided by any of the borough Acts any sums which they are by any such Act authorised to borrow and which they do not think it expedient to raise by means of Corporation stock.

[NOTE.—*This section is amended by the Provisional Orders of 1890 and 1895, pages 128, 135, which authorise loans by the Corporation to the School Board, the Guardians of the Poor of the Kingston-upon-Hull Incorporation, and the Hull and Goole Port Sanitary Authority. Article 4 of the Order of 1890 also provides as follows:*

Art. IV. Section 4 of the Local Act shall be deemed to have been altered as from the passing of the Local Act by the insertion of the following provisions; viz.,—

" For raising

" (1.) Any sum required for the payment off or redemption of "any Corporation Stock, mortgage, bond, debenture, "debenture stock, annuity, rentcharge, or other "security granted or created, or redeemable, or payable "by them, which sum may include the amount of any "payment made to the holder of any such security for "his consent, or for compensating him for such payment "off or redemption, or for the substitution of Corporation "Stock for his secuity ;

" (2.) Any sum payable under Article V. of this Order; and

" (3.) Any sums properly chargeable to capital and paid as "commissions, discounts, or expenses in respect of any "Corporation Stock."]

5. Where any Corporation stock has been created under this Act for the purpose of raising moneys or paying off or converting any security for moneys borrowed for any of the purposes of any of the borough Acts or for repaying any moneys temporarily borrowed for any such purposes such Corporation stock shall be deemed to have been created for the said purposes of such Act and any moneys raised thereby shall be deemed to have been raised for such purposes and shall subject to the provisions of this Act be applied accordingly. *Application of Corporation stock.*

6. After any moneys have been raised by the Corporation by the issue of Corporation stock or after the conversion of any securities into Corporation stock the Corporation shall not issue any mortgages or other securities for the amounts so raised or converted and shall not again borrow the same and to the extent of such amount as aforesaid the powers of the Corporation to borrow and re-borrow moneys shall be extinguished. *Restriction on exercise of borrowing powers after issue of Corporation stock.*

7. All Corporation stock and the interest thereon and the sums required for the redemption thereof shall be charged indifferently on the whole revenues of the lands waterworks and other property belonging to the Corporation under the borough Acts or otherwise howsoever and on the funds accounts revenues and rates formed received and leviable by the Corporation under the borough Acts and on the borough fund and borough rate subject to all charges existing at the passing of this Act on such lands waterworks funds accounts revenues and rates respectively and shall be a first charge on the said revenues funds accounts and rates after those charges. *Security for Corporation stock.*

8. No holder of any portion of Corporation stock shall have any priority or preference by reason of the prior creation of such stock or otherwise. *No preference among holders.*

9. (1) The Corporation may enter into an arrangement with the holder of any security granted by them under any of the borough Acts for the conversion thereof into such amount of Corporation stock as may be agreed on ; *Conversion of existing securities into Corporation stock.*

(2) Any person who holds any such security and who is one of the persons enabled by the Lands Clauses Consolidation Act 1845 to sell land under that Act may consent to any arrangement under this Act for the conversion of such security into Corporation stock or to the payment of the moneys secured thereby before the *8 & 9 Vict. c. 18.*

time limited for the payment thereof as if such person were the absolute owner in his own right of such security, and such person is hereby indemnified for so doing ;

(3) All Corporation stock and moneys issued or paid in substitution for or on account of any such security or the moneys secured thereby shall be subject and liable to the same trusts powers provisions declarations agreements charges liens and incumbrances as immediately before the conversion or payment thereof affected such security or the moneys secured thereby and so as to give effect to and not to annul any testamentary or other disposition of or affecting the same and every such disposition shall take effect with reference to a proportionate amount of the substituted stock and moneys.

[NOTE.—*This section is amended by the Provisional Order of 1890, Art. V., page 129, which provides*

> Art. V. Section 9 of the Local Act shall be deemed to have authorised as from the passing of the Local Act, and to authorise the Corporation to enter into an arrangement with the holder of any security legally granted, or redeemable, or payable by them for the redemption thereof by payment of such an amount in money or Corporation Stock, or partly in one and partly in the other, as may be mutually agreed upon.]

Trustees may invest in Corporation stock.
38 & 39 Vict. c. 83.

10. Subject to the provisions of this Act as to stock certificates to bearer and as to coupons trustees or other persons for the time being having power to invest any moneys in nominal debentures or nominal debenture stock issued under the Local Loans Act 1875 shall have power to invest such moneys in Corporation stock issued under this Act.

Nature and incidents of Corporation stock.

11. (1) Corporation stock shall be personal estate ;

(2) Corporation stock shall not be redeemable except by agreement between the Corporation and the holder of any portion of such stock.

[*This section is amended by the Provisional Order of 1888, Art. I., page 123, which provides*

> Art. I. Section 11 of the Act of 1881 shall be altered so as to provide that, notwithstanding sub-section (2.) of that section, any resolution for the creation of Corporation Stock passed after the commencement of

this Order may provide that such stock shall be redeemable by the Corporation at par, that is to say, at the rate of one hundred pounds sterling for every nominal amount of one hundred pounds stock issued, at or after such time and in such manner as the Corporation by that resolution declare. Such stock shall be designated by the Corporation as Hull Corporation Redeemable Stock. Any certificate of stock granted in respect of Corporation Redeemable Stock created after the commencement of this Order shall have endorsed upon it the conditions upon which such stock is redeemable.]

12. (1) The Corporation shall cause to be kept a register in which shall be entered the names and addresses of the persons from time to time entitled to Corporation stock and the amounts to which they are respectively entitled and the transfers from time to time made of such stock; *Register of Corporation stock.*

(2) No notice of any trust express implied or constructive shall be entered on the register or be receivable by or affect the registrar;

(3) The register kept in pursuance of this Act shall be primâ facie evidence of all matters entered therein and as regards persons entered therein as holders of stock of the title of those persons to that stock;

(4) The Corporation may from time to time appoint such person or bank as they may think fit to be the registrar for the purposes of this Act and may from time to time rescind any such appointment and the person or bank so appointed shall have all the powers and duties of the registrar under this Act subject to any directions which may from time to time be given by the Corporation.

13. (1) Corporation stock shall bear such fixed and perpetual interest as the Corporation by the resolution creating the same may determine; *Interest on Corporation stock.*

(2) The interest shall be payable half-yearly on the first day of January and the first day of July or on such other days as the Corporation may from time to time determine;

(3) If a day fixed for the half-yearly payment of interest falls on a Saturday or Sunday or a day observed as a public holiday at the Bank of England the interest shall in that case be payable on the first of the following days which is not one of the days excepted as aforesaid.

Receipt of interest by executors &c.

14. The Corporation shall not be required to allow any executors or administrators to receive any interest on Corporation stock held by their testator or intestate until the probate of the will or the letters of administration has or have been left with the registrar for registration.

Receipts for interest of joint holders.

15. If two or more persons are registered as joint holders of any stock any one of such persons may give effectual receipts for any interest on such stock unless notice to the contrary shall have been given to the registrar by any other holder.

Interest warrants by post.

16. (1) The registrar may from time to time make arrangements for payment of interest on Corporation stock by sending warrants through the post and every warrant so sent shall be deemed a cheque within the meaning assigned to that term in

39 & 40 Vict. c. 81.

the Crossed Cheques Act 1876;

(2) Where a holder of Corporation stock desires to have his interest warrants sent to him by post he shall make a request for that purpose to the registrar in writing signed by him in a form approved by the registrar and shall give to the registrar an address in the United Kingdom or in the Channel Islands or the Isle of Man to which the letters containing the warrants are from time to time to be sent;

(3) The posting by the registrar of a letter containing an interest warrant addressed to the holder of Corporation stock on his request under this Act at the address given by him to the registrar shall as respects the liability of the Corporation and registrar be equivalent to the delivery of the warrant to the said holder of Corporation stock himself.

Transfer of Corporation stock.

17. (1) Transfers of Corporation stock shall be made only in the register and shall be signed by the transferor or by his attorney thereunto lawfully authorised by writing under his hand attested by at least one witness;

(2) The transferee may if he thinks fit underwrite his acceptance of the transfer;

(3) The instrument of transfer may be in the form in the second schedule to this Act.

Losing register for transfers.

18. (1) The register may be closed for transfers during such time (not exceeding fifteen days) immediately preceding each half-yearly payment of interest on the Corporation stock as may be directed by the Corporation on their giving not less than seven days' notice of such closing in one or more local newspapers circulating generally in the borough ;

(2) The persons who on the day of such closing are inscribed in the register as holders of stock shall as between them and their transferees of any stock be entitled to the interest then next payable on such stock.

19. (1) The executors or administrators of a deceased holder of Corporation stock shall be the only persons recognised as having any title to the stock of such holder or to any interest thereon ; *Transmission of Corporation stock.*

(2) Any person becoming entitled to any stock in consequence of the death bankruptcy or insolvency of any holder of Corporation stock or in consequence of the marriage of any female holder of Corporation stock or otherwise than by transfer of the stock shall produce such evidence of his title as may reasonably be required by the registrar and the person so becoming entitled to any stock may transfer such stock to another person without being registered himself ;

(3) The Corporation shall not be required to allow any executors or administrators to transfer any Corporation stock until the probate of the will or the letters of administration to the deceased has or have been left with the registrar for registration.

20. (1) The registrar shall issue to the holder of any Corporation stock on his application and on payment of the fees chargeable in pursuance of this Act a stock receipt specifying the name and address of such holder and the amount of stock to which he is entitled and such stock receipt shall be primâ facie evidence of the title of the holder at the date of the stock receipt to the amount of stock stated therein but the want of such stock receipt shall not prevent the owner of any Corporation stock from transferring the same ; *Stock receipts.*

(2) If any such stock receipt be worn out or damaged then the same may on production thereof be cancelled and another similar stock receipt may be given to the holder of the stock specified in the stock receipt so worn out or damaged or if such stock receipt be lost or destroyed then on proof thereof to the satisfaction of the registrar a similar stock receipt may be given

to the holder of the stock specified in the stock receipt so lost or destroyed and in either case a due entry of the substituted stock receipt shall be made in the register.

Stock certificates to bearer.

21. (1) Subject to the provisions of this Act with respect to trustees and to the conditions hereinafter mentioned the registrar if so authorised by the Corporation may on the application of any holder of Corporation stock and payment of the fees chargeable in pursuance of this Act issue to such holder a certificate (in this Act called a "stock certificate to bearer") which shall entitle the bearer to the stock therein specified and shall be transferable by delivery;

(2) A stock certificate to bearer shall not be granted in respect of any sum of Corporation stock not being twenty-five pounds fifty pounds one hundred pounds two hundred pounds five hundred pounds or one thousand pounds:

(3) Any stock in respect of which a stock certificate to bearer has been so issued shall not so long as such certificate is outstanding be transferable in the register;

(4) Every stock certificate to bearer of Corporation stock in respect of the transfers whereof a composition has not been paid

43 & 44 Vict. c. 20.

under the provisions of Part 5 of the Inland Revenue Act 1880 shall be charged with a stamp duty of seven shillings and sixpence for every full sum of one hundred pounds and the like for every fraction of one hundred pounds of the nominal amount of the stock described in such certificate.

Coupons attached to stock certificates to bearer.

22. (1) There shall be attached to every stock certificate to bearer coupons entitling the bearer of the coupons to the interest on the stock described in such stock certificate for a limited period;

(2) On the expiration of the period for which the coupons attached to a stock certificate to bearer have been issued the registrar may issue fresh coupons for a further limited period in respect of such certificate or may exchange the certificate for another certificate with coupons for a further limited period and so for successive periods:

(3) Coupons shall be payable on presentation at the office of the registrar or at any bank in that behalf mentioned in the coupon within three clear days from the day of presentation:

(4) The payment to the bearer of any coupon of the amount

expressed therein shall be a full discharge to the registrar and the Corporation from all liability in respect of that coupon and the interest represented thereby.

23. On delivery to the registrar of a stock certificate to bearer issued under this Act and of all unpaid coupons belonging thereto and on payment of the fees chargeable in pursuance of this Act the registrar shall enter the bearer in the register as holder of the stock described in the certificate and thereupon that stock shall become transferable in the register and the interest thereon shall thenceforth be payable as if no stock certificate to bearer had been issued in respect thereof. *Registration of bearer of stock certificates to bearer.*

24. A trustee shall not apply for or hold a stock certificate to bearer unless authorised so to do by the terms of his trust and any contravention of this provision shall be deemed a breach of trust but this provision shall not impose on the registrar an obligation to enquire whether a person applying for or holding a stock certificate to bearer or coupon is or is not a trustee or subject the registrar or the Corporation to any liability in the event of his issuing to a trustee a stock certificate to bearer or coupon or dealing with a trustee as the holder of a stock certificate to bearer or coupon or invalidate any stock certificate to bearer or coupon issued to a trustee. *Trustees not to hold stock certificates to bearer.*

25. If any stock certificate to bearer or coupon issued under this Act is lost or destroyed the registrar may on receiving indemnity to his satisfaction issue a fresh stock certificate to bearer or coupon. *Loss or destruction of stock certificate to bearer or coupon.*

26. Save in so far as relates to the mode of transfer and payment of interest thereon any Corporation stock described in a stock certificate to bearer issued under this Act shall be a charge on the same securities and shall be subject to the same powers of redemption and (save in so far as such stock certificate is a negotiable security) to the same incidents in all respects as if such stock had continued registered in the register as stock transferable therein. *General provision as to stock described in stock certificate to bearer.*

27. There shall be charged with respect to the several proceedings in relation to stock receipts and stock certificates to bearer the fees specified in the third schedule to this Act annexed or such other reasonable fees as may be from time to time determined by the Corporation: Provided that where the registrar in *Fees in respect of stock receipts and stock certificates to bearer.*

lieu of issuing fresh coupons in respect of a stock certificate to bearer gives in exchange a fresh stock certificate to bearer with coupons annexed no fee shall be charged in respect of such fresh stock certificate to bearer or coupons :

All fees payable in pursuance of this section shall be payable to the registrar and shall be carried to the account of the Corporation Loans Fund.

Arrangements with bank.

28. The Corporation may from time to time enter into such arrangements with the Bank of England or with any other bank as they think proper for carrying into effect the provisions of this Act with reference to the issue and transfer of Corporation stock and the management thereof and the keeping of the register and any other matters and for the proper remuneration of the bank with reference thereto :

In the event of the Bank of England becoming the registrar under this Act then so long as the Bank continue to act as registrar the following provisions shall have effect (namely) :—

(a) The Bank as registrar may if they see fit require every power authorising an attorney to transfer stock to be under the seal of the person executing the power and attested by two or more credible witnesses ;

42 & 43 Vict c. 11.

(b) The Bankers' Books Evidence Act 1879 shall apply to the register and to all other books accounts and documents kept by the registrar in pursuance of this Act ;

(c) The Bank as registrar before paying interest on any Corporation stock may if the circumstances of the case appear to make it expedient require evidence by a statutory declaration made under the Act 5 & 6 Will. 4 c. 62 or otherwise of the title of any person claiming a right to receive the interest ;

(d) Where Corporation stock is standing in the name of an infant or person of unsound mind jointly with any person not under legal disability a letter of attorney for the receipt of the interest on the stock shall be sufficient authority in that behalf if given under the hand and seal of the person not under disability attested by two or more credible witnesses The Bank as registrar before acting on the letter of attorney may require proof to their satisfaction of the alleged infancy or unsoundness of mind by statutory declaration made under the Act 5 & 6 Will. 4 c. 62 or otherwise ;

(c) Where the executors of the will of a deceased holder of stock purpose to transfer his stock or part thereof the Bank as registrar may if they see fit require all the executors who have proved the will to join in the transfer.

29. (1) The Corporation may from time to time make alter and rescind with respect to the transfer of Corporation stock the issue of stock certificates to bearer and coupons and otherwise in relation to such stock reasonable regulations not inconsistent with the provisions of this Act ; *Corporation may make regulations as to Corporation stock.*

(2) A printed copy of all such regulations shall be entered in the register and any such regulations for the time being in force shall be duly observed.

30. The expenses from time to time incurred by the Corporation in the execution of the provisions of this Act and any payment of composition for stamp duty in respect of Corporation stock created and issued for any of the purposes of any of the borough Acts and otherwise in relation to such stock shall be deemed to be expenses incurred by the Corporation in the execution of the said Acts respectively and shall be defrayed out of the funds accounts revenues and rates applicable under the said Acts respectively to the redemption of Corporation stock or in the case of any such composition for stamp duty out of moneys borrowed on the security of such funds accounts revenues and rates respectively and the Corporation are hereby authorised to borrow such moneys as they may from time to time require for the purpose of such composition and any moneys so borrowed shall be deemed to be borrowed under the borough Acts. *Expenses of execution of Act.*

31. The Corporation shall cause to be kept proper accounts showing the several purposes of the borough Acts for which from time to time Corporation stock has been created and distinguishing the amounts of Corporation stock created for such purposes respectively and such accounts shall be from time to time audited in like manner as other accounts of the Corporation are from time to time audited. *Accounts to be kept by Corporation.*

32. For the purpose of paying the interest on and redeeming Corporation stock created under this Act there shall be *Corporation loans fund.*

established a fund to be called "the Hull Corporation Loans Fund" (in this Act referred to as "the Corporation Loans Fund") which shall be formed in manner following (that is to say) :—

(1) The Corporation shall carry to the Corporation Loans Fund any moneys which may arise from the issue of any Corporation stock at a premium ;

(2) The Corporation shall also carry to the said fund any sums standing to the credit of any sinking fund applicable to the discharge of any securities converted into Corporation stock under this Act ;

(3) The Corporation shall also carry to the said fund all moneys in the nature of capital arising from the sale of lands and property acquired by the Corporation under any of the borough Acts but not required for the purposes of such Act remaining to the credit of the Corporation after providing for all charges on such moneys existing at the time of the passing of this Act and to which the same are for the time being applicable exclusive of any portion of such moneys which the Corporation may be authorised or required from time to time to reinvest or to apply to the purposes of any of the borough Acts as aforesaid ;

(4) The Corporation shall also in every year carry to the said fund :—

(a) Such sum as shall be equal to the amount of all the interest payable as by this Act provided on Corporation stock for that year : and

(b) Such sum as shall be equal to the amount of all the moneys payable as by this Act provided towards the redemption of Corporation stock for that year.

33.   The Corporation shall provide the sums directed by this Act to be carried in every year to the Corporation Loans Fund for payment of interest and towards redemption of stock respectively by means of contributions from and out of the several funds accounts revenues and rates from and out of which such contributions are respectively payable under this Act : Provided that where in any case any such fund account revenue or rate is by reason of any deficiency in such fund account or revenue or of any limit to such rate wholly or partially insufficient to yield the amount required

Contributions for providing sums to be carried in every year to Corporation loans fund.

for any contribution the Corporation shall provide the amount required to make up such insufficiency from the borough fund or borough rate : Provided further that no occupier of any lands covered with water or used only as a dock or as a canal or the towing path thereof or as a railway constructed under the powers of any Act of Parliament for public conveyance shall be rated in respect of any such lands to any increase of or addition to the borough rate for the purposes or under the authority of this Act in any greater proportion of the net annual value of such lands than the proportion in which such occupier would have been liable to be rated in respect of such lands to such insufficient rate and that in the event of any such occupier being rated in any greater proportion the Corporation shall repay or allow to such occupier a drawback equal to the amount overpaid by such occupier and the same may be recovered by action at law or may be deducted out of any other rate to which such occupier may be liable.

34. (1) The contributions required from time to time to provide the sums directed by this Act to be carried to the Corporation Loans Fund as aforesaid for payment of the interest on Corporation stock issued for raising moneys or paying off or converting any security for moneys raised for the purposes of any of the borough Acts shall from time to time be payable out of the several funds accounts revenues and rates which by such Act would be charged or chargeable with the payment of the interest on such moneys if the same were secured in manner provided by such Act :

Funds and rates out of which contributions to be payable.

(2) The contributions required to provide the sums directed by this Act to be carried to the Corporation Loans Fund towards the redemption of stock shall be paid as follows :—

(a) As regards stock issued for the conversion of securities granted under the borough Acts before the passing of this Act from and out of the several funds accounts revenues and rates from and out of which respectively a yearly or other sum would have been payable for the purpose of forming a sinking fund for the repayment of or of repaying by instalments or otherwise the moneys secured by the securities so granted if such securities had not been converted :

(b) As regards stock issued to secure moneys borrowed under the borough Acts after the passing of this Act from and out of the several funds accounts revenues and rates from and out of which respectively a yearly or other sum would have been payable for the purpose of forming a sinking fund for the repayment of or of repaying by instalments or otherwise the moneys so borrowed if such moneys had been secured in manner provided by the borough Acts :

(3) Nothing in this section contained shall alter or affect the securities on which Corporation stock is by this Act indifferently charged or the order in which Corporation stock is charged on such securities nor shall anything in this section contained discharge or relieve any of such securities from any liability in respect of such Corporation stock or of the moneys required for the payment of interest thereon and the redemption thereof.

Amounts of contributions.

35. (1) The amounts of the several contributions to any sum directed by this Act to be carried to the Corporation Loans Fund for payment of interest as aforesaid shall be the several sums from time to time ascertained to be payable in respect thereof by the apportionment of such sum among the several funds accounts revenues and rates respectively out of which such contributions are payable having regard to the amount of Corporation stock in respect of which interest is payable out of such funds accounts revenues and rates respectively : Provided that the amounts of the several contributions required for payment of interest as aforesaid in any year shall be reduced by the amount of income resulting from investment of the Corporation Loans Fund which is applied in that year in payment of such interest and all interest resulting from such investment and not otherwise specifically applicable may be applied accordingly :

(2) The amounts of the several contributions to any sum directed by this Act to be carried to the Corporation Loans Fund for redemption of stock as aforesaid shall be such amounts as with accumulations at the rate of three pounds ten shillings per centum per annum will be sufficient to redeem at par the stock towards the redemption of which such contributions are respectively made payable by this Act in the case of the loans of the Corporation already authorised by any existing Act or provisional order or order of any Government Department within sixty years from the time

when the moneys represented by such stock were first respectively borrowed in the case of any loan to be hereafter authorised within such period as may be prescribed for paying off such loan by the Act or provisional order or order of any Government Department authorising such loan : But if any part of the Corporation Loans Fund is applied in redemption of stock before the expiration of the period aforesaid then a sum equivalent to interest at the rate of three pounds ten shillings on the stock so redeemed shall thenceforth be annually paid into the said fund out of the funds accounts revenues or rates chargeable with payment of the interest on such stock.

[NOTE.—*Sections 34 and 35 are altered by the Provisional Order of 1890, Art. VI. page 129, so as to apply the provisions of those sections to stock issued for the purposes mentioned in Articles IV. and V. of that Order.*]

36. (1) The Corporation shall from time to time raise the amount of such contributions as aforesaid respectively out of the funds accounts and revenues and by means of the rates out of which the same are respectively payable under this Act in every respect as though such contributions respectively were on account of interest on and for the repayment of moneys raised for the same purposes respectively and charged on such funds accounts revenues and rates respectively by securities granted under the authority of the borough Acts respectively ;

Raising of contributions.

(2) The Corporation shall for the raising of such contributions respectively perform all such acts and exercise all such powers and when necessary collect the same rents and make and levy the same rates respectively as they would have been required to do for the benefit and security of the holders of such securities as aforesaid ;

(3) If in any case any such fund account revenue or rate is wholly or partly insufficient to yield the amount required for any contributions to be provided thereout or by means thereof and the amount required to make up such insufficiency is provided as by this Act prescribed out of the borough fund or borough rate the amount so provided shall be deemed to be a debt due from such fund account revenue or rate to the borough fund in respect of which interest shall be payable at the rate of four pounds per centum per annum until repayment of the same and the amount of such debt together with the interest thereon until repayment thereof

at the rate aforesaid shall as soon as may be and when the Corporation are of opinion that such fund account revenue or rate will be sufficient for such purpose be raised and levied as part of and together with the then next contribution out of such fund account revenue or rate and when so raised the same shall be carried to the credit of the borough fund.

Application of Corporation Loans Fund.

37. (1) The Corporation shall from time to time apply the Corporation Loans Fund first in payment of the interest on Corporation stock and then in purchasing Corporation stock for redemption :

(2) The Corporation shall in the meantime invest so much of such fund as shall remain unapplied and uninvested on the thirty-first day of December in any year and as shall not have been paid into the fund for the purpose of paying interest on the Corporation stock in any securities in which trustees are for the time being authorised to invest trust funds or in any mortgages bonds debentures debenture stock or other securities authorised by Parliament of any municipal Corporation (including the Corporation) or local board and the interest on such investments and the resulting income thereof shall form part of the Corporation Loans Fund and shall be applied and may be invested in the same manner.

Purchase and cancellation of Corporation stock.

38. (1) Where any Corporation stock is created by the Corporation a like amount of Corporation stock shall be purchased by the Corporation for redemption and cancelled in the case of loans under any of the borough Acts within a period of sixty years from the time when the moneys represented by such stock were first borrowed and in the case of any other loans within the period prescribed in that behalf by the Acts or provisional orders authorising the respective loans : Provided that (subject to the discretionary power herein-after conferred on the Local Government Board) the Corporation shall not be bound to purchase any Corporation stock for such purpose unless they can do so at or below par but if the whole or any part of such amount of Corporation stock shall not be redeemed and cancelled within such periods respectively then and in such case the interest from time to time payable on the whole or any part of such amount of Corporation stock remaining unredeemed after such period shall so long as any part of such amount remains unredeemed be paid out of the moneys for the time being forming the Corporation Loans Fund and save in so far as such moneys may be insufficient for such purpose no further moneys shall be carried to the Corporation Loans Fund from the fund account revenue or rate liable to contributions for payment of such interest : Provided further that if at any time after the expiration of such respective periods as aforesaid the Local Government Board are of opinion that the Corporation can without incurring any material loss redeem any Corporation stock remaining unredeemed they may after hearing the Corporation (if desirous of being heard) by order give such directions as they think fit for ensuring the redemption of such stock and any such order shall be enforceable by writ of mandamus to be obtained by the Local Government Board out of the High Court of Justice :

(2) All Corporation stock purchased for redemption shall be cancelled and thereupon all interest in respect thereof shall be extinguished : Provided that in the case of Corporation stock comprised in a stock certificate to bearer all outstanding coupons belonging thereto shall previously have been delivered up to be cancelled.

39. The Corporation may from time to time invest all moneys which may be raised by the issue of Corporation stock and which may not for the time being be required for the purposes of this Act in any securities in which trustees are for the time being authorised to invest trust funds or in any mortgages bonds debentures debenture stock or other securities authorised by Parliament of any municipal Corporation (including the Corporation) or Local Board and shall from time to time carry the interest arising therefrom to the Corporation Loans Fund on account of the sums from time to time required to be carried thereto in respect of such Corporation stock.

Application of moneys raised by Corporation stock and not for the time being required.

40. (1) Any person entitled to any Corporation stock may if default be made for a period of two months after demand in writing in the payment of interest on such stock apply to the Chancery Division of the High Court of Justice in a summary manner by motion or petition without the issue of a writ for the appointment of a receiver and the Chancery Division may if it think fit on such application appoint a receiver on such terms and conditions and with such power as it may think fit ;

Appointment of receiver in certain cases.

(2) Any receiver so appointed shall have the same power of collecting and receiving and recovering and applying all moneys

liable to be carried under this Act to the Corporation Loans Fund and of assessing and raising and recovering all rates for the purpose of obtaining such moneys as the Corporation or any of their officers may have and shall apply all such moneys after payment of expenses and costs under the direction of the Chancery Division for the purposes of and in conformity with this Act ;

(3) The Chancery Division may at any time discharge such receiver and shall have full jurisdiction over such receiver and the applicant and all persons interested in the acts of the receiver in the same manner and to the same extent as if such receiver had been appointed in an action duly instituted therein.

Exemption of purchasers of stock from inquiries into application of moneys &c.

41. A person purchasing any Corporation stock or advancing money to the Corporation on the security of such stock or accepting such stock in lieu of and by way of conversion of any security under this Act shall not be bound to see or inquire whether such stock is created or such advances are required for the purposes of the borough Acts or is or are within the borrowing powers of the Corporation or otherwise in accordance with the provisions of this Act or any regulations made thereunder and shall not be prejudiced by the same not being so and shall not be bound to see to or inquire into the application of the moneys or any part of the moneys arising from such stock or of any such security or advances or be in any way responsible for the non-application or misapplication thereof and shall not be bound to inquire whether the council or any meeting thereof when creating such Corporation stock was properly constituted or convened or that the proceedings at any meeting of the council were legal or regular.

Land disposed of to be freed from charges.

42. Where the Corporation sell or lease or otherwise dispose of to any person any land or property the revenues of which are charged under the provisions of this Act as security for any Corporation stock such lands and property shall in the hands of such person be absolutely freed from every such charge and such person shall not be bound to see to or inquire into the application of the money arising from such sale lease or other disposition or be in any way responsible for the non-application or misapplication thereof.

Corporation may dispose of land

43. Nothing in this Act shall affect any power or duty of the Corporation to sell lease or otherwise dispose of land or any property belonging to them or to apply the moneys arising from such sale lease or disposition in discharge of such liabilities and securities as are a charge on the same in priority to the charge created by this Act or to apply any part of such moneys received by way of fines in the same manner as they might have done if this Act had not been passed or affect the claim of any person under any such prior charge to such moneys or any part thereof.

44. *The treasurer of the borough shall within forty-two days after the thirty-first day of December in each year during which any payment is required to be made into the Corporation Loans Fund under the provisions of this Act transmit to the Local Government Board a return showing:*

(a) The amounts which have been paid into the Corporation Loans Fund during the year in accordance with the provisions of this Act for the purpose of paying the interest on the Corporation stock and towards redeeming such stock respectively ;

(b) The amounts of the contributions so paid in accordance with the provisions of this Act from and out of the several funds accounts revenues and rates charged with payment of the same by this Act :

(c) The amounts which have been so paid in accordance with the provisions of this Act in respect of the sale of any lands and other property on the revenues of which the Corporation stock is charged ;

(d) The amounts which have been carried to the credit of the Corporation Loans Fund during the year in accordance with the provisions of this Act in respect of any premium or sinking fund ;

(e) The amounts which have accumulated during the year on the investments of the Corporation Loans Fund ;

(f) The amounts which have been applied during the year for the purpose of paying the interest on the Corporation stock and towards redeeming such stock respectively ;

(g) The amounts which have been invested during the year and the description of the securities on which any investment has been made ;

(h) The total amount (if any) remaining uninvested at the end of the year :

(i) The total amount of the Corporation stock then remaining unredeemed.

Annual return to Local Government Board.

In the event of any wilful default in making such return the said treasurer shall be liable to a penalty not exceeding twenty pounds If it appears to the Local Government Board by that return or otherwise that the Corporation have made default in complying with any of the provisions of this Act relating to the payments to be made into the Corporation Loans Fund or the application and investment of the same they may after hearing the Corporation if desirous of being heard by order require such default to be made good within a period to be limited by such order and any such order may contain such directions as in the opinion of the Local Government Board may be necessary for giving effect thereto and shall be enforceable by writ of mandamus to be obtained by the Local Government Board out of Her Majesty's High Court of Justice.

[NOTE.—*The words in italics are repealed by the Provisional Order of 1890, Art. VII., page 130, and the Provisional Order of 1895, Art. II., page 135, and the following words enacted in lieu thereof :*

> The Treasurer of the Borough shall, within forty-two days after the Twenty-fifth day of March in each year, transmit to the Local Government Board an abstract (verified by statutory declaration if so required by that Board) of the accounts of the Corporation relating to Corporation Stock and the Loans Fund in a form prescribed by that Board which they shall have power from time to time to alter.]

Saving rights of holders of existing securities.

45. Nothing in this Act shall affect the security or rights of any person who may before the passing of this Act have advanced money to the Corporation or who may for the time being hold any security granted by the Corporation under any of the Borough Acts so long as such person has not been paid the principal and interest due in respect of such advance or security or made an arrangement for the conversion of such security under this Act and the Corporation shall during the same period (whenever so required by the holder of any such security) apply the funds accounts revenues and moneys under their control in such manner and perform all such acts and exercise all such powers and if necessary levy the same rates as they would have been required to do for the benefit and security of such holder if this Act had not passed.

46. All moneys which the Corporation may *under any of the Borough Acts be authorised to borrow at any time after the passing of this Act* may be raised by the Corporation by the creation and issue of Corporation stock and such further stock shall rank pari passu with the stock created and issued under the foregoing provisions of this Act and all the provisions of this Act shall extend and apply to the creation and issue of such further stock and to the security for the same and otherwise in relation thereto and this Act and all deeds securities instruments and documents in which this Act is mentioned or referred to shall be construed accordingly.

Issue of stock in exercise of future borrowing powers under borough Acts.

Where the Corporation issue any stock to raise moneys borrowed with the sanction of the Local Government Board or of any other Government Department given after the passing of this Act the period for redemption of such stock shall notwithstanding any of the foregoing provisions of this Act be the period for which the loan is sanctioned and the provisions of this Act shall as respects the redemption of such stock be read and have effect accordingly.

[NOTE.—*The words in italics are repealed by the Provisional Order of 1890, Art. VIII., page 130, and the following words enacted in lieu thereof :*

For the time being be authorised to borrow, re-borrow, or continue on loan, or, being in the nature of an annuity or rent charge, to redeem or pay off or continue payment of.]

47. Where by any Act or provisional order passed or confirmed after the passing of this Act the Corporation are empowered to borrow any moneys and it is by such Act or order provided that for the purpose of raising or securing the moneys thereby authorised to be borrowed the Corporation may create and issue Corporation stock then and in every such case any further stock created and issued under the authority of such Act or order shall rank pari passu with the stock created and issued under the authority of the foregoing provisions of this Act and all the provisions of this Act shall extend and apply to the creation and issue of such further stock and to the security for the same and otherwise in relation thereto as if such Act or order were mentioned in the first schedule to this Act annexed and were included in the expression " the borough Acts " and this Act and

Issue of stock in exercise of borrowing powers under future Acts.

all deeds securities instruments and documents in which this Act is mentioned or referred to shall be construed accordingly.

Forgery &c. of transfer of stock.

48. For the purposes of the Act of the session of the twenty-fourth and twenty-fifth years of the reign of Her present Majesty chapter ninety-eight "to consolidate and amend the "statute law of England and Ireland relating to indictable "offences by forgery" all Corporation stock shall be deemed to be capital stock of a body corporate and for the purposes of the Forgery Act 1870 the terms stock certificate and coupon in that Act shall be deemed to include a stock receipt and a stock certificate to bearer and a coupon under this Act.

33 & 34 Vic. c. 58.

Expenses of Act.

49. The costs charges and expenses of and incidental to the preparing applying for and obtaining this Act shall be paid by the Corporation out of the borough fund and borough rate or out of moneys borrowed on the security thereof and the Corporation are hereby authorised to borrow such moneys as they may require for that purpose and any moneys so borrowed shall be deemed to be borrowed under the borough Acts.

SCHEDULES referred to in the foregoing Act.

FIRST SCHEDULE.

Setting forth the several Acts and Orders in the foregoing Act referred to collectively as " The Borough Acts."

An Act of the 41st year of the reign of King George the Third chapter 65 " For enlarging and improving the market-place of the town of Kingston-upon-Hull and for making a commodious street from thence to the river Humber with a dock and wharf or landing-place for the ferry and market boats belonging and resorting to the said town."

The Kingston-upon-Hull Improvement Act 1854.

An Act of the 6th and 7th years of the reign of Her Majesty Queen Victoria chapter 73 " For better supplying with water the borough of Kingston-upon-Hull."

An Act of the 35th and 36th years of the reign of Her Majesty Queen Victoria chapter 200 " For making further provision respecting the supply of water to the borough of Kingston-upon-Hull and for other purposes."

The Hull (Corporation) Electric Lighting Act 1880.

The Kingston-upon-Hull Order confirmed by the Local Government Supplemental Act 1863.

The Kingston-upon-Hull Order confirmed by the Local Government Supplemental Act 1865 (No. 5).

The Kingston-upon-Hull Order confirmed by the Local Government Supplemental Act 1871 (No. 2).

The Kingston-upon-Hull Order confirmed by the Local Government Supplemental Act 1871 (No. 4).

The Kingston-upon-Hull Order confirmed by the Local Government Supplemental Act 1872.

The Kingston-upon-Hull Order confirmed by the Local Government Board's Provisional Orders Confirmation (Belper Union &c.) Act 1877.

The Kingston-upon-Hull Order confirmed by the Local Government Board's Provisional Orders Confirmation (Aspull &c.) Act 1879.

The Kingston-upon-Hull Order confirmed by the Local Government Board's Provisional Orders Confirmation (Kingston-upon-Hull &c.) Act 1880.

The Municipal Corporation Acts as defined by the foregoing Act so far as they relate to the borough.

The Acts 9 & 10 Vict. c. 74 and 10 & 11 Vict. c. 61 and the Baths and Washhouses Act 1878 so far as the same relate to the borough.

The Burial Acts 1852 to 1871 and the Acts altering amending or affecting the same for the time being in force so far as the same relate to the borough.

The Lunatic Asylums Act 1853 and the Acts altering amending or affecting the same for the time being in force so far as the same relate to the borough.

The Public Libraries Act 1855 and the Acts altering amending or affecting the same for the time being in force so far as the same relate to the borough.

The Tramways Act 1870 and the Acts altering amending or affecting the same for the time being in force so far as the same relate to the borough.

The Artizans' and Labourers' Dwellings Improvement Act 1875 and the Acts altering amending or affecting the same for the time being in force so far as the same relate to the borough.

The Public Health Act 1875 and the Acts altering amending or affecting the same for the time being in force so far as the same relate to the borough : and

All public Acts passed before the passing of the foregoing Act so far as the same relate to the borough and authorise the borrowing of money by the Corporation and any Acts altering amending or affecting the same for the time being in force.

SECOND SCHEDULE.

Form of Transfer of Corporation Stock.

I A. B. of   in consideration of the sum of
pounds paid to me by C. D. do hereby
transfer to the said C. D. his executors administrators and assigns
the sum of   Hull Corporation stock
standing in my name in the register of such stock and all my right
and interest in and to the same and the interest thereon.

In witness whereof I have hereunto set my hand this
day of   18   .

Name

Address

Signed by the above named A. B. in my presence.

Name

Address

THIRD SCHEDULE.

Schedule of Fees.

On the issue of a stock receipt or of a substituted stock receipt in lieu of a stock receipt lost or destroyed a fee not exceeding two shillings and sixpence.

On the issue of a stock certificate to bearer or of a new stock certificate to bearer in lieu of a stock certificate to bearer lost or destroyed a fee not exceeding five shillings on every hundred pounds of Corporation stock included in the stock certificate to bearer and a proportional sum for any less sum.

If the applicant is the registered holder of an amount of Corporation stock divisible into several sums of twenty-five pounds fifty pounds or multiples of fifty pounds he may subject to the provisions of this Act as to the sums for which stock certificates to bearer may be granted require such sums of twenty-five pounds fifty pounds or such multiples of fifty pounds to be distributed among different stock certificates to bearer as he thinks fit subject to this proviso that if the number of certificates required by him exceed the proportion of five to a thousand pounds he shall in respect of each certificate constituting that excess pay a sum of sixpence in addition to the percentage fee.

On the entry in the register of the Corporation stock included in a stock certificate to bearer there shall be charged a fee not exceeding five shillings.

HULL EXTENSION AND IMPROVEMENT ACT, 1882.
45 AND 46 VICT., CH. CXV.

Royal Assent, 12th July, 1882.

PART I.
PRELIMINARY.

1. This Act may be cited as the Hull Extension and Improvement Act 1882. *Short title of Act.*

2. For the purposes of proceedings preliminary to the municipal elections of 1882 this Act shall take effect on its passing but except for those purposes and except as herein-after otherwise expressly provided this Act shall commence and take effect from and immediately after the thirty-first day of March 1883 (which last-mentioned time is in this Act referred to as the commencement of this Act). *Commencement of Act.*

3. This Act is divided into parts as follows :— *Division of Act into parts.*
Part I.—Preliminary.
Part II.—Extension of Borough.
Part III.—Lands.
Part IV.—Lighting.
Part V.—Lunatic Asylum.
Part VI.—Rating and Borrowing Provisions.
Part VII.—New Road and Streets Improvement.
Part VIII.—Water.
Part IX.—Procedure and Miscellaneous.

4. The Lands Clauses Consolidation Acts 1845 1860 and 1869 (in this Act referred to as the Lands Clauses Acts) so far as the same are applicable for the purposes of and not varied by or inconsistent with this Act are hereby incorporated with this Act. *Incorporation of 8 & 9 Vict. c. 18. 23 & 24 Vict. c. 106. and 32 & 33 Vict. c. 18.*

5. In this Act unless the context otherwise requires— *Interpretation of terms.*

" The existing borough " means the borough and county of the town of Kingston-upon-Hull as existing immediately before the passing of this Act :

" The added part of the borough " means the area added to the existing borough by this Act :

" The borough " used without any qualification or " the extended borough " means the existing borough with the added part of the borough :

"The Corporation" means the mayor aldermen and burgesses of the existing borough or of the extended borough (as the case may require):

"The borough fund" and "the borough rate" and "the district fund" and "general district rate" mean respectively the borough fund borough rate and district fund and general district rate of the borough:

"The town clerk" and "the borough engineer" mean respectively the town clerk and the borough engineer of the borough:

5 & 6 W. 4.
c. 76.
"The Municipal Corporation Acts" means the Municipal Corporation Act 1835 and all Acts for the time being in force amending the same or otherwise relating to municipal corporations in England:

17 & 18 Vict.
c. ci.
"The Improvement Act" means the Kingston-upon-Hull Improvement Act 1854:

"The Public Health Act 1875" includes any Act for the time being in force amending the same:

15 & 16 Vict.
c. 85, &c.
"The Burial Acts" means the Burial Acts 1852 to 1871 and all Acts for the time being in force amending or extending the same:

"The Treasury" means the Lords Commissioners of Her Majesty's Treasury:

"The Education Department" means the Lords of the Committee of Her Majesty's Privy Council on Education:

"The dock company" means the dock company at Kingston-upon-Hull:

The expressions "parish" "lands" "premises" "owner" and "street" have in this Act the meanings respectively assigned to them by the Public Health Act 1875:

"Person" includes a corporation:

Words and expressions to which meanings are assigned by the Acts incorporated herewith have in this Act the same respective meanings provided that the expression "superior court" or "court of competent jurisdiction" or any other like term shall have effect as if the debt or demand with respect to which it is used were a common simple contract debt and not a debt or demand created by statute.

6. (1.) The Improvement Act and the several other Acts Repeal of Acts. and orders which are enumerated in the First Schedule to this Act are hereby repealed as from the commencement of this Act to the extent and with the exceptions set forth in the second column of that schedule specified ;

(2.) Notwithstanding this repeal—

(*a*) All acts and things before the commencement of this Act done or commenced under the powers of any of the said Acts or orders and which were at the commencement of this Act valid or in progress and all awards deeds instruments securities contracts agreements obligations rights and remedies at the commencement of this Act existing under the same shall subject to the provisions of this Act be and continue as valid and for all purposes and for and against all parties and may be continued and completed as if this Act had not been passed.

(*b*) All actions prosecutions arbitrations or other proceedings by with or against the Corporation by reason of any matter or thing done before the commencement of this Act in execution of or in relation to any of the said Acts and orders may be continued commenced or prosecuted by or against the Corporation as if this Act had not been passed.

(*c*) All rates rents tolls and other sums at the passing of this Act due or accruing due to the Corporation may be collected and recovered by the Corporation as if this Act had not been passed.

(*d*) All books and documents which under any of the said Acts or orders or otherwise would have been receivable in evidence shall be receivable in evidence as if this Act had not been passed.

7. This Act shall be carried into execution by the Cor- Act to be executed by council. poration acting by the Council in and for the extended borough and according to the Municipal Corporation Acts and the Acts for the time being affecting the Corporation as a municipal body and as a sanitary authority respectively and with all the rights powers privileges exemptions and authorities conferred by those Acts respectively on the Corporation and on the council and committees of the council and the officers agents and servants of the Corporation with respect to matters provided for or comprised in the Municipal Corporation Acts and the Public Health Act 1875 respectively and as nearly as may be in all respects as if the powers duties exemptions and property vested in imposed on or enjoyed by the Corporation by or under this Act were vested in imposed on or enjoyed by them by or under the Municipal Corporation Acts and the Public Health Act 1875 respectively.

Committees of council.

8. (1) The Corporation may from time to time appoint committees of their members and may delegate to each such committee such of the powers and duties of the Corporation whether as a municipal body or as an urban sanitary authority or otherwise as the council think fit and the acts and proceedings of every such committee within the limits of their delegation shall be deemed the acts and proceedings of the council and the quorum of any committee in this section provided for shall be such as the council direct and the council may from time to time make such regulations as they think fit with respect to the confirmation of the proceedings of a committee and otherwise for the guidance of a committee and the council may from time to time remove any member of a committee and fill any casual vacancy in a committee arising by death resignation removal or otherwise.

(2) A committee may appoint a sub-committee of its members to execute and discharge any of the powers and duties of the committee but the acts of such sub-committee shall unless the council on the appointment of the committee otherwise direct be submitted for approval to the committee by which such sub-committee was appointed Provided that in no case shall a committee be authorised to borrow any money or to make any rate.

PART II.

EXTENSION OF BOROUGH.

(i.) *Extension of Boundaries and of Powers of Corporation &c.*

Extension of boundaries of borough.

9. The boundaries of the existing borough are hereby extended so as to comprise and the borough shall accordingly comprise in addition to the existing borough the district of the Newington Local Board and the said township and parish of

Marfleet so much of the district of the Cottingham Local Board and of the township of Sutton and Stoneferry in the parish of Sutton (all in the east riding of the county of York) as is described in the Second Schedule to this Act.

10. Subject to the provisions of this Act the powers rights privileges authorities and duties of the Corporation acting by the Council as a municipal body and of the Corporation acting by the Council as the sanitary authority for the district of the existing borough and of the Corporation acting in the execution of the Public and Local Acts and provisional orders in force within the existing borough or otherwise and of all officers and servants of the Corporation save as herein-after provided shall extend to and throughout the extended borough. *Authority of Corporation extended.*

11. [Exception as to area within limits of supply of Newington Water Company Limited. 38 & 39 Vict. c. 169.]

[See Water Acts.]

12. The jurisdiction powers authorities rights privileges and duties of the sheriff recorder clerk of the peace and coroner of the existing borough and of the Ancient Court of Record of the existing borough and its officers and of the justices of the peace appointed for the existing borough whether acting in general or quarter sessions or in petty Sessions or out of sessions or otherwise and of the police constables and other peace officers of the existing borough shall extend throughout the extended borough Provided always that nothing in this Act contained shall in any way diminish take away alter or affect the jurisdiction rights power or authority of any coroner acting under lawful authority for the wapentake liberty or hundred of Holderness but such jurisdiction rights power and authority shall continue to be held used and enjoyed as fully and freely in all respects as if this Act had not been passed. *Jurisdiction of the sheriff recorder and other officers extended.*

13. Lands and other property in the added part of the borough shall not be liable to be rated or be rated to any county or hundred rate police highway or sanitary rate made after the commencement of this Act in or for the east riding of the county of York or any part thereof or by or in accordance with the precept of any rural sanitary authority but orders or precepts of county justices or other authorities respecting rates and matters connected therewith made before the commencement of this Act shall be *Extinction of liability to county and other rates and collection of arrears.*

executed in and with respect to the added part of the borough and arrears of rates existing at the commencement of this Act may be collected and recovered therein as if this Act had not been passed and every person committing an offence in the added part of the borough before the commencement of this Act shall be tried adjudicated on and dealt with as if this Act had not been passed.

Added part of borough to be part of county of town of Hull.

14. Subject to the provisions of this Act the added part of the borough shall to and for all intents and purposes be part of the borough and county of the town of Kingston-upon-Hull and all the rights privileges benefits and advantages held used or enjoyed by the burgesses and inhabitants of the existing borough shall be and the same are hereby extended to the burgesses and inhabitants of the extended borough.

Limits of parliamentary borough not affected.

15. Nothing in this Act shall extend limit alter or affect the parliamentary boundaries of the borough of Kingston-upon-Hull.

Vesting property of Corporation.

16. All estates and property of every description vested in the Corporation at the commencement of this Act for the benefit of the existing borough shall vest in the Corporation for the benefit of the extended borough and the Corporation shall hold enjoy and exercise for the benefit of the extended borough all the powers rights and privileges which at the commencement of this Act are vested in the Corporation for the benefit of the existing borough but subject to all debts liabilities and engagements affecting the same.

Officers of Corporation continued.

17. Subject to any re-arrangement of offices and duties in consequence of the passing of this Act the town clerk and all other officers and servants of the Corporation shall continue to be the town clerk officers and servants of the Corporation upon such and the same terms as they now hold their respective offices except such officers and servants as may under this Act be or become entitled to compensation for ceasing to hold their offices provided that in case any officer or servant of the Corporation shall under this Act be or become entitled to compensation for the partial loss of his emoluments then the salary of every such officer or servant shall be liable to such reduction as the Corporation may see fit.

Deposit of borough map.

18. A map of the borough as altered and extended by this Act signed in duplicate by the Chairman of Committees of the House of Lords shall within two weeks after the passing of this

Act be deposited in the Office of the Clerk of the Parliaments and with the town clerk of the borough at his office.

19. Copies of the said map deposited with the town clerk or any extract therefrom certified by him or by the borough engineer to be true shall be received by all courts of justice and elsewhere as primâ facie evidence of the contents of such map and such map shall at all reasonable times be open to inspection on payment of one shilling and any person shall be entitled to a copy of or extract from such map certified by the town clerk or borough engineer on payment of the costs of every such copy or extract All sums received under this section shall be carried to the credit of the borough fund.

Copies of deposited borough map to be evidence.

20. All byelaws orders and regulations made by the Corporation and at the commencement of this Act in force within the existing borough shall extend and apply to the extended borough (subject to any future repeal or amendment of the same) and byelaws orders and regulations made by any local board county justices rural sanitary authority or highway authority shall on the commencement of this Act cease to be in force or to have any effect within the added part of the borough Provided that any person may be tried and punished for any offence against the same committed before the commencement of this Act as if this Act had not been passed. Provided also that no such byelaws orders and regulations made or to be made by the Corporation and relating to water supply shall extend to or be applicable within the area comprised as aforesaid within the limits of supply of the Newington Water Company Limited.

Byelaws &c. to apply to extended borough.

(ii.) *Election of Councillors and Aldermen.*

21. On and from the thirtieth day of October 1882 the extended borough shall be divided into wards not being less than seven or more than fourteen and the number names or distinguishing numbers and boundaries of such wards shall be fixed and determined by order of the Local Government Board made on the report of a commissioner to be for that purpose appointed by the said Board within three weeks after the passing of this Act.

Division of borough into wards.

22. The Newington District as at present defined shall not be divided but shall with any portion of the existing borough of Hull added to it be one of the wards of the extended borough and shall be called "Newington Ward."

Newington district to be named "Newington Ward."

Provisions for existing councillors continuing to represent their former constituents.
23. The commissioner shall include in his report a scheme for allocating all the existing councillors among the new wards described in his report so as to provide (as far as practicable) for each councillor continuing to represent as large a number as possible of his former constituents and such councillors shall be allocated by the order of the Local Government Board accordingly.

Commissioner to report before first of August.
24. The commissioner shall commence and proceed with the duties of his appointment with all practicable despatch and so as to make his report to the Local Government Board before the first day of August one thousand eight hundred and eighty-two or such later day as may on his application be fixed by the said Board. Such report shall be subject to revision by the said Board who shall make such order therein as they think fit.

Order of Local Government Board to be published.
25. The said order shall be published within ten days of the making thereof or on such later day as may be fixed by the said Board in the "London Gazette" and in a local newspaper circulating in the Borough and on and from the thirtieth day of October one thousand eight hundred and eighty-two the names or numbers and boundaries of the wards as set forth in such order shall be the names or numbers and boundaries thereof for all purposes as if they had been specially set forth in this Act and every councillor shall hold his office in the ward to which he may be allocated by such order for the same time as he would have held office if this Act had not been passed.

Constitution and number of the Council.
26. After the division of the borough into wards the council for the borough shall continue to consist (including the mayor) of fourteen aldermen and forty-two councillors and each ward shall return at least three councillors.

As to burgess roll, &c.
27. For the purposes of the burgess list burgess roll and other lists to be made after the passing of this Act under the Municipal Corporation Acts and in relation to the functions and offices of the mayor town clerk and other officers under those Acts the added part of the borough shall be deemed to have always been part of the borough.

General saving for elections of councillors, &c.
28. Subject to the provisions of this Act respecting the division of the borough into wards the allocation of councillors among the new wards and other relative matters the retirement and elections of mayor aldermen and councillors shall take effect and be held in like manner as if this Act had not been passed.

29. Any commissioner appointed under this Act shall have the same power with regard to the examination of witnesses and production of documents as an inspector of the Local Government Board under the Public Health Act 1875 and the costs of any inquiry held by any such commissioner (including the remuneration of such commissioner to be fixed by the said Board) shall be paid by the Corporation.

Powers of commissioner and costs of inquiry.

(iii.) *Provisions respecting Local Boards School Boards and Burial Board.*

30. From and after the commencement of this Act the local board for the district of Newington shall be dissolved but notwithstanding such dissolution the accounts of the local board up to the commencement of this Act shall be audited in like manner as they would have been audited if this Act had not been passed subject to any special directions that may be given in the matter by the Local Government Board.

Dissolution of Newington Local Board.

31. From and after the commencement of this Act all powers jurisdiction and duties which immediately before the commencement of this Act were exercisable by or attached to the Newington Local Board shall wholly cease and all property real and personal of every description (including things in action) which at the commencement of this Act belongs to or is vested in the Newington Local Board shall be transferred to and vested in the Corporation and may be held recovered and enjoyed accordingly.

Cesser of powers and transfer to Corporation of property of Newington Local Board.

32. Subject to the provisions of this Act all deeds contracts documents securities orders notices and proceedings made or entered into with in favour of or by for or on behalf of the Newington Local Board or any person on their behalf and in force at the commencement of this Act shall be and remain as valid and effectual in favour of against and with reference to the Corporation and may be proceeded on and enforced in like manner to all intents and purposes as if the Corporation instead of the said local board had been party or privy thereto.

Saving for deeds securities &c.

33. Any action cause of action prosecution or other proceeding whatsoever commenced or existing either by or against the Newington Local Board before the commencement of this Act shall not abate or be discontinued or prejudicially affected by this Act but on the contrary may be maintained commenced prosecuted or continued by in favour of or against the Corporation in like

Actions &c. not to abate.

manner to all intents and purposes as if the Corporation instead of the said local board were parties to such action prosecution or proceeding.

Rates and debts payable to and by Newington Board to be recoverable by and from Corporation.

34. All rates tolls dues rents and moneys which immediately before the commencement of this Act are due and payable or accruing due and payable to the Newington Local Board shall from and after the commencement of this Act be payable to and may be collected and recovered by the Corporation and all moneys which immediately before the commencement of this Act are due and payable or accruing due and payable by the said local board or which at any time thereafter would but for the passing of this Act have become due and payable under any Act of Parliament or order of the Local Government Board shall from and after the commencement of this Act be paid by and be recoverable from the Corporation.

Books to be evidence.

35. All books and other documents directed or authorised to be kept by the Newington Local Board by any Act of Parliament and which at the passing of this Act would be receivable in evidence shall notwithstanding the dissolution of that board be admitted as evidence in Her Majesty's High Court of Justice and all other courts accordingly.

Cesser of jurisdiction of Cottingham Board and Sculcoates Rural Sanitary Authority over parts of their districts.

36. (1) The Cottingham Local Board and the Sculcoates Rural Sanitary Authority shall respectively cease from and after the commencement of this Act to have or exercise any powers rights or jurisdiction in or in relation to the parts of their respective districts which are by this Act added to the borough   But nothing in this Act shall be construed to prevent the Cottingham Local Board from suing for and recovering any rates or sums of money due to them at or immediately before the commencement of this Act and the said board may accordingly sue for and recover all such rates and sums in the same manner as if this Act had not been passed.

(2) All buildings sewers lamps lamp-posts pipes mains and other property of the said local board and rural sanitary authority situate in the said parts shall from and after the commencement of this Act be transferred to and vest in the Corporation for all the estate and interest therein of the said local board and rural sanitary authority respectively   Provided that the Corporation shall not be at liberty to remove the water pipes in the Saint John's

Wood district of the Cottingham Local Board so as to interfere with the supply of water by the Newington Waterworks Company to the remainder of the Newland Ward.

(3) The Corporation shall pay to the said local board and rural sanitary authority respectively for the property by this section transferred to the Corporation such sum as may be agreed on or as in default of agreement may be determined by the Local Government Board.

37. Notwithstanding any of the foregoing provisions of this Act it shall be lawful for the Corporation on the one hand and for the Cottingham Local Board and the Sculcoates Rural Sanitary Authority or either of them on the other hand at any time after the passing of this Act with the approval of the Local Government Board to make and carry into effect agreements with respect to the transfer of any property liabilities or powers from the said local board and rural sanitary authority respectively to the Corporation and for settling and adjusting any doubt or difference arising in relation thereto and generally with respect to the execution of the provisions of this Act relating to any such agreement and any such agreement may provide for the reference of any matter to the decision of the Local Government Board and the provisions of any such agreement shall be deemed to be within the powers of the Corporation and of the said local board and rural sanitary authority respectively and shall be carried into effect accordingly.

Power of Cottingham Board and Sculcoates Rural Sanitary Authority to enter into agreement with Corporation.

38. The agreement dated the eighteenth day of July 1874 and made between the local board for the district of Newington in the east riding of the county of York of the first part the local board for the district of Cottingham in the same riding of the second part the mayor aldermen and burgesses of the borough of Kingston-upon-Hull acting and being by the town council thereof the local board of health and urban sanitary authority within and for the said borough of the third part and the Local Government Board of the fourth part shall be modified as follows :—

Provision as to outfall sewers.

(1.) The Corporation shall provide within a reasonable time after the commencement of this Act and thereafter maintain pumping engines and other appliances for raising and disposing of the sewage at the outfall mentioned in the said agreement and the Cottingham Local Board shall contribute towards the cost from time to time incurred in the providing maintenance and working of such pumping engines or other appliances and of all buildings required therefor :

(2.) The cost of the said pumping engines appliances and buildings and the proportion thereof to be contributed by the Cottingham Local Board in respect of that portion of their district not added to the borough shall be the subject of agreement between the Corporation and the Cottingham Local Board or in case of a difference shall be settled by the Local Government Board the amount of the contribution by the Cottingham Local Board being determined by the proportion which the rateable value of the remaining portion of their district bears to the rateable value of the rest of the district the sewage of which is dealt with by the said pumping engines appliances and buildings and for the purpose of determining such values the rateable value of lands and property of the nature specified in subsection 1 (*b*) of section 211 of the Public Health Act 1875 in the district of Cottingham shall be taken at one-fourth part only of the full value thereof.

(3.) Instead of contributing one third of the cost of the maintenance of the outfall sewer constructed under the said agreement the Cottingham Local Board shall from and after the commencement of this Act be liable to contribute only the same proportion of such cost as they have to contribute to the cost of the construction and maintenance of the said pumping engines appliances and buildings.

39. The existing sewers or drains of the Cottingham Local Board in that part of the Cottingham Road included within the borough and in the Clough Road shall from and after the passing of this Act be maintained and kept in a proper and sufficient state of repair by and at the expense of the Corporation and notwithstanding anything in this Act the Cottingham Local Board shall at all times after the commencement of this Act have full and free right and liberty to cause the drainage of their district or any part thereof to be discharged into and to use the said sewers or drains but the Corporation shall not be compelled to enlarge or incur extra expenditure on the said sewers or drains by reason of this provision.

As to use and maintenance of outfall and other sewers.

40. The Corporation shall as from the commencement of this Act undertake and become liable for the following loans of the Cottingham Local Board and shall indemnify the Cottingham

Liability of Corporation to debts of Cottingham Local Board.

Local Board in respect thereof namely : The balance unpaid at the commencement of this Act of the sum of eight thousand two hundred pounds borrowed in 1875 from the Public Works Loan Commissioners for the purpose of providing street improvements in Saint John's Wood Newland and of the sum of one thousand five hundred pounds borrowed in 1871 from the Public Works Loan Commissioners for the purpose of water supply   Also such proportion of the part of the balance remaining unpaid at the commencement of this Act charged in the accounts of the Cottingham Local Board against the Newland Ward of the sum of seventeen thousand pounds borrowed in 1876 from the Public Works Loan Commissioners for works of main drainage in the Cottingham Local Board District and such proportion of the part of the balance then remaining unpaid charged to the Newland Ward as aforesaid of the sum of four thousand four hundred pounds borrowed from the said Public Works Loan Commissioners in 1875 for the purpose of works of outfall drainage as shall be agreed between the Corporation and the said Cottingham Local Board or in case of dispute shall be settled by the Local Government Board who in adjusting such dispute shall settle the same on the basis that the said balances shall be paid in such proportions as the rateable value of the portion of Newland Ward taken by the Corporation bears to the remainder of the ward land and property of the nature specified in sub-section 1 (*b*) of section 211 of the Public Health Act 1875 in the district of Cottingham being taken at one-fourth of its rateable value   Provided that the Cottingham Local Board shall pay all instalments on the said loans payable up to the commencement of this Act   Provided also that nothing herein contained shall affect the liability of the Cottingham Local Board to the Public Works Loan Commissioners or the securities given by the local board for such loans.

41. Nothing in this Act contained shall lessen prejudice or affect the right of the Cottingham Local Board to the free and unobstructed use of the public landing place on the River Hull at Stoneferry as heretofore enjoyed by them or lessen prejudice or affect their rights and interests in the ferry over the said river at Stoneferry.

Saving certain rights of the Cottingham Local Board.

Saving for
Cottingham
Board
Sculcoates
Rural
Sanitary
Authority and
Sutton School
Board.

42. Subject to the provisions of this Act and of any agreement made in pursuance thereof the powers rights jurisdictions property and liabilities of the Cottingham Local Board the Sculcoates Rural Sanitary Authority and the Sutton School Board are not impaired altered or affected by the passing of this Act.

Borough to be
a school
district.
33 & 34 Vict.
c. 75.

43. (1) For the purposes of the Elementary Education Act 1870 and the Acts amending the same the extended borough shall be a school district and the school board for the existing borough shall be the school board for that district to the exclusion of any other school authority.

(2) The members of the school board for the existing borough who are in office at the commencement of this Act shall constitute the school board for the school district of the extended borough and shall be deemed to have been elected therefor and shall hold office subject to the provisions of the said Acts and of this Act and of any order for holding a new election or otherwise which may be made by the Education Department.

As to bye-
laws of school
board.

44. From and after the commencement of this Act all byelaws and regulations made by the school board of the existing borough and then in force shall apply to and be in force within the extended borough (subject to any future repeal or amendment of the same) and all byelaws and regulations made by any other school authority shall cease to be of any force or effect in the added part of the borough.

Dissolution of
school board
of Newington.

45. From and after the commencement of this Act the school board for the school district of Newington shall be dissolved and the buildings fittings books and other property of such board shall be transferred to and vest in the school board for the extended borough and all the debts liabilities contracts and engagements of the said school board existing at the commencement of this Act shall be transferred to and be discharged satisfied and performed by the school board for the extended borough.

Transfer of
jurisdiction
of Cottingham
and of Sutton
and
Stoneferry
School Boards
over parts of
their districts
added to the
borough, &c.

46. From and after the commencement of this Act all powers and jurisdiction of the school boards for the school districts of Cottingham and of Sutton and Stoneferry shall cease as respects so much of their respective districts as is by this Act added to the existing borough and all buildings with their fittings belonging to any of those school boards and situate within the parts added as aforesaid shall be transferred to and vest in the school board for the extended borough for all the estate and interest of the said boards respectively and so much of the debt of the school board for the school district of Cottingham as is at the commencement of this Act owing in respect of the erection of the Londesborough Street Board School and is also charged upon the school fund and local rate of the said school district of Cottingham and so much of the debt of the school board for the school district of Sutton and Stoneferry as is at the commencement of this Act owing in respect of the erection of the Stoneferry Infants Board School and is also charged upon the school fund and local rate of the said school district of Sutton and Stoneferry shall be discharged and satisfied by the school board for the extended borough.

Any doubt or difference arising under this section shall on the application of either of the school boards interested stand referred to and be determined by the Education Department.

47. As soon as practicable after the commencement of this Act the Education Department shall issue an order for the election of fifteen persons to serve as members of the school board of the extended borough in the place of the persons who at the time of making such order shall be members of the said school board under the provisions of this Act.

Order for election of new school board.

48. The Corporation may from time to time if they see fit sell or lease and dispose of any buildings or other property transferred to them by or under this part of this Act and they shall apply the proceeds of any sale towards paying off any debt of the local board or other body to which the property belonged unless the amount realised is less than one hundred pounds in which case the proceeds of the sale shall be carried to the borough fund.

Power to sell property transferred to Corporation.

49. (1) The Corporation shall pay compensation to any clerk or officer to or of any county justices local board or school board who by reason of the dissolution of such board or of any other provision of this Act loses his office or is deprived of the whole or part of the emoluments of his office within two years after the commencement of this Act and does not receive remuneration to an equal amount in respect of some office or employment under the Corporation or school board for the extended borough and also to any officer of the Corporation who may cease to hold his office or who may lose any part of the

Compensation to officers for loss of emoluments.

emoluments of his office in consequence of the passing of this Act:

(2) Such compensation may be by way of annuity or otherwise and the amount thereof shall be determined subject to the following conditions:

(3) That such officer or other person shall have been in the actual employment of such body or person for a continuous period of not less than two years previous to the first day of November one thousand eight hundred and eighty-two;

(4) That the amount of such compensation shall be such as would be payable on retirement to such officer or other person under section two of the Superannuation Act, 1859, in the event of his having served in an established capacity in the permanent civil service of the State for the same time as in the service of such body or person and as if ten years were added to the number of years he may have actually served;

22 Vict. c. 26.

(5) That in estimating such compensation the amount of the salary and fees upon which the same shall be calculated shall be taken on the average of the salary and fees actually received during the two years next preceding such first day of November one thousand eight hundred and eighty-two by such officer or other person as and for his own use after deducting therefrom any payments or allowances usually made by him;

(6) That no such compensation shall exceed two-thirds of the salary and fees upon which the same shall be estimated;

(7) Every such compensation shall be payable by two equal half-yearly payments the first of such payments to be made at the expiration of six months from the date when such officer or other person shall by reason of the passing of this Act cease to receive such salary or fees.

(8) Provided always that the Corporation may at any time agree with any officer or other person entitled to any annuity under this enactment for the commutation of such annuity and may pay the same out of the same fund and rate or rates as such annuity is payable or any moneys borrowed on the security thereof.

(9) Provided always that in case the Corporation shall within six months after the commencement of this Act tender to any such officer or person any office or employment of equal or greater value

entailing the same or similar duties to the office or employment in respect of which he derived the salary and fees in respect of the loss of which compensation is by this Act payable to him and such officer or person accepts such office or employment or declines within one month after such tender to accept such office or employment or neglects to execute the duties thereof satisfactorily (being in a competent state of health) he shall forfeit his right to any compensation under this Act.

50. Where any land in the Newington District as at present defined has been or shall hereafter be excavated for obtaining brick-earth or for any other purpose no dwelling-house shall be erected on any part of such excavated land until the excavation has been re-filled with proper material to within two feet of the original level and the surface covered with a layer of concrete of four inches in thickness at the least.

Not to erect buildings on excavated land until properly filled up.

51. If the Corporation at any time make assess and levy any general district rate or any highway or other rate under the Improvement Act or any other Act enabling them in that behalf the owners and occupiers of such property in the added part of the borough as is mentioned in sub-section (*b*) of section 211 of the Public Health Act 1875 shall be entitled to such exemption in respect of that property as is by that sub-section granted in the case of the general district rate leviable under that Act.

Exemptions under section 211 of Public Health Act to apply to property in added part of borough.

52. The Corporation shall be the burial board for the extended borough and shall have and may exercise within the extended borough to the exclusion of any other burial board or authority all the powers rights and privileges and be subject to all the liabilities of a burial board beyond the Metropolis under the Burial Acts as defined by this Act.

Corporation to be burial board.

53. Nothing in this Act contained shall be deemed or construed to impose any liability on the owners or occupiers of premises adjoining the turnpike or high roads from Kingston-upon-Hull to Beverley from the River Hull to Newland and from thence to Cottingham within the borough to flag or form any causeway footway or sideway abutting on any of the said turnpike or high roads respectively.

Protection of owners of property adjoining highways.

PART III.

LANDS.

Power to appropriate lands for purposes of Act.

54. Subject to the provisions of this Act the Corporation may from time to time appropriate and use for any of the purposes of this Act any lands for the time being vested in them as part of their corporate estates or in their capacity of a sanitary authority and which are not required for the purposes for which the same were acquired or are at present generally applied.

Corporation may acquire easements only.

55. Instead of purchasing the lands required for purposes of this Act the Corporation may if they think fit by agreement purchase only such easements as they may require for those purposes and any easement so acquired shall be land within the meaning of the Lands Clauses Acts.

Persons empowered by Lands Clauses Acts to sell lands may grant easements.

56. Persons empowered by the Lands Clauses Consolidation Act 1845 to sell and convey or release land may if they think fit subject to the provisions of that Act and of the Lands Clauses Consolidation Acts 1860 and 1869 and of this Act grant to the Corporation any easement right or privilege (not being an easement of water) required for the purposes of this Act in over or affecting any such lands and the provisions of the said Acts with respect to lands and rentcharges so far as the same are applicable in this behalf shall extend and apply to such grants and to such easements rights and privileges as aforesaid respectively.

Power to sell lands.

57. The Corporation may with the consent of the Treasury after due notice in accordance with the Municipal Corporation Acts sell any lands belonging to them and not required for the purpose for which the same were acquired   The Corporation may also if they think fit with such consent as aforesaid sell land for building purposes and also houses and buildings subject to an annual rent or perpetual charge to be fixed by the Corporation.

Corporation may lease lands not required for purposes of Act.

58. The Corporation from time to time if and when they think fit may lay out for building purposes all or any part of any lands acquired by them under any former Act or under this Act and not required for the purposes of this Act and may from time to time demise or grant on building or other leases with or without fine for any term not exceeding ninety-nine years all or any part of such lands to such persons and subject to such reservations covenants terms and conditions as the Corporation think fit and the Corporation may make any such lease by public auction or tender or by private contract and with or without any special conditions and stipulations and may accept a surrender of any lease and either before or after a lease is granted may in like manner sell and dispose of any rent reserved or agreed to be reserved for any such lands and may execute and do all deeds and things necessary to effect the several purposes aforesaid.

59. Any purchase money received on any sale of land and any money received as a fine on the granting of any lease by the Corporation shall be distinguished as capital in the accounts of the Corporation and shall be applied exclusively for purposes for which money borrowed by the Corporation is for the time being applicable or in discharge of borrowed moneys and any money so discharged shall not be re-borrowed.

Application of purchase money of land.

PART IV.

LIGHTING.

60. [Extension of electric lighting powers.]

61. [Provision for the protection of the Postmaster General.]

[Superseded. See Electric Lighting Acts.]

PART V.

LUNATIC ASYLUM.

62. (1) The council of the borough may at any time within six months after the first day of September one thousand eight hundred and eighty-three give notice by writing under their common seal to one of Her Majesty's Principal Secretaries of State of the intention of the council to take on themselves the duties powers and authorities imposed or conferred on or given to the justices of the borough by the Lunatic Asylums Act 1853 and the Acts amending the same and from and after the giving of such notice the council shall be subject to and have and exercise all the duties powers and authorities of the said justices and of any committee of visitors appointed by them under the said Acts and

Power of Corporation to undertake duties of visiting justices.

all liabilities and contracts incurred or entered into by the said justices or committee shall thereupon become transferred to and obligatory on such council to the same extent as they would have been binding or obligatory on such justices or committee and all matters and things which by the said Acts are required to be done at any meeting of such justices shall be done at any meeting of the council and all notices which by the said Acts are required to be given to or by the clerk of the peace shall thenceforth be given to or by the town clerk.

(2) If the Corporation elect within the time above mentioned to undertake the duties of the justices as above provided the new asylum at or near Willerby shall thereupon vest in and become the property of the Corporation.

(3) When the new asylum at Willerby shall be completed and occupied the old asylum within the borough and the lands adjacent thereto shall vest in and become the property of the Corporation and shall be sold by them in one or more lots or otherwise disposed of and the net proceeds of such sale or disposal shall be carried to the borough fund.

Committee appointed by council to have same powers as committee of visitors.

63. The council may from time to time confer on any committee appointed by them such of the powers and authorities which by the Lunatic Asylums Act 1853 and the Acts amending the same are conferred on any committee of visitors appointed thereunder as the council may see fit.

PART VI.
RATING AND BORROWING PROVISIONS.

Expenses of executing Act

64. All expenses incurred by the Corporation in carrying into execution the provisions of this Act except such of those expenses as are payable out of borrowed moneys or out of the borough fund and borough rate under any general Act of Parliament or this Act and except so far as any such expenses may be defrayed out of revenue derived from the water undertaking of the Corporation or from any other property of the Corporation or be recovered from the owners or occupiers of premises or other persons shall be paid out of the district fund and general district rate leviable under the Public Health Act 1875.

65. (1) The Corporation may make any rate which they are for the time being authorised to make either prospectively in order to raise money to pay charges and expenses to be incurred after the making of the rate or retrospectively in order to raise money to pay charges and expenses incurred at any time within six months before the making of the rate or partly prospectively and partly retrospectively ; *Making and assessment of rates and power to rate owner in certain cases.*

(2) The Corporation may include in one rate book the assessments of all or any of the rates and water rents which they are authorised to levy ;

(3) In the case of all rates leviable by the Corporation the owner instead of the occupier may at the option of the Corporation be rated in cases where he might be rated under section two hundred and eleven subsection one of the Public Health Act 1875.

66. [Exception of an area so far as regards rates in connection with water.]

[See Water Acts.]

67. As regards all rates which after the commencement of this Act are made and levied by the Corporation the North-eastern Railway Company shall in respect of their railways in the added part of the borough be assessed thereto in the proportion of one-fourth part only of the net annual value thereof and as regards all rates which after the commencement of this Act are made and levied by the Corporation the dock company shall in respect of their docks in the added part of the borough be assessed thereto in the proportion of one-fourth part only of the net annual value thereof. *As to rating of railway and dock properties in the added part of the borough.*

68. All borough general district burial cemetery library and other rates which the Corporation are entitled to levy and raise under this Act or any other Act shall be recoverable and the payment thereof may be enforced in like manner as if they were poor rates and with the like right of appeal. *Recovery of rates.*

69. No lands or other property within the added part of the borough shall be reassessed and the existing assessment in the added part of the borough shall remain in force until a general reassessment of the whole borough as extended shall be made. *Present assessment of added area not to be altered until the extended borough is reassessed.*

70. (1) The Corporation may from time to time borrow for the purposes of the new road and streets improvement authorised by this Act any sums not exceeding eighteen thousand pounds *Power to borrow and create Corporation stock for purposes of Act.*

and for waterworks purposes any sums not exceeding twenty thousand pounds but moneys borrowed under this enactment shall be applied only to purposes to which capital is properly applicable;

(2) For the purpose of raising or securing all or any of the moneys authorised to be borrowed for the above purposes or for defraying the costs charges and expenses of obtaining this Act the Corporation may from time to time create and issue Hull Corporation Stock under the Hull Corporation Loans Act 1881 ;

(3) For the purposes of section thirty-five of the said Corporation Loans Act the period prescribed for paying off moneys borrowed by the Corporation for purposes of this Act shall be sixty years from the time or respective times when the same are first respectively borrowed ;

(4) The contributions to the sums directed by the said Corporation Loans Act to be carried to the Corporation Loans Fund in respect of interest on and of redemption of stock shall be payable in the case of stock created and issued under this section for the purposes of the water undertaking of the Corporation out of the revenue of the water undertaking for the time being of the Corporation and in the case of stock created and issued under this section for any other purpose of this Act out of the district fund and general district rate.

Power to create Corporation stock for discharge of debts transferred to Corporation.

71. The Corporation may from time to time borrow such moneys as they from time to time require for effecting the discharge of any outstanding loans or portion of any outstanding loan which by or under the provisions of this Act are transferred to the Corporation from the Newington Local Board or the Cottingham Local Board or the Sculcoates Rural Sanitary Authority and may raise or secure any such moneys by the creation and issue of Hull Corporation Stock under the Hull Corporation Loans Act 1881 subject to the provisions following (that is to say) :

(i) The contributions to the sums directed by the said Corporation Loans Act to be carried to the Corporation Loans Fund in respect of interest on and of redemption of stock shall in the case of stock created and issued under this section be payable out of the district fund and general district rate ;

(ii) For the purposes of section thirty-five of the said Corporation Loans Act the amount of contributions in respect of redemption of such stock shall be such as to provide for its redemption within a period of thirty years from the time or respective times when the moneys represented by such stock were first respectively borrowed ;

(iii) In the case of any loan contracted by either of the said local boards for works of private improvement of any premises the Corporation shall recoup to the district fund and general district rate the amount of contributions paid in respect of that loan to the Corporation Loans Fund as aforesaid and shall for that purpose from time to time make and levy on the owners or occupiers of such premises such rate or rates as but for the passing of this Act would have been in respect of that loan leviable by the said local boards or either of them.

72. (1) The Corporation are hereby authorised from time to time to borrow and raise by the creation and issue of Hull Corporation Stock under the Hull Corporation Loans Act 1881 all or any of the sums not exceeding one hundred thousand pounds which they are under the Hull Barnsley and West Riding Junction Railway and Dock Act 1880 empowered to subscribe and contribute towards the undertaking of the Hull Barnsley and West Riding Junction Railway and Dock Company ;

Power to raise by issue of Corporation stock sums authorised to be borrowed under 43 and 44 Vict. c. cxcix.

(2) For the purposes of section thirty-five of the said Corporation Loans Act the period prescribed for paying off any moneys borrowed and raised by the creation and issue of Corporation stock under this section shall be one hundred years from the time or respective times when the same were respectively borrowed ;

(3) The contributions to the sums directed by the said Corporation Loans Act to be carried to the Corporation Loans Fund in respect of interest on and of redemption of stock shall in the case of stock created and issued under this section be payable out of the district fund and general district rate.

PART VII.

NEW ROAD AND STREETS IMPROVEMENT.

73. The Corporation are hereby authorised in the lines and on the lands in that behalf delineated and described in the

Power to make new road from Trinity Street to Lunatic Asylum Grounds, to widen and improve Carr Lane, &c.

deposited plans and book of reference and according to the levels shown on the deposited sections to execute the following works (that is to say):—

1. A new road or approach from Trinity Street to the borough lunatic asylum grounds commencing on the south side of Trinity Street opposite to Derringham Street and terminating at the northern side of such grounds all in the parish of Holy Trinity within the borough ;

2. A widening and improvement of Carr Lane on the south side thereof from No. 4 Ocean Place in the occupation of William Hickling to No. 26 Ocean Place in the occupation of Thomas Hunter and William Thompson all in the parish of Holy Trinity aforesaid.

And for those purposes may enter upon take and use such of the lands delineated on the said deposited plans and described in the deposited book of reference to such plans as shall be necessary for such purposes and for the purpose of the completion of a new road leading from Church Street to Fountain Road in the parish of Sculcoates and for the completion of King Street improvement in the parish of Holy Trinity may enter upon take and use the lands delineated on the deposited plans and described in the deposited book of reference to such plans that is to say :—

A piece or parcel of land and building used now or lately used as an oil refinery situate on the northern side of Egginton Lane and bounded on the west by land belonging or reputed to belong to the charity trustees and on the north and east by land belonging or reputed to belong to Messieurs Grotrian and Hearfield ;

Two dwelling-houses with offices cellars and other premises belonging to Thomas Keyworth and in the occupation of the said Thomas Keyworth or of Thomas Keyworth and Company and situate at the street-crossing between King Street and Trinity House Lane and Postern Gate and North Church Side.

Limits of deviation.

74. In executing the said works the Corporation may deviate vertically to any extent not exceeding five feet from the levels defined on the deposited sections and may deviate laterally to any extent within the limits of deviation defined on the deposited plans.

75. And whereas in the execution of the said improvement of Carr Lane it may happen that portions only of certain of the lands and buildings shown on the deposited plans may be sufficient for the purposes of the same and that such portions may be severed from the remainder of the said properties without material detriment thereto Therefore notwithstanding section ninety-two of the Lands Clauses Consolidation Act 1845 the owners of and persons interested in the lands and buildings described in the Third Schedule to this Act and whereof parts only are required for the purposes of this Act may (if such portions can in the judgment of the jury arbitrators or other authority assessing or determining the compensation under that Act be severed from such properties without material detriment thereto) be required to sell and convey to the Corporation the portions only of the premises so required without the Corporation being obliged or compellable to purchase the whole or any greater portion thereof the Corporation paying for the portions required by them and making compensation for any damage sustained by the owners thereof or other parties interested therein by severance or otherwise.

Owners may be required to sell parts only of certain lands and buildings.

76. The provisions of any Act or Acts or of any byelaws from time to time in force in the borough shall not except as regards any building used or occupied exclusively as a dwelling-house apply to any building erected or about to be erected or altered and used or intended to be used by the North-eastern Railway Company for the purposes of their business as a railway company Provided that no building shall be erected by the railway company beyond the frontage line of buildings in any street except gatekeepers lodges and signal boxes or signal cabins for the protection of the railway traffic and the public safety.

Byelaws and provisions as to erection of buildings not to apply to railway buildings.

PART VIII.

Water.

[See Water Acts.]

PART IX.

PROCEDURE AND MISCELLANEOUS.

(i.) *General Provisions as to Procedure.*

Prosecution and recovery of offences and penalties.

88. All offences penalties forfeitures damages costs and expenses by this Act or any Act incorporated herewith or any byelaw thereunder authorised or directed to be prosecuted or recovered summarily or before any justices or justice or the prosecution or recovery of which is not otherwise expressly provided for may be prosecuted and recovered in manner provided by the Summary Jurisdiction Acts and all penalties recovered summarily by the Corporation within the borough under this Act or any Act incorporated herewith or any byelaw thereunder shall be paid to the Corporation and carried to the borough fund.

Appeal to quarter sessions.

89. Any person who deems himself aggrieved by any rate made under the provisions of this Act or by any order conviction judgment or determination of or by any matter or thing done by any court of summary jurisdiction or by the Corporation under the powers of this Act may appeal to the borough court of quarter sessions.

Restriction on informations.

90. No information shall be laid for the recovery of any penalty under this Act except by the party aggrieved or by the authority of the Corporation.

Proceedings not to be quashed for want of form.

91. No order verdict rate assessment judgment conviction or other proceeding touching or concerning any offence against this Act or against any rule order or byelaw made by authority thereof shall be quashed or vacated for want of form only.

Proceedings against several persons for the same offence.

92. In the case of any joint act or default by several persons contravening the provisions of this or of any other Act or of any byelaw in force within the borough the Corporation may if they think fit include all or any of those persons in one information or complaint and a justice may if he thinks fit include all or any of them in one summons and any conviction judgment or order made in such a case may include all or any one or more of the persons included in the summons and the costs may be distributed as to the court appears fair.

Judges not disqualified.

93. A judge of any court or a justice shall not be disqualified from acting in the execution of this Act by reason of his being a member of the Corporation or liable to any rate or other charge under this Act or being interested in any contract under this Act for a supply of water or means of lighting.

94. If any person against whom the Corporation have any claim or demand become bankrupt or enter into any arrangement for the liquidation of his affairs or composition with creditors it shall be lawful for the town clerk in all proceedings against or in the matter of the estate of such bankrupt or insolvent to represent the Corporation and act in their behalf in proving the debt and in all other respects as if such claim or demand had been the claim or demand of the town clerk and not of the Corporation.

Proofs of debts in bankruptcy.

95. Any constable or other officer of the Corporation and such person or persons as he may call to his assistance may without any warrant or other authority than this Act seize or detain any person being unknown to such constable or other officer who shall be found committing any offence against this Act and take him as soon as conveniently may be before the nearest justice of the peace for the borough.

For securing transient offenders.

96. Whenever any expenses are payable to the Corporation by the owner of any buildings or lands in respect thereof and such buildings or lands are in lease such expenses may be apportioned between the lessees and the reversioners of such lands in such proportions as the Corporation may deem equitable provided that nothing in this section shall alter the liabilities respecting the payment of expenses as between owner and lessee under any special contract relative thereto.

Apportionment where lands are leased.

97. The Corporation from time to time may direct any prosecution for any public nuisance whatsoever created permitted or suffered in the borough and may order proceedings to be taken for the recovery of any penalties and for the punishment of any persons offending against any of the provisions of this Act or of any Act incorporated herewith or of any bye-law in force in the borough and may defray the expenses of such prosecution or other proceedings as part of their general expenditure in the execution of this Act.

Corporation may order prosecutions and expenses thereof.

(ii.) *Notices.*

98. (1) Any instrument (including a notice order resolution requisition declaration requisition consent approval disapproval demand or other document) made given delivered or served by the Corporation under this or any other Act or any byelaw may be

Form and service of notices by Corporation.

either in print or in writing (including lithograph) or partly in print and partly in writing (including lithograph) and shall be sufficiently authenticated by the name of the town clerk or of the Surveyor or other proper officer (according to the subject of the particular instrument) being affixed thereto in print or writing or by a stamp on behalf of the Corporation ;

(2) Subject to any express provision of this or of any other Act it shall be sufficient where any such instrument is required to be given to or served on the owner or occupier of any premises to address it to such owner or occupier by his description as owner or occupier (as the case may be) of the premises (naming them) in respect of which it is given or served without further name or description and any such instrument may be addressed to owners or occupiers of any adjoining or neighbouring premises collectively and when so addressed may be served on more owners or occupiers than one so that separate copies be served on the respective owners and occupiers of the premises concerned ;

(3) Any such instrument may be served on any such owner occupier or other person either personally or by sending the same through the post in a registered letter addressed to him by name at his last known place of abode or business or by delivering the same to some inmate at his last known or usual place of abode or business or in case of an occupier to any inmate of the premises in respect of which it is given or served or if the premises are un-occupied and the place of abode of the person to be served is after diligent inquiry unknown it shall be sufficient to affix it or a copy thereof upon some conspicuous part of such premises.

(4) Service by a registered letter under this section shall be deemed to be effected on the day on which such letter would be delivered in the ordinary course of post.

(iii.) *Byelaws, &c.*

Provisions as
to byelaws
of the
Corporation. **99.** All byelaws authorised by this Act or by any other Act and at any time in force within the borough may be altered or re-pealed from time to time by the Corporation.

Sections one hundred and eighty-two to one hundred and eighty-six (both inclusive) of the Public Health Act 1875 (except so much of section one hundred and eighty-five as applies ex-clusively to byelaws made by a rural authority) shall apply to the alteration and repeal of any existing byelaws and to the making alteration and repeal of the byelaws made by the Corporation under this Act or any Act incorporated with this Act (except byelaws required by this Act to be confirmed by the Board of Trade) as if they were byelaws made by a local authority under that Act.

100. The Corporation may from time to time make alter and repeal byelaws for all or any of the following purposes—

Byelaws as to corn and other meters and weighers

For licensing corn and other meters and weighers (that is to say persons measuring and weighing or supervising the measuring and weighing of cargoes of vessels on their discharge); and

For charging any fee not exceeding five shillings for any such license for twelve months and in the like proportion for any shorter period; and

For imposing penalties on persons acting as corn or other meters and weighers without being licensed.

All moneys received from corn and other meters under this section shall be paid over at such time and times in every year as the Corporation direct to the borough treasurer and be carried to the credit of the district fund;

Such byelaws shall not extend or apply to or in relation to any person appointed or employed as a meter or weigher by or in or upon the property of the dock company or by or in or upon the property of the undertakers of the navigation of the rivers Aire and Calder.

The making alteration and repeal of such byelaws shall be subject to confirmation by the Board of Trade.

101. Any license granted by the Corporation either before or after the passing of this Act may be revoked by the Corporation on the conviction summarily or otherwise for any offence of the grantee of the license.

Power to revoke licenses.

(iv.) *Private Improvement Expenses.*

102. The expression " private improvement expenses " means and includes all private improvement expenses expressly declared to be such by or under the Public Health Act 1875 or this Act or any byelaw made in pursuance of either of those Acts (whether incurred before or after the passing of this Act) also all other expenses at any time incurred by the Corporation for the repayment whereof the owner of the building or lands in respect whereof such expenses may have been or may be incurred is liable

What to be deemed private improvement expenses.

under any enactment or byelaw or under any agreement with or by reason of any application of such owner.

Apportion-
ment of
private
improvement
expenses.

103. (1) Where any private improvement expenses are recoverable by the Corporation from owners or occupiers of premises under the Public Health Act 1875 or this Act in respect of works executed by the Corporation in any street the Corporation may apportion such expenses among such owners or occupiers as the Corporation having regard to all the circumstances of the case and not merely to frontage may deem most just;

(2) The North-eastern Railway Company shall not be liable in respect of any of their premises fronting adjoining or abutting on any street within the extended borough to sewer level pave metal flag channel or make good such street or to pay any part of the expenses of the execution of such works in cases where such premises shall be used by such company solely as a part of their actual line of railway and shall have no communication with such street. Provided nevertheless that nothing in this section shall affect the liability of the said company to contribute towards the expenses of the repair of any such street where such expenses are chargeable on and payable out of the general district rates.

(3) A person aggrieved by a decision of the Corporation under this section may appeal within twenty-one days after notice in writing of such decision to the police magistrate who may summon all parties interested to appear before him and may make an order confirming or varying the apportionment in whole or in part and with or without costs to any party as may appear to him just.

Recovery of
expenses.

104. All private improvement expenses and all other expenses by this Act or any byelaw thereunder made payable by or recoverable from the owner or occupier of any building or lands or from any other person shall if not paid on demand be recoverable by the Corporation with interest thereon from the expiration of one month after such demand at the rate to be determined by the Corporation not exceeding five pounds per centum per annum in addition to any other mode of recovery which the Corporation may possess either as a debt from such owner or occupier or other person (as the case may be) in any court of competent jurisdiction or by distress and sale of the goods and chattels of such owner or occupier or other person (as the case may be) and any justice may issue his warrant accordingly.

105. Summary or other proceedings for the recovery of any amount or instalment of any private improvement expenses or other expenses recoverable by the Corporation may be commenced at any time within twelve months from the date of service of a demand for payment of the same. *Limit of time for recovery of expenses by Corporation extended.*

106. When any private improvement expenses are recoverable from the owners or occupiers of buildings or lands the Corporation may by resolution allow to the owners or occupiers or any of them time for repayment thereof or of any part thereof and may order the same or any part thereof to be paid either in one sum or by such instalments as the Corporation think fit with interest for the principal money from time to time remaining unpaid after such rate as the Corporation determine but all sums so remaining due notwithstanding that the Corporation agree so to allow time shall from time to time at the expiration of the several times allowed be recoverable from the respective owners and occupiers for the time being both present and future in succession one after another as the same would have been recoverable from the original owner or occupier if no such time had been allowed and with respect to any such instalment the time limited by this Act or otherwise for the recovery of expenses shall be deemed to run only from the time when such instalment becomes due but the Corporation shall not in any case allow under this section a term exceeding twenty years for the payment of any expenses or of any part thereof. *Power to allow time for repayment of expenses.*

107. All private improvement expenses and other expenses by this Act or any byelaw thereunder made payable by or recoverable from the owner of any building or lands with such interest thereon as by this Act or any such byelaw is provided for shall be a charge on such building or lands in priority to any incumbrance or charge on or affecting the same and created subsequently to the time when the works are commenced. *Expenses to be a charge on premises.*

108. Where any premises are in the possession of any mortgagee or other person having in his own right any charge or incumbrance thereon such mortgagee or other person shall have and exercise the same powers and remedies for the recovery of any moneys paid by him in accordance with the provisions of this Act in respect of such premises for forming constructing sewering levelling paving flagging and channelling or otherwise completing *Recovery by mortgagees in possession of moneys paid by them.*

any street or footway as he has and may exercise for the recovery of the principal money secured by such mortgage or the interest thereof.

Saving for special contracts as to expenses of works.

109. Nothing in this Act shall alter the liabilities as between owner and occupier respecting the payment of any private improvement expenses or other expenses made payable or recoverable by this Act or any byelaw thereunder of any owner or occupier under any special contract relative thereto made before or after the commencement of the Act.

Persons having partial interests may raise expenses by mortgage.

110. All owners of buildings or lands being tenants for life only and all committees of the estates of lunatics and all trustees seized possessed of or entitled to any estate or interest in any buildings or lands for or on behalf of any person or charity may charge such buildings or lands with such sum as may be necessary to defray the whole or any part of any private improvement expenses which the owners of such buildings or lands for the time being are liable to pay and the expenses of making such charge and for securing the repayment of such sum with interest may mortgage such buildings or lands to any person advancing such sum but so that the principal money due on any such mortgage shall be repaid within twenty years.

Corporation may charge supervision in addition to costs.

111. Whenever under this Act or the Public Health Act 1875 the Corporation either on the application or in consequence of the default of the owners or occupiers of any premises execute any work the cost of which is payable by such owners or occupiers they may if they see fit in addition to the actual cost of such works charge and recover in respect of plans sections measuring supervision and all other matters an amount not exceeding five per centum of the amount of the actual cost of such works.

(v.) Saving Clauses.

Continuing exemption of dock company from rates.

112. The dock company may from time to time claim and shall be entitled to any exemption from liability to rates and assessments which if this Act were not passed they might claim and be entitled to under the provisions of the enactments by this Act repealed or any of them.

As to streets, &c. repaired, &c. under the Hull Dock Acts.

113. All streets quays and other places in the borough now lighted repaired maintained cleansed or drained by and at the expense of the dock company under and by virtue of the Hull Docks Acts or any of them or otherwise shall continue to be lighted repaired maintained cleansed and drained by such company as heretofore. Provided that the Corporation may by agreement with the said company undertake such lighting cleansing repairing and maintenance on such terms as to payment to the Corporation of a gross or annual sum or otherwise as the Corporation and the said company may agree and any such agreement shall be valid and bind the parties.

114. This Act shall not by implication or otherwise take away alter abridge or prejudicially affect any estate rights and titles to property power or privilege of the dock company which they now have or might have had or have availed themselves of or have been entitled to in case this Act had not been passed. *Saving rights of dock company.*

115. This Act shall not by implication or otherwise prejudice alter or impair any estate right title interest property power or privilege of the Guild or Brotherhood of Masters and Pilots Seamen of the Trinity House in Kingston-upon-Hull which they might have had availed themselves of or been entitled to in case this Act had not been passed. *Saving rights of Trinity House.*

116. If at any time the Corporation shall construct any work within the limits of the borough as defined by this Act on any part of the shore or bed of the River Humber where and so far up the same as the tide flows and reflows they shall not less than two months before commencing any such work deliver to the Humber Conservancy Commissioners plans defining the nature and extent of the works so proposed to be carried out and the Corporation shall not in the exercise of any of the powers conferred on them by this Act or any part thereof prejudicially affect the navigation or the channel or roadstead of the River Humber. *Plans of works to be delivered to Humber Conservancy Commissioners.*

117. Except as in this Act otherwise expressly provided nothing contained in this Act or in any of the schedules thereto shall prejudice or alter any of the provisions of the Humber Conservancy Acts 1852 to 1876 or any of those Acts. *Saving rights of Humber Conservancy Commissioners 15 & 16 Vict. c. cxxx. &c.*

118. Nothing in this Act contained shall extend or be construed to extend to take away lessen prejudice or alter any of the property powers rights privileges or jurisdiction of the Beverley and Barmston Drainage Commissioners under " The Beverley and Barmston Drainage Acts 1798 and 1880 " but all such powers rights and jurisdiction shall remain and be as good valid and effectual as if this Act had not been passed. *Saving rights of Beverley and Barmston Drainage Commissioners 38 G. 3. c. lxiii. 43 & 44 Vict. c. cxxviii.*

Saving
rights of the
trustees
of the
Beverley
and Skidby
drainage.

25 O. 3. c. 92.
48 G. 3. c. xl.

119. Nothing in this Act contained shall extend or be construed to extend to take away lessen prejudice or alter any of the powers rights or jurisdiction of the trustees of the Beverley and Skidby drainage acting under an Act passed in the twenty-fifth year of His late Majesty King George the Third intituled " An Act " for draining preserving and improving certain low grounds and " carrs in the several parishes of Saint John in Beverley and of " Skidby in the east riding of the county of York " and another Act passed in the fourty-eighth year of His said Majesty intituled " An Act to alter and amend an Act passed in the twenty-fifth year " of His present Majesty for draining preserving and improving " certain low grounds and carrs in the several parishes of Saint " John of Beverley and of Skidby in the east riding of the county " of York " but all such powers rights and jurisdictions shall remain and be as good valid and effectual as if this Act had not been passed.

Saving
rights of
the trustees
of Cotting-
ham drain-
age.

6 G. 3. c.
lxxviii.

31 G. 3. c. 20.

120. Nothing in this Act contained shall extend or be construed to extend to take away lessen prejudice or alter any of the powers rights or jurisdiction of the trustees of the Cottingham drainage acting under an Act of Parliament made and passed in the 6th year of the reign of His late Majesty King George III. entitled " An " Act for dividing enclosing and draining certain lands grounds and " common pastures in the parish of Cottingham in the east riding " of the county of York " and of a certain other Act of Parliament made and passed in the 31st year of the said reign entitled " An " Act for dividing and enclosing certain open fields lands and grounds " in the parish of Cottingham in the east riding of the county of " York and for amending an Act passed in the sixth year of the " reign of His present Majesty for dividing enclosing and draining " certain land ground and common pasture in the said parish " but all such powers rights and jurisdiction thereunder shall remain and be as good valid and effectual as if this Act had not been passed.

Saving
rights of the
trustees of
the Holder-
ness drain-
age.

2 & 3. W. 4.
c. l.

121. Nothing in this Act contained shall extend or be construed to extend to take away lessen prejudice or alter any of the powers rights or jurisdiction of the trustees acting under an Act passed in the second year of the reign of His late Majesty King William the Fourth intituled " An Act to alter and enlarge " the powers of two Acts passed in the fourth and sixth years of " the reign of His Majesty King George the Third for draining and " improving certain low grounds and carrs in Holderness in the "east riding of the county of York" and the two said several Acts recited in that Act but all such powers rights and jurisdiction shall remain and be as good valid and effectual as if this Act had not been passed.

122. [Saving rights of Newington Water Company.]

[See Water Acts.]

123. Nothing in this Act contained shall in any way diminish take away alter prejudice or affect any right title estate or interest jurisdiction power franchise or royalty which Sir Frederick Augustus Talbot Clifford Constable Baronet or his successors in title or any person or persons claiming through or under Sir Thomas Aston Clifford Constable deceased may have or be entitled to at the time of the passing of this Act but all such rights title estate interest jurisdiction powers franchises and royalties shall continue to be held used and enjoyed by the said Sir Frederick Augustus Talbot Clifford Constable and his successors in title and by all persons claiming under the will of the said Sir Thomas Aston Clifford Constable deceased as fully and freely as if this Act had not been passed. *(margin: Saving for Sir Frederick Augustus Talbot Clifford Constable, Bart.)*

124. No litigation as to foreshore or other property pending at the passing of this Act and no title to any such foreshore or other property shall be altered or affected by any of the provisions of this Act. *(margin: Saving for lis pendens)*

125. All powers rights and remedies given to the Corporation by this Act shall (except where otherwise expressly provided) be deemed to be in addition to and not in derogation of any other powers conferred on them by Act of Parliament law or custom and the Corporation may exercise such other powers as if this Act had not passed. *(margin: Powers of Act cumulative.)*

126. All the preliminary and other costs charges and expenses of and incident to the preparing for obtaining and passing of this Act shall at the option of the Corporation be paid by the Corporation out of the district fund and general district rate and the Corporation are hereby authorised to borrow such moneys as they may require for that purpose and to raise the same by the creation and issue of Hull Corporation Stock under the Hull Corporation Loans Act 1881 and to exercise the powers of this section at any time after the passing of this Act. *(margin: Costs of Act.)*

THE FIRST SCHEDULE.

Acts and Orders Repealed.

Title or Short Title.	Extent of Repeal.
"An Act for enlarging and improving the market place of the town of Kingston-upon-Hull and for making a commodious street from thence to the River Humber with a dock and wharf or landing-place for the ferry and market boats belonging and resorting to the said town."— (41 Geo. 3. c. 65.)	The whole Act.
The Kingston-upon-Hull Improvement Act 1854.—(17 & 18 Vict. c. 101.)	The whole Act except the proviso to section 8 and Schedule (C) which save from repeal certain provisions of 23 Geo. 3 c. 55, and sections 22, 31, 33, 69, 74, 75, 79, 80, 83, 84, 87, 88, 90, 92 to 94, 97 to 102, 104 to 107, 109, 111, 114, 115, 120, 121, 122, 123, 126, 135, 151, 154 to 158, 161, 165 to 168, 176 all numbers inclusive.
The Local Government Supplemental Act 1863.—(26 & 27 Vict. c. 32.)	So much as confirms the provisional order altering the Kingston-upon-Hull Improvement Act 1854, and the whole of the said order, except articles 5 to 17 inclusive.

[Note.—*Articles V. to XXII. (both inclusive) of this Order are re-enacted by the Provisional Order of 1886, page 122.*]

The Local Government Supplemental Act 1865 (No. 5).— (28 & 29 Vict. c. 108).	So much as confirms the provisional order altering the Kingston-upon-Hull Improvement Act 1854, and the whole of the said order.

TITLE OR SHORT TITLE.	EXTENT OF REPEAL.
The Local Government Supplemental Act 1871 (No. 2).— (34 & 35 Vict. c. 59.)	So much as confirms the provisional order for the repeal and alteration of Local Acts in force within the district of the Kingston-upon-Hull Local Board of Health and section 2 of the said Act, and the whole of the said order, except articles 5, 6, 7 and 11.

[NOTE.—*Articles VI. and IX. to XV. (both inclusive) of this Order are re-enacted by the Provisional Order of 1886, page 122.*]

The Local Government Supplemental Act 1871 (No. 4).— (34 & 35 Vict. c. 187.)	So much as confirms the provisional order putting in force the Lands Clauses Consolidation Act 1845 within the borough of Kingston-upon-Hull, and the whole of the said order.
The Local Government Supplemental Act 1872 (35 & 36 Vict. c. 45.)	The whole Act and the whole of the order scheduled thereto, except articles 6, 9 to 12 and 15 inclusive.
The Local Government Board's Provisional Orders Confirmation (Belper Union &c.) Act 1877.— (40 & 41 Vict. c. 132.)	So much as confirms the provisional order for altering the Kingston-upon-Hull Improvement Act 1854 and section 4 of the said Act, and the whole of the said order, except article 3.

[NOTE.—*Article III. of this Order is re-enacted by the Provisional Order of 1886, page 122, and partially repealed by the Provisional Order of 1893, page 132.*]

The Local Government Board's Provisional Orders Confirmation (Kingston-upon-Hull &c.) Act 1880.—(43 & 44 Vict. c. 84.)	So much as confirms the provisional order for partially repealing altering and amending a confirming Act, and the whole of the said order, except articles 2 to 8 and 19 inclusive.

[NOTE.—*Articles II. to XIX. (both inclusive) of this Order are re-enacted by the Provisional Order of 1886, page 122.*]

THE SECOND SCHEDULE.

DESCRIPTION OF THE BOUNDARIES OF THE BOROUGH AS EXTENDED.

A boundary line commencing on the bed or shore of the River Humber at the south-western point of the present boundary of the town and county of Kingston-upon-Hull as shown on the 6-inch Ordnance map and proceeding thence in a westerly direction along the line shown on the said map or plan as the boundary of the wapentake and county to a point on such line opposite the south-western extremity of the district of the Newington Local Board thence in a northerly direction to the south-western extremity of the local board district of Newington and thence in a northerly direction along the existing boundary of the said local board district of Newington to the point where the said boundary adjoins the present boundary of the borough thence in an easterly direction along the boundary between the present borough and the Cottingham Ward of the Cottingham Local Board to the point where the same is intersected by the Bridlington Branch of the North-eastern Railway and the boundary between the Cottingham and Newland Wards of the Cottingham Local Board and thence in a northerly direction and continuing along the boundary between the Cottingham and Newland Wards of the Cottingham Local Board to the road leading from Newland to Cottingham and thence across such road to the northern side thereof and thence in an easterly direction along the northern side of such road to and across the road leading from Hull to Beverley called the Beverley Road and thence along the north side of the road leading to Stoneferry called the Clough Road to the eastern boundary of the said Newland Ward in the centre of the River Hull and thence in a northerly direction along such boundary to a point opposite to where the drain which flows from near the Beverley and Hull road opposite Endike Lane enters the River Hull between certain lands belonging respectively to William Henry Harrison Broadley Esq. M.P. and Colonel Benjamin Blaydes Haworth Booth and from thence in a straight line in an easterly direction to the north-east corner of the Leads Bridge carrying the Stoneferry Road over the Holderness drain thence in a straight line in a south-easterly direction to a point on the present boundary line of the borough at the south-western corner of a field in the parish of Sutton

belonging to John Edward Lee and others on the northern side of
such boundary and opposite to a field in the parish of Drypool on
the southern side of such boundary being part of a farm called
Summergangs belonging to the Corporation thence in an easterly
direction along the present boundary of the borough to the north-
eastern corner of the present borough at Bilton drain thence
northward along the boundary between the parishes of Sutton and
Marfleet to the point where the same joins the boundary between
the parish of Marfleet and the parish of Bilton thence along the
said boundary between the parishes of Marfleet and Bilton to a
point on the Old Fleet drain where such boundary joins the
boundary line between the parishes of Marfleet and Preston thence
in a southerly direction along the said boundary between the
parishes of Marfleet and Preston to the point where the Old Fleet
drain discharges into the Humber and thence in a south-westerly
direction to a point on the boundary line shown on the Ordnance
map as the boundary line of the wapentake and county one mile
and six hundred and thirty yards east of the point where the same
meets a line shown on such map as the eastern boundary of the
town and county of Kingston-upon-Hull thence westward along
such boundary line to the said eastern boundary of the town and
county of Kingston-upon-Hull thence along the line shown on such
map as the southern boundary of the town and county of Kingston-
upon-Hull to a point where the same meets a line shown on such
map as the western boundary of the town and county of Kingston-
upon-Hull being the point firstly described as the commencement
of the extended boundary.

THE THIRD SCHEDULE.

PREMISES OF WHICH PART ONLY MAY BE TAKEN.

Carr Lane Widening and Improvement.—Parish of Holy Trinity.

[*Works executed.*]

BOROUGH OF KINGSTON-UPON-HULL.
PROVISIONAL ORDER,

Dated 25th May, 1883.

Confirmed by the Local Government Board's Provisional Orders Confirmation (No. 8) Act, 1883, 46 & 47 Vict., Ch. XCIX.

Royal Assent, 16th July, 1883.

Art. I. [*Waterworks. See Water Acts.*]

Art. II. Section 6 of the Act of 1882, and the first Schedule to that Act shall be altered and amended so as to provide as follows :

(*a*.) No house or building shall be occupied as a dwelling-house until the drainage thereof has been completed, and the house or building has been examined by the Surveyor or other Officer appointed by the Corporation for that purpose, and has been certified by such Surveyor or other Officer as having been built in accordance with plans approved by them, and as being in every respect fit for human habitation.

(*b*.) The Surveyor or other Officer as aforesaid shall, not later than seven days after notice in writing has been given to the Corporation or to such Surveyor or other Officer by the owner of any such house or building that he is desirous of receiving a certificate as aforesaid, examine the house or building and shall within seven days after such examination, either give to such owner a certificate that the house or building has been built in accordance with plans approved by the said Corporation, and is in every respect fit for human habitation, or shall signify in writing to such owner the reasons for withholding such certificate.

(*c*.) No fee shall be payable in respect of any such examination or certificate.

(*d*.) Any person deeming himself aggrieved by the refusal of any such certificate may appeal from the decision of the Corporation to the next court of quarter sessions in the same manner and subject to the same provisions as in the case of an appeal from the decision of a court of summary jurisdiction under Section 269 of the Public Health Act, 1875, and, for the purposes of such appeal, the decision of the Surveyor or other Officer of the Corporation shall be deemed to be the decision of the Corporation.

KINGSTON-UPON-HULL CORPORATION WATER ACT, 1884.

47 AND 48 VICT., CH. LX.

Royal Assent, 23rd June, 1884.

The following section amends Article II. (d) of the Provisional Order of 1883 page 98.]

Amending Article II. of Kingston-upon-Hull Order 1883.

16. Any person deeming himself aggrieved by the refusal of the Corporation or their surveyor or other officer to grant him a certificate under Article II (subsection (d)) of the Order of 1883 may appeal within twenty-one days after such refusal to the police magistrate of the borough who may summon all parties to appear before him and make an order confirming reversing or modifying the decision of the Corporation and with or without costs to any party as he thinks just.

(*e.*) Every person knowingly occupying or permitting to be occupied as a dwelling-house any building in contravention of any provision contained in this Article, shall be liable to a penalty not exceeding forty shillings, and to a like penalty for every day on or during which the offence shall continue, and every such penalty shall be recovered summarily, and applied as if it were a penalty authorised or directed by the Act of 1882, to be recovered summarily.

Art. III.   (1.) The Confirming Act of 1879, so far as it relates to the Order of 1879*, and the Confirming Act of 1880, so far as it relates to the Order of 1880, shall be altered and amended so as to provide as follows :—

The Corporation may from time to time apply or invest temporarily in the purchase for redemption, within the meaning of Section 38 of the Act of 1881, of Corporation Stock issued or to be issued under that Act, the whole or any part of any sinking fund which they have set apart or may from time to time set apart, in pursuance of the provisions of Article I. of the Order of 1879, and of Section 13 of the Local Loans Act, 1875, and the whole or any part of any sinking fund created under Article X. of the Order of 1880.

(2.) Where the Corporation in pursuance of the provisions of this Article apply or invest temporarily the whole or any part of any sinking fund in the purchase for redemption of Corporation Stock, the amount so applied or invested shall be deemed to be a debt due to such sinking fund from the Hull Corporation Loans Fund established under Section 32 of the Act of 1881.

In respect of the said debt, interest shall be payable at the rate of four pounds per centum per annum from the date of the cancellation of the Corporation Stock so purchased for redemption until repayment of the same ; and the amount of such debt, together with the interest thereon until repayment thereof at the rate aforesaid, shall be paid, as soon as may be out of the Hull Corporation Loans Fund, to the credit of the said sinking fund, for the purpose of being applied in discharge of the borrowed moneys in respect of which such sinking fund has been created.

* *Relates to Waterworks.*

HULL (DRYPOOL) BRIDGE & IMPROVEMENTS ACT, 1885.

48 AND 49 VICT., CH. CLXXXI.

Royal Assent, 6th August, 1885.

Short title.   **1.** This Act may be cited as the Hull (Drypool) Bridge and Improvements Act 1885.

Incorporation of Acts.   **2.** The Lands Clauses Consolidation Acts 1845 1860 and 1869 the Lands Clauses (Umpire) Act 1883 and the sections of the Railways Clauses Consolidation Act 1845 numbered fifty-three fifty-four fifty-five fifty-six fifty-seven and fifty-eight relating to the substitution of other roads for roads interfered with and to the restoration of roads interfered with are (except where expressly varied by this Act) incorporated with and form part of this Act and in the said incorporated Acts or any of them or in any Acts incorporated therewith or with this Act unless there be something in the subject or context repugnant to the respective constructions herein-after defined the expression " the special Act " means this Act the expressions " the promoters " " the promoters of the undertaking " " the undertakers " and " the company " mean respectively the Corporation and the expressions " the railway " and " the undertaking " mean respectively the bridge over the River Hull and approaches and the street and street improvements and other works authorised by this Act.

Interpretation.   **3.** In this Act the several words and expressions to which meanings are assigned by the Acts wholly or partially incorporated herewith have the same respective meanings unless there be something in the subject or context repugnant to such construction :

> " The borough " means the borough of Kingston-upon-Hull :
>
> " The Corporation " means the mayor aldermen and burgesses of the Borough :
>
> " The council " means the council of the borough :
>
> " The improvements " means the bridge over the River Hull and approaches and the new street and street improvements and other works authorised by this Act :
>
> " Person " includes corporation :
>
> " The general district rate " means the general district rate of the borough :

"The Trinity House" means the Guild or Brotherhood of Masters and Pilots Seamen of the Trinity House of Kingston-upon-Hull:

"The Dock Company" means the Dock Company at Kingston-upon-Hull:

and for the purposes of this Act the expression "superior courts" or "court of competent jurisdiction" or any other like expression in this Act or any Act wholly or partially incorporated herewith shall be read and have effect as if the debt or demand with respect to which the expression is used were a simple contract debt and not a debt or demand created by statute.

4. Subject to the provisions of this Act the Corporation may make and maintain the bridge over the River Hull and approaches thereto and the new street and the diversion widening and improvement of existing streets and other works hereinafter described with all necessary arches embankments and approaches hydraulic lifts capstans mooring-posts dolphins buildings works machinery and conveniences connected therewith respectively and may enter upon take and use such of the lands delineated on the deposited plans and described in the deposited books of reference as may be required for that purpose (that is to say): *Power to make bridge over River Hull new street and street improvements*

1. A swing or opening bridge across the River Hull commencing in the parish of Saint Mary on the western side of the river at the east end of Salthouse Lane Staith at a point five yards or thereabouts measuring along the timber edging of the staith in a southerly direction from the wooden pillar or support at the south-east corner of the warehouse and wharf belonging or reputed to belong to Messrs. James T. and N. Hill and terminating in the parish or extra-parochial place of Garrison Side on the eastern side of the said river at the west end of Clarence Street at a point three yards or thereabouts measuring in a northerly direction from the south-west corner of the landing steps belonging or reputed to belong to and occupied by John Fisher;

2. An approach road commencing in High Street at or near a point three yards or thereabouts measuring in a southerly direction from the junction of Salthouse Lane with that street thence passing in an easterly direction

along lands south of Salthouse Lane Staith and the said staith and terminating at the west end of the intended bridge at the point of commencement thereof above described which approach road will be wholly situate in the parish of Saint Mary;

3.   An approach road commencing at the west end of Clarence Street at the point of termination of the intended bridge above described thence passing along Clarence Street and terminating at a point opposite the house No. 8 in that street in the occupation of Samuel Jessop which approach road will be wholly situate within the said parish or extra-parochial place of Garrison Side;

4.   The diversion widening and improvement of Argyle Street (marked "1" on the deposited plans) commencing at a point in Argyle Street opposite the house No. 10 in that street in the occupation of George Wright and terminating at a point ten feet or thereabouts measuring in an easterly direction from the north-west corner of the boundary wall surrounding the Hull Workhouse all in the parish of Holy Trinity;

5.   A new bridge over the North-eastern Railway and a street or road in continuation of Argyle Street (marked "2" on the deposited plans) commencing at the termination of the diversion widening and improvement of Argyle Street above described thence proceeding in a northerly direction crossing Londesborough Street and terminating one hundred and sixty-seven yards or thereabouts from the commencement of such new bridge above described all in the parish of Holy Trinity;

6.   The widening alteration and improvement of Londesborough Street (marked "3" on the deposited plans) for a distance of fifty-five yards or thereabouts on the east side and forty-two yards or thereabouts on the west side of the crossing of that street by the intended new street or road No. 5 immediately before described all in the parish of Holy Trinity;

7.   The widening alteration and improvement of Day Street on the west side at the northern end thereof for a distance of thirty-one yards or thereabouts measuring in a

southerly direction from the junction of that street with the Anlaby Road all in the parish of Holy Trinity.

5. The bridge across the River Hull by this Act authorised shall be constructed with an opening arch of eighty feet clear span measured at right angles with the direction of the piers as shown upon the deposited plans the western termination of which span shall be not more than sixty feet from the western shore of the said river and one arch of twenty feet clear span on the western side of the river and one arch of not less than twenty feet clear span on the eastern side of the river : Provided always that the foundations of the cylinders of the bridge shall be placed at such a depth not being less than fifteen feet below the bed of the river as will allow of a reasonable deepening of the river at any future time : Provided also that none of the permanent works of the bridge shall be constructed so as to project to the southward more than seventy feet from the centre line of the bridge as shown upon the deposited plans nor so as to project in front of the line of waterway of the piers.

As to construction of bridge over the River Hull.

6. Subject to the other provisions of this Act the enactments following shall be in force and have effect for the protection of the Commissioners of Sewers for the east parts of the east riding of the county of York (that is to say) :—

For protection of Commissioners of Sewers for the east riding of the county of York.

(A) The Corporation in building the said bridge over the River Hull shall not construct any stone or brick pier in the channel of the said river but such bridge and the machinery thereof shall be erected so far as regards the said river upon iron cylinders protected by wooden fenders so as to interfere as little as possible with the stream and flow of the said river ;

(B) During the construction of the said bridge the Corporation shall use every means in their power to prevent any avoidable obstruction in the stream or to the navigation of the said river And they shall not fix or allow to be fixed any pile work erection or scaffolding which shall or may tend to prevent the free passage of the said stream or flow of water beyond what is absolutely necessary for the proper construction of the said bridge ;

(c) Except as in this Act otherwise expressly provided nothing herein contained shall extend or be construed to prejudice or affect the powers or authorities of Her Majesty's said Commissioners of Sewers for the east parts of the east riding of the county of York.

7. Previously to commencing the bridge over the River Hull or the works connected therewith the Corporation shall deposit at the Board of Trade plans sections and working drawings of the bridge and works for the approval of the Board The approval of the Board of Trade shall be signified in writing under the hand of the secretary or an assistant secretary of the Board and the bridge and works respectively shall be constructed only in accordance with such approval and when the bridge or works shall have been commenced or constructed the Corporation shall not at any time alter or extend the same without obtaining previously to making any such alteration or extension the like consent or approval and if the bridge or works shall be commenced or completed or be altered extended or constructed contrary to the provisions of this Act the Board of Trade may abate alter and remove the same and restore the site thereof to its former condition at the cost and charge of the Corporation and the amount thereof shall be a debt due from the Corporation to the Crown and be recoverable accordingly with costs of suit or may be recovered with costs as a penalty is or may be recoverable from the Corporation.

8. The Corporation shall provide erect and maintain for the assistance and use of vessels passing through or under the bridge such mooring posts dolphins or other works as the Trinity House may from time to time direct.

9. The Corporation shall on or near the works below high-water mark hereby authorised during the whole time of the constructing altering or extending exhibit and keep burning at their own expense every night from sunset to sunrise such lights (if any) as the Board of Trade from time to time require or approve. If the Corporation fail to comply in any respect with the provisions of the present section they shall for each night in which they so fail be liable to a penalty not exceeding twenty pounds.

10. The Corporation shall exhibit and keep burning from sunset to sunrise such lights (if any) on each side of the said bridge over the River Hull as the Trinity House shall from time to time direct. If the Corporation fail to comply in any respect with the provisions of the present section they shall for each night

in which they so fail be liable to a penalty not exceeding twenty pounds.

11. The bridge over the River Hull shall be deemed part of the streets of the borough and the provisions of any Act for the prevention or removal of nuisances obstructions and annoyances shall be applicable to the bridge and penalties for offences may be enforced and recovered in the same manner as penalties for offences in any public street in the Borough could be enforced and recovered. *Bridge and approaches to be deemed part of the streets of the borough.*

12. For the space of four hours before high water and three hours and a half after high water of every tide the bridge shall be open for the passage of vessels at such times and in such manner and for such period not exceeding fifteen minutes at any one time as the harbour master appointed by the Trinity House shall either verbally or in writing direct and subject thereto the bridge shall be opened and shut at such times and in such manner and shall continue open for such period as shall be prescribed by byelaws and regulations to be from time to time made by the Corporation and which byelaws and regulations the Corporation are hereby from time to time authorised to make and alter at their discretion Provided always that all such byelaws and regulations shall be submitted to and approved by the Board of Trade under the hand of the secretary or an assistant secretary of the Board of Trade for the time being and if any disagreement arise as to the framing or alteration of any such byelaws and regulations the Board of Trade may determine any matters in difference in such manner as they from time to time think fit Provided always that in case of storm tempest or other emergency affecting the safety of shipping the harbour master may when necessary in consequence thereof extend the time for keeping the bridge open beyond fifteen minutes And the Corporation shall provide at their own expense a bridge master and also servants and labourers for properly and efficiently opening and shutting the bridge at all times whether by night or day when necessary in accordance with the provisions of this Act. *Regulations as to opening bridge.*

13. The Corporation may by any byelaws made by them under this Act impose on offenders against the same such reasonable penalties as they think fit not exceeding the sum of ten *Penalty for breach of byelaws.*

pounds for each offence but all such byelaws imposing any penalty shall be so framed as to allow of the recovery of any sum less than the full amount of the penalty.

Penalty if bridge master exercise powers unfairly.

14. If any bridge master appointed by the Corporation or any of his assistants without reasonable cause or in an unreasonable and unfair manner exercise any of the powers or authorities vested in him the person so offending shall for every such offence be liable to a penalty not exceeding five pounds.

Penalty if persons offer rewards or bribes to bridge master.

15. If any person give or offer any sum of money or anything whatsoever by way of reward or bribe to the bridge master appointed by the Corporation or any of his assistants or any person employed by the Corporation on or about the bridge for the purpose of gaining an undue preference in the execution of his office or for the purpose of inducing such bridge master or other assistant or person as aforesaid to do or omit to do anything relating to his office or if such bridge master or other assistant or person as aforesaid receive any such reward or bribe as aforesaid every person so offending shall be liable for every such offence to a penalty of twenty pounds.

Board of Trade may order local survey.

16. If at any time or times it shall be deemed expedient by the Board of Trade to order a local survey and examination of any works of the Corporation authorised by this Act in over or affecting any tidal or navigable water or river or of the intended site thereof the Corporation shall defray the costs of every such local survey and examination and the amount thereof shall be a debt due to the Crown from the Corporation and if not paid upon demand may be recovered as a debt due to the Crown with the costs of suit or may be recovered with costs as a penalty is or may be recoverable from the Corporation.

If any works be abandoned &c. Board of Trade may direct removal.

17. If any works by this Act authorised to be constructed by the Corporation in under over through or across any tidal water or navigable river or if any portion of any work which affects or may affect any such water or river or access thereto shall be abandoned or suffered to fall into disuse or decay the Board of Trade may abate and remove the same or such part or parts thereof as that Board may at any time or times deem fit and proper and restore the site thereof to its former condition at the cost and charge of the Corporation and the amount thereof shall be a debt due from the Corporation to the Crown and if not paid upon demand may be recovered as a debt due to the Crown with the costs of suit or may be recovered with costs as a penalty is or may be recoverable from the Corporation.

18. Nothing in this Act shall extend or be construed to extend to defeat lessen diminish take away prejudice or affect all or any of the rights privileges liabilities or powers liberties or authorities given to or vested in the Trinity House or the dock company under or by virtue of all or any of the Acts of Parliament relating to the River Hull and every clause matter and thing therein contained shall be and continue in full force and shall and may be carried into execution under such Acts of Parliament in such and the like manner to all intents and purposes as if this Act had not been passed save only and except so as not in any manner to prevent injure or prejudice the due execution of this Act or of all or any of the powers and authorities hereby given to and vested in the Corporation.

Saving the rights of the Trinity House and Dock Company.

19. In the construction and execution of the improvements the Corporation may subject to the provisions of this Act deviate laterally from the lines thereof as shown on the deposited plans to any extent within the limits of lateral deviation marked thereon and the Corporation may deviate from the levels shown on the deposited sections to any extent not exceeding five feet   Provided that any such deviations so far as the same affect the bridge over the River Hull shall only be made to such extent as shall be approved by the Board of Trade after such inquiry (if any) as the said Board may think necessary.

Power to deviate.

20. The Corporation may stop up and discontinue as public streets or thoroughfares :—

Streets to be stopped up.

So much of Argyle Street and Asylum Lane including the existing level crossing over the North-eastern Railway as will be rendered unnecessary by the diversion widening and improvement of Argyle Street and the new bridge and street or road in continuation thereof by this Act authorised.

21. The Corporation during the making of the improvements may in or upon the lands shown upon the deposited plans temporarily stop up or cause to be stopped up all or any part of the carriageways or footways of streets which they shall think necessary for the purposes of this Act to be temporarily stopped up and

Power to stop up ways during the execution of the improvements.

for that purpose may from time to time put or cause to be put up sufficient palisades bars posts and other erections and may make from time to time such orders for regulating the traffic as to them shall seem proper.

Power to make subsidiary works

22. Subject to the provisions of this Act and within the limits defined on the deposited plans the Corporation in connection with the improvements and as part and for the purposes thereof may make junctions and communications with any existing streets intersected or interfered with by or contiguous to the works and may make diversions widenings or alterations of the lines or levels of any existing street for the purpose of connecting the same with the works or of crossing under or over the same or otherwise and may alter divert stop up or appropriate all or any part of any street square place court alley or passage whether a thoroughfare or not and the paving metalling or materials therein thereon or forming part of the same shall vest in the Corporation and the Corporation may also alter and interfere with any drain or sewer but the Corporation shall provide a proper substitute before interrupting the flow of sewage in any such drain or sewer and the materials obtained in such alterations and interference shall vest in the Corporation and all substituted drains and sewers shall be under the same jurisdiction care management and direction as the existing drains and sewers for which they may be so substituted   Provided that the Corporation shall make full compensation to all persons whose property shall be injuriously affected by the exercise of the powers of this section.

Period for compulsory purchase of lands.

23. The powers of the Corporation for the compulsory purchase of lands for the purposes of this Act shall not be exercised after the expiration of three years from the passing of this Act.

Period for completion of works

24. If the improvements are not completed within five years from the passing of this Act then on the expiration of that period the powers by this Act granted to the Corporation for making and completing the improvements or otherwise in relation thereto shall cease to be exercised except as to so much thereof as is then completed.

Errors and omissions in plans &c. to be corrected by justices who shall certify the same.

25. If there be any omission misstatement or wrong description of any lands or of the owners lessees or occupiers of any lands shown on the deposited plans or specified in the deposited books of reference the Corporation after giving ten days' notice to the owners lessees and occupiers of the lands in question may apply to two justices for the correction thereof and if it appear to the justices that the omission misstatement or wrong description arose from mistake they shall certify the same accordingly and they shall in their certificate state the particulars of the omission and in what respect any such matter is misstated or wrongly described and such certificate shall be deposited with the clerk of the peace for the county of the town of Kingston-upon-Hull and with the clerk of the peace for the East Riding of the county of York and a duplicate thereof shall also be deposited with the parish clerks of the several parishes in which the lands affected thereby are situate and such certificate and duplicate respectively shall be kept by such clerks of the peace and parish clerks respectively with the other documents to which the same relate and thereupon the deposited plans and books of reference shall be deemed to be corrected according to such certificate and the Corporation may take the lands and execute the works in accordance with such certificate.

26. Persons empowered by The Lands Clauses Consolidation Act 1845 to sell and convey or release lands may if they think fit subject to the provisions of that Act and of the Lands Clauses Consolidations Acts Amendment Act 1860 and of this Act grant to the Corporation any easement right or privilege not being an easement of water required for the purposes of this Act in over or affecting any such lands and the provisions of the said Acts with respect to lands and rent charges so far as the same are applicable in this behalf shall extend and apply to such grants and to such easements rights and privileges as aforesaid respectively.

Power to take easements &c by agreement

27. (1) The Corporation shall not under the powers of this Act purchase or acquire in any city borough or other urban sanitary district or any parish or part of a parish not being within an urban sanitary district ten or more houses which after the passing of this Act have been or on the fifteenth day of December last were occupied either wholly or partially by persons belonging to the labouring class as tenants or lodgers unless and until—

Restriction as to houses of the labouring class.

    (A) They shall have obtained the approval of the Local Government Board to a scheme for providing new dwellings for such number of persons as were residing in such houses on the fifteenth day of December last or for such number of persons as the Local Government Board shall after inquiry deem necessary having regard to the number of persons on or after that date residing in such houses and working within one mile therefrom and to the amount of vacant suitable accommodation in the immediate neighbourhood of such houses or to the place of employment of such persons and to all the circumstances of the cases ; and

(n)   They shall have given security to the satisfaction of the Local Government Board for the carrying out of the scheme.

(2)   The approval of the Local Government Board to any scheme under this section may be given either absolutely or conditionally and after the Local Government Board have approved of any such scheme they may from time to time approve either absolutely or conditionally of any modifications in the scheme ;

(3)   Every scheme under this section shall contain provisions prescribing the time within which it shall be carried out and shall require the new dwellings proposed to be provided under the scheme to be completed fit for occupation before the persons residing in the houses in respect of which the scheme is made are displaced :

Provided that the Local Government Board may dispense with the last-mentioned requirement subject to such conditions (if any) as they may see fit.

(4)   Any conditions subject to which the Local Governmen Board may have approved of any scheme or of any modifications of any scheme under this section or subject to which they may have dispensed with the above-mentioned requirement shall be enforceable by a writ of mandamus to be obtained by the Local Government Board out of the Queen's Bench Division of the High Court of Justice.

(5)   If the Corporation acquire or appropriate any house or houses for the purposes of this Act in contravention of the foregoing provisions or displace or cause to be displaced the persons residing in any house or houses in contravention of the requirements of the scheme they shall be liable to a penalty of five hundred pounds in respect of every such house which penalty shall be recoverable by the Local Government Board by action in the High Court of Justice and shall be carried to and form part of the Consolidated Fund of the United Kingdom :

Provided that the court may if it think fit reduce such penalty.

(6) Subject to the provisions of this section the Corporation and the Local Government Board and their inspectors shall have and may exercise for any purpose in connection with any scheme under this section all or any of the powers vested in them under The Public Health Act 1875 in the same manner in every respect as if the preparation and carrying into effect of such scheme were one of the general purposes of that Act :

Provided that all lands on which any buildings have been erected or provided by the Corporation in pursuance of any scheme under this section shall for a period of twenty-five years from the passing of this Act be appropriated for the purpose of dwellings and every conveyance demise or lease of such lands and buildings shall be endorsed with notice of this enactment :

Provided also that the Local Government Board may at any time dispense with all or any of the requirements of this sub-section subject to such conditions (if any) as they may see fit.

(7) The Corporation shall pay to the Local Government Board a sum to be fixed by that Board in respect of the preparation and issue of any Provisional Order in pursuance of this section and any expenses incurred by that Board in relation to any inquiries under this section including the expenses of any witnesses summoned by the inspector holding the inquiry and a sum to be fixed by that Board not exceeding three guineas a day for the services of such inspector.

(8) For the purposes of this section the expression "labouring class " includes mechanics artizans labourers and others working for wages hawkers costermongers persons not working for wages but working at some trade or handicraft without employing others except members of their own family and persons other than domestic servants whose income does not exceed an average of thirty shillings a week and the families of any of such persons who may be residing with them.

28. The Corporation may for any purpose in connection with the improvements upon the lands acquired by them under the powers of this Act and also in any street within the limits of deviation defined on the deposited plans raise sink or otherwise alter the position of any watercourse water pipe gas pipe or hydraulic pipe belonging to or connected with any house or building adjoining or near to the improvements and also any main or other pipe laid down or used by any company or person for

Alteration of position of water gas and other pipes.

carrying a supply of water or gas or hydraulic power and also any pipe tube wire or apparatus laid down for telegraphic or other purposes and any pipe tube wire or apparatus laid down for supplying electricity and may remove any other obstruction making in cases of alteration proper substituted works in the meantime and causing as little detriment and inconvenience as circumstances admit to any company or person and making reasonable compensation to any company or person who suffers damage by any such alteration   Provided always that before the Corporation alter the position of any main or other pipe laid down or used by any such company or person they shall (except in cases of emergency) give to the company or person to whom the same belongs notice of their intention to do so specifying the time at which they will begin such notice to be given twenty-four hours at least before the commencement of the work for effecting such alteration and such work shall·be done under the superintendence (at the expense of the Corporation) of the company or person to whom such pipe belongs unless such company or person refuses or neglects to give such superintendence at the time specified in the notice for the commencement of such work or discontinues the same during the execution of such work and the Corporation shall execute such work to the reasonable satisfaction of the engineer of such company or person   Provided also that the Corporation shall not cause any street to be lowered or raised or the position of any water or gas main or other pipe to be altered so as to leave over such main or other pipe in any part a covering of less than two feet where the covering now existing is not less than two feet unless the Corporation shall in such case protect the same pipes from frost or injury by artificial covering to the satisfaction of the engineer of such company or person or more than six feet where the covering now existing does not exceed six feet or more than such existing covering where the same exceeds six feet unless the Corporation in such case provide special means of access to the same to the satisfaction of the engineer of such company or person.

If any difference arises between the Corporation or their engineer and any such company or person or their or his engineer touching the amount of any costs expenses or charges under the provisions of this Act to be paid by the Corporation to any such company or person or touching any work matter or thing with reference to such mains or other pipes under such provisions to be done or executed by the Corporation or the mode of doing or executing the same such difference shall be settled by an engineer to be agreed upon by the engineers of the Corporation and of any such company or person respectively or failing agreement by such engineer as shall on the application of either the engineer of the Corporation or of any such company or person be named by the President for the time being of the Institute of Civil Engineers and whose decision shall be final and binding and the expenses of the reference shall be borne as the referee may direct   Provided that any difference which in the exercise of the powers conferred by this section may arise between the Corporation and any undertakers authorised by any license or order under the Electric Lighting Act 1882 may on the requisition of such undertakers be determined by an engineer or other fit person to be nominated as arbitrator by the Board of Trade subject to and in accordance with the provisions of section twenty-eight of that Act.

Nothing in this section shall extend to or authorise any interference with any works of any undertakers within the meaning of the Electric Lighting Act 1882 to which the provisions of section fifteen of the said Act apply:

Provided also : That the Corporation shall not raise sink or otherwise alter the position of any pipe tube wire or apparatus laid down for telegraphic or other purposes and belonging to the Postmaster General except in accordance with and subject to the provisions of the Telegraph Act 1878.

29. The Corporation may cause such parts of the improvements to be laid out for carriageways and such parts thereof for footways as they think proper and may construct erect and provide such vaults cellars arches sewers drains subways and other works and conveniences as they think proper for the purposes of the improvements within the limits of deviation defined on the deposited plans and in laying out or forming such carriageways and footways and works the Corporation may in addition to the powers by this Act conferred exercise the same powers and authorities as are vested in and shall be subject to the same liabilities only (if any) as are imposed upon any local board or urban sanitary authority when they stop up temporarily any thoroughfare or any part thereof in the repairing or repaving of any street within the borough.

Corporation empowered to lay out carriage ways &c.

Owners may be required to sell to Corporation parts only of certain buildings.

30. And whereas in the construction of the improvements or otherwise in exercise of the powers of this Act it may happen that portions only of the houses or other buildings or manufactories shown on the deposited plans may be sufficient for the purposes of the same and that such portions may be severed from the remainder of the said properties without material detriment thereto   Therefore notwithstanding section ninety-two of " The Lands Clauses Consolidation Act 1845 " the owners of and other persons interested in the lands and buildings described in the Schedule (A) to this Act and whereof parts only are required for the purposes of this Act may if such portions can in the opinion of the jury arbitrators or other authority to whom the question of disputed compensation shall be submitted be severed from the remainder of such properties without material detriment thereto be required to sell and convey to the Corporation the portions only of the premises so required without the Corporation being obliged or compellable to purchase the whole or any greater portion thereof the Corporation paying for the portions required by them and making compensation for any damage sustained by the owners thereof or other parties interested therein by severance or otherwise.

Corporation may let or exchange lands.

31. The Corporation may from time to time let either from year to year or for a less period or for a term at rack rent or exchange or otherwise dispose of any building or lands or any part thereof acquired by them under the powers of this Act and not required for any of the purposes of this Act and may execute and do any deed act or thing proper for effectuating any such lease exchange or other disposition.

Receipts of Corporation to be effectual discharges.

32. The receipt of the Corporation or the treasurer thereof or of any person duly authorised by the Corporation for any purchase moneys rents or profits or money payable to them by virtue of this Act shall be a sufficient and effectual discharge for the money in such receipt expressed or acknowledged to be received and the person to whom the same shall be given shall not afterwards be answerable or accountable for the misapplication or non-application of the money in such receipt expressed or acknowledged to be received and such money shall be applied by the Corporation towards the expenses of the Corporation in executing the works by this Act authorised.

33. The Corporation may subject to the provisions of this Act from time to time enter into and carry into effect agreements with any person being the owner of or interested in any lands houses or property abutting on any portion of any of the works authorised by this Act with respect to the sale by the Corporation to such person of any lands or property (including any street or thoroughfare or any part of a street or thoroughfare acquired by the Corporation under the powers of this Act and not required for any of the purposes of this Act) for such consideration as may be agreed upon between the Corporation and such person not being a rent charge annuity or other payment extending over a period of more than sixty years and the Corporation may accept as satisfaction of the whole or any part of such consideration by such person the grant of any lands or other property required by the Corporation for the purposes of this Act.

Power to Corporation to make agreements with owners of property &c.

34.—(1) The Corporation may from time to time borrow for the purposes of this Act including the costs charges and expenses in relation to and in obtaining this Act any sum not exceeding fifty thousand pounds and in order to raise or secure the money so borrowed the Corporation may from time to time create and issue Hull Corporation stock under the Hull Corporation Loans Act 1881.

Power to borrow and create Corporation Stock for purposes of Act.

(2) For the purposes of section thirty-five of that Act the period prescribed for paying off moneys borrowed under this section except for the payment of the said costs charges and expenses shall be sixty years from the time or respective times when the same are first respectively borrowed and in respect of moneys borrowed for payment of the said costs charges and expenses shall be twenty years from such time or respective times and the contributions to the sums directed by the said Corporation Loans Act to be carried to the Corporation loans fund in respect of interest on and of redemption of stock shall be payable in the case of stock created and issued under this section out of the general district rate.

35. All money borrowed by the Corporation under this Act shall be applied for the purposes of this Act to which capital is properly applicable and not otherwise.

Application of money.

36. The agreement contained in the Schedule (B) to this Act made the twenty-sixth day of November one thousand eight hundred and eighty-four between the Corporation and the North-

Confirming agreement with North-eastern Railway Company.

eastern Railway Company is hereby confirmed and made binding on the parties thereto and the Corporation shall from time to time on the request of the North-eastern Railway Company and at the cost of that company exercise such of the powers conferred on them by this Act as may be necessary or requisite to enable the railway company to fulfil the obligations undertaken by them in the agreement hereby confirmed.

For protection of the North-eastern Railway Company

37. Notwithstanding anything contained in this Act or shown upon the deposited plans and sections the Corporation shall not for the purposes of this Act either temporarily or permanently enter upon take occupy use or interfere with any railway or lands or property of the North-eastern Railway Company except such of the lands of the said Company as under the said agreement contained in the Schedule (B) to this Act are to be appropriated by the said company for the purpose of carrying out the works comprised in the said agreement.

Saving rights of the Crown in the foreshore.

38. Nothing in this Act shall authorise the Corporation to take use or in any manner interfere with any portion of the shore or bed of the sea or of any river channel creek bay or estuary or any right in respect thereof belonging to the Queen's Most excellent Majesty in right of Her Crown and under the management of the Board of Trade without the previous consent in writing of the Board of Trade on behalf of her Majesty (which consent the Board of Trade may give) neither shall anything in this Act extend to take away prejudice diminish or alter any of the estates rights privileges powers or authorities vested in or enjoyed or exercisable by the Queen's Majesty Her heirs or successors.

Saving rights of the Crown.

39. Nothing in this Act shall authorise the Corporation to take use or in any manner interfere with any land or hereditaments or any rights of whatsoever description belonging to the Queen's Most Excellent Majesty in right of Her Crown and under the management of the Commissioners of Her Majesty's Woods Forests and Land Revenues or either of them without the consent in writing of the same Commissioners or one of them on behalf of Her Majesty first had and obtained for that purpose (which consent such Commissioners are hereby respectively authorised to give) neither shall anything in this Act extend to take away prejudice diminish or alter any of the estates rights privileges powers or authorities vested in or enjoyed or exercisable by the Queen's Majesty Her heirs or successors.

40. All the preliminary and other costs charges and ex- Costs of Act. penses of and incident to the preparing for obtaining and passing of this Act including the costs incurred by the Corporation in complying with the provisions of the Act 35 and 36 Vict. c. 91 with respect to the Bill for this Act as taxed and ascertained by the taxing officer of the House of Lords or House of Commons shall be paid by the Corporation out of moneys borrowed by the Corporation under the provisions of this Act.

SCHEDULES REFERRED TO IN THE FOREGOING ACT.

SCHEDULE (A).

Describing LANDS and BUILDINGS of which portions only
may be required.

[*Improvement carried out.*]

SCHEDULE (B).

AN AGREEMENT made this twenty-sixth day of November 1884
between the NORTH-EASTERN RAILWAY COMPANY (herein-after
called "the Company") of the one part and the MAYOR
ALDERMEN and BURGESSES of the borough of Kingston-upon-
Hull acting as the Urban Sanitary Authority within and for
the same borough (herein-after called "the Authority") of
the other part.

WHEREAS the Authority are desirous of making certain
improvements in and about Argyle Street and Londesborough
Street in the said borough involving alterations of the levels and
the widening and diversion of parts of such streets and for the
purpose of carrying out the proposed works the arrangements
herein-after expressed have been made between the Company and
the Authority.

Now therefore it is hereby mutually declared and agreed
by and between the parties hereto as follows :—

1. The Company shall execute the works between the letters
A B C D and E shown on the plans and drawings marked Plan
No. 1 and Plan No. 2 and signed by the respective solicitors for
the Company and the Authority.

2. The land required for the purpose of carrying out the said
works shall be provided as follows viz. the Company shall provide free of cost to the Authority the land shown on the said Plan
No. 1 and thereon coloured yellow (except so much thereof as will
lie between the side walls of the arches through the embankment
shown on the said Plan No. 1 and Plan No. 2 over which last-
mentioned piece of land the Authority will be entitled to an ease-

ment for the purposes of the maintenance of the said arches and the embankment to be made thereon) and the Authority shall at their own cost acquire or provide all the residue of the land shown upon the said Plan No. 1 coloured red as necessary for the said works. In consideration of the Company providing the said land firstly mentioned the Authority will upon the completion of the said works convey or procure to be conveyed to the Company in fee simple such parts of the sites of the existing streets as are coloured green on the said plan No. 1 freed and discharged from any rights of way or other easements or incumbrances.

3. The Company shall also convey to the Authority free of cost for the purpose of their street improvement works beyond the limits of the works referred to in this agreement the pieces of land between the letters B and G and D and F respectively shown on the said Plan No. 1 and thereon coloured brown.

4. The Authority shall at their own cost compensate the owners lessees and occupiers (other than the Company their lessees or tenants) of the dwelling-houses lands and hereditaments which shall be injuriously affected by the execution of the said works and shall undertake at their own cost the defence or settlement of any actions or claims for such compensation and indemnify the Company against any liability in respect thereof.

5. The Company shall at all times for all purposes and for all descriptions of traffic have the right of passage with horses or carriages or on foot through the arches under the embankment which will be made on the land coloured red on the said Plan No. 1 and shall also have the right of using the drains or sewers in the said streets for the purpose of draining the bridge on which Argyle Street is to be carried over the North-eastern Railway.

6. All works under this agreement shall be executed in accordance with the said plans and drawings and shall be let by public tender in one contract which shall contain a stipulation that the same shall be completed within eighteen months from the date thereof.

7. The cost of executing the said works and all costs and expenses connected therewith or incident thereto (except as herein otherwise expressly provided) including interest at the rate of five per cent. per annum on the moneys from time to time expended by the Company from the dates of the expenditure thereof until the

final completion of the works shall be borne and paid as follows that is to say two thirds thereof by the Company and one third thereof by the Authority   A certificate signed by the engineer of the Company and the engineer of the Authority or in the event of their difference by an umpire to be appointed by them or if they shall disagree by the Board of Trade shall be final and conclusive as to the completion of the works and as to the amount of such cost and the Authority shall pay to the Company their aforesaid proportion of the sum named in such certificate on demand upon the completion of the works.

8.   The bridge over the North-eastern Railway and the roadway thereon shall after the completion thereof be maintained by the Company at their own cost and the rest of the said works shall after the completion thereof be maintained by the Authority at their own cost.

9.   If hereafter it shall be deemed advisable by the Authority to erect upon their land abutting on the approaches to the bridge houses shops or other buildings with frontages to the approaches they shall be at liberty so to do and may for such purpose use the retaining walls or other portions of the works executed under this agreement so far as may be necessary and may also authorise the owners of any property fronting or abutting such approaches to do likewise   Provided that the Company shall in like manner be at liberty to use the retaining walls or other portions of the said works in building upon their land.

10.   If and whenever any dispute or question shall arise between the Company and the Authority touching this agreement or anything herein contained or the construction hereof or the rights duties or liabilities in relation to the premises the matter in difference shall (except as otherwise herein provided) be referred to two arbitrators or their umpire in all respects pursuant to the Common Law Procedure Act 1854 or any Act amending the same   And such submission may be made a rule of Her Majesty's High Court of Justice at the instance of either the Company or the Authority without any notice to the other of them.

11.   The Authority will at their own expense take any steps which may be necessary for obtaining proper legal authority for the execution of the said works if the execution of the same is not within the powers of the Company or of the Authority and for

extinguishing all rights of way if any over the said land coloured green on the said Plan No. 1 and if it should be found that the said works cannot be carried out without new statutory powers this agreement is made subject to such alterations as Parliament may think fit to make therein.

In witness whereof the Company and the Authority have hereunto set their respective common seals the day and year first above written.

The common seal of the North-eastern Railway Company was hereunto affixed in the presence of

Seal of the
North-eastern
Railway
Company.

W. FAIRLAMB,

Secretary's Office, York.   C.N.W.

Sealed with the common seal of the Corporation in the presence of

Seal of the
Mayor, Aldermen
and Burgesses of
the Borough of
Kingston-upon-
Hull.

S. GEO. DUNCAN,

Town Clerk's Department,

Town Hall, Hull.

BOROUGH OF KINGSTON-UPON-HULL.

PROVISIONAL ORDER,

Dated 8th June, 1886.

Confirmed by the Local Government Board's Provisional Orders Confirmation (No. 10) Act, 1886, 50 Vict., Ch. XVI.

Royal Assent, 25th September, 1886.

From and after the date of the Act of Parliament confirming this Order, the Act of 1882 shall be altered so as to provide that, notwithstanding anything in Section 6 or in the First Schedule contained, the following portions of the said Provisional Orders and so much of the Confirming Acts as relate thereto shall be deemed to have remained in force as from the passing of the Act of 1882, and to be in force in the Borough ; viz.,—

Articles 5 to 22 (both inclusive) of the Order of 1862.

Articles 6, and 9 to 15 (both inclusive) of the Order of 1871.

* Article 3 of the Order of 1877.

Articles 2 to 19 (both inclusive) of the Order of 1880.

* *This Article was partially repealed by the Provisional Order of 1893, Art. II. p. 132.*

BOROUGH OF KINGSTON-UPON-HULL.

PROVISIONAL ORDER,

Dated 29th May, 1888.

Confirmed by the Local Government Board's Provisional Orders Confirmation (No. 11) Act, 1888, 51 & 52 Vict., Ch. CXXXI.

Royal Assent, 24th July, 1888.

Art. I.   Section 11 of the * Act of 1881 shall be altered so as to provide that, notwithstanding sub-section (2.) of that section, any resolution for the creation of Corporation Stock passed after the commencement of this Order may provide that such stock shall be redeemable by the Corporation at par, that is to say, at the rate of one hundred pounds sterling for every nominal amount of one hundred pounds stock issued, at or after such time and in such manner as the Corporation by that resolution declare.   Such stock shall be designated by the Corporation as Hull Corporation Redeemable Stock.   Any certificate of stock granted in respect of Corporation Redeemable Stock created after the commencement of this Order shall have endorsed upon it the conditions upon which such stock is redeemable.

* *Hull Corporation Loans Act,* 1881.

BOROUGH OF KINGSTON-UPON-HULL.

PROVISIONAL ORDER,

Dated 21st January, 1889.

Confirmed by the Local Government Board's Provisional Order Confirmation (No. 7) Act, 1889, 52 & 53 Vict., Ch. CVII.

Royal Assent, 26th July, 1889.

Art. I.   The * Local Act shall be altered so as to provide tha it may be cited for any purpose as "The Kingston-upon-Hull Improvement Act, 1854."

Art. II.   The Local Act shall be further altered so that the provisions of the Town Police Clauses Act, 1847, with respect to hackney carriages, shall be incorporated therewith.

Art. III.   The Local Act shall be further altered so as to provide as follows :—

(1.) The terms "hackney coaches," "hackney carriages," "hackney carriage," "carriages," or "carriage," whenever used in such of the provisions of the Town Police Clauses Act, 1847, by this Order incorporated with the Local Act, as are referred to in subdivision (2) of this Article, shall, anything in Section 38 of the Town Police Clauses Act, 1847, notwithstanding, be deemed to include every omnibus ; and such provisions shall apply to the owners and drivers of every omnibus, and the provisions of Section 39 of the last-mentioned Act shall apply to omnibus licenses.

(2.) The following are the provisions of the Town Police Clauses Act, 1847, to which reference is made in subdivision (1) of this Article, viz., Sections 37, 40 to 52, both inclusive, 54, 58, and 60 to 67, both inclusive, and so much of Section 68 as enables the Corporation from time to time to make byelaws for all or any of the following purposes ; that is to say,—

For regulating the conduct of the proprietors and drivers of hackney carriages plying within the prescribed distance in their several employments, and determin-

* *An Act for the further improvement of Kingston-upon-Hull, and for other purposes.*

ing whether such drivers shall wear any and what badges ;

For regulating the manner in which the number of each carriage, corresponding with the number of its license, shall be displayed ;

For regulating the number of persons to be carried by such hackney carriages, and in what manner such number is to be shown on such carriage ;

For fixing the stands for such hackney carriages ;

For securing the safe custody and re-delivery of any property accidentally left in hackney carriages, and fixing the charges to be made in respect thereof.

Provided that the expression " within the prescribed distance" in Sections 37, 45, 46, 51, and 68 of the Town Police Clauses Act, 1847, shall, for the purposes of the Local Act, as hereby altered, mean within the Borough, and whenever the word "driver" or "drivers" occurs in any of the sections of the Town Police Clauses Act, 1847, mentioned in this Article, it shall be deemed to include every conductor of any omnibus.

Provided further, that, for the purposes of Sections 54, 58, and 66 of the Town Police Clauses Act, 1847, the fare, according to the statement of fares exhibited on any omnibus, shall be deemed to be the fare allowed by the special Act, or the fare authorised by a byelaw under the special Act.

Provided also, that nothing in this Order contained shall empower the Corporation to fix the site of the stand of any omnibus in any railway station or in any yard adjoining or connected therewith, except with the consent of the railway company owning such site.

(3.) A license granted to a driver or conductor under the Local Act, as hereby altered, shall only authorise the holder thereof to act as driver or conductor of the class or description of carriage specified in such license, and shall be in force for one year only from the date thereof, or until the next general licensing meeting, in case any annual licensing day be appointed, and shall be subject to the power of suspension or revocation provided for by Section 50 of the Town Police Clauses Act, 1847.

Art. IV. The Local Act shall be further altered so as to provide that the Corporation may make byelaws for all or any of the following purposes : viz.,—

(1.) To provide for the exhibition on some conspicious part of any omnibus of a statement, in legible letters and figures, of fares to be demanded and received from the persons using, or carried for hire in, such omnibus ;

(2.) To prevent within the Borough—

(a.) The owner, driver, or conductor of any omnibus, or any other person on their behalf, by touting, calling out, or otherwise, from importuning any person to use, or to be carried in, such omnibus, to the annoyance of such person, or of any other person ;

(b.) The blowing of, or playing upon, horns or other musical instruments, or the ringing of bells, by the driver or conductor of any omnibus, or by any person travelling by or using any such omnibus ;

(3.) To fix the points within the Borough at which any omnibus shall or may take up and set down passengers.

Art. V. The Local Act shall be further altered so as to provide that,

(1.) For the purposes of that Act, as altered by this Order, the term "omnibus" shall mean every omnibus, char-a-banc, waggonette, stage-coach, and other carriage, plying, or standing for hire by, or used to carry passengers at separate fares to or from any part of the Borough (except tramway cars and carriages licensed by the Corporation under the provisions of the Tramways Act, 1870, or of any Provisional Order made thereunder and confirmed by Parliament), but nothing in this Order contained shall affect any omnibus bringing into the Borough passengers carried at separate fares, but not plying or standing for hire in the Borough, or the owner, driver, and conductor of any such last-mentioned omnibus.

(2.) The provisions contained in the Public Health Act, 1875, with respect to byelaws, and the penalties which may be imposed thereby, and the recovery and application of ponalties, shall apply to all byelaws made, altered, or repealed by the Corporation under the provisions of the Local Act as hereby altered, or of this Order, and to all penalties imposed thereby, and to all penalties imposed by any of the sections of the Town Police Clauses Act, 1847, mentioned in this Order, so far as they are by this Order rendered applicable to omnibuses, and their owners, drivers, and conductors.

BOROUGH OF KINGSTON-UPON-HULL.

PROVISIONAL ORDER,

Dated 9th June, 1890.

*Confirmed by the Local Government Board's Provisional Order
Confirmation (No. 14) Act, 1890, 53 and 54, Vict., Ch. CCIII.*

Royal Assent, 14th August, 1890.

Art. I.   The Corporation may from time to time by resolution
determine that any sum or sums which the Kingston-upon-Hull
School Board or the Guardians of the Poor of the Kingston-upon-
Hull Incorporation (hereinafter respectively referred to as " the
borrowing authority ") may be authorised to borrow or re-borrow
upon the security of any rates or funds, and which the borrowing
authority may be desirous of borrowing from the Corporation, shall
be lent by the Corporation accordingly.

[Note.—*This Article is amended by the Provisional Order of
1895, Art. I., page 135, by the insertion, after the word " Incorporation," of the words " or the Hull and Goole Port Sanitary
Authority."*]

Art. II.   Any sum or sums which the Corporation shall resolve
to lend as aforesaid shall, if borrowed by the Corporation, be raised
by the issue of Hull Corporation Redeemable Stock according to
the provisions of the Local *Act, as altered by the †Order.

Art. III.   (1.) When, under the authority of this Order, the
Corporation lend any money to the borrowing authority, the
consent or sanction of the Local Government Board or of the
Education Department, as the case may be, to the borrowing of
such money shall be conclusive evidence that at the date of such
consent or sanction the borrowing authority had power to borrow
such money.

(2.) Where any sum is lent by the Corporation under this
Order to the borrowing authority it shall be lent for a period not
exceeding that for which the borrowing authority is authorised to
borrow or re-borrow the same, and with a provision for repayment
by instalments.

(3.) If any sum payable to the Corporation for principal shall
not be received within six months of the time appointed for the

---

* *Hull Corporation Loans Act,* 1881.
' *Provisional Order of* 1888.

payment thereof, a like sum shall be set apart out of the borough fund, and applied or invested in place thereof by the Corporation ; and if after such application or investment the sum, or any part thereof, shall be received by the Corporation, the same shall be carried to the credit of the borough fund.

Provided that where any money is raised under Article 2 of this Order by the issue of Hull Corporation Redeemable Stock, all sums received for interest and principal, or to be set apart out of the borough fund under paragraph (3) of this Article, shall be paid into the loans fund under the Local Act.

Art. IV.   Section 4 of the Local Act shall be deemed to have been altered as from the passing of the Local Act by the insertion of the following provisions ; viz.,—

" For raising

" (1.) Any sum required for the payment off or redemption " of any Corporation Stock, mortgage, bond, debenture, " debenture stock, annuity, rentcharge, or other security " granted or created, or redeemable, or payable by them, " which sum may include the amount of any payment " made to the holder of any such security for his consent, " or for compensating him for such payment off or " redemption, or for the substitution of Corporation Stock " for his security ;

" (2.) Any sum payable under Article V. of this Order ; and

" (3.) Any sums properly chargeable to capital and paid as " commissions, discounts, or expenses in respect of any " Corporation Stock."

Art. V.   Section 9 of the Local Act shall be deemed to have authorised as from the passing of the Local Act, and to authorise the Corporation to enter into an arrangement with the holder of any security legally granted, or redeemable, or payable by them for the redemption thereof by payment of such an amount in money or Corporation Stock, or partly in one and partly in the other, as may be mutually agreed upon.

Art. VI.   Sections 34 and 35 of the Local Act shall be altered so as to provide that any stock issued for the purposes mentioned in Articles IV. and V. of this Order shall be deemed to have been raised by virtue of the statutory borrowing powers under which the security or stock in respect of which the premium, commission, discount, or expense to be paid out of the moneys raised by such issue of stock was paid or incurred was granted or created, and shall be redeemable accordingly.

Art. VII.   Section 44 of the *Local Act from its commencement to and including *sub-section* (1), and so much of the Confirming Act as relates to Article II. of the †Order are hereby repealed, except so far as they have been acted upon, and in lieu of the repealed enactments the following provisions shall have effect as if they were inserted before the unrepealed part of the said Section 44; viz.,—

> " The treasurer of the borough shall, within forty-two days
> " after the Twenty-fifth day of March in each year,
> " transmit to the Local Government Board an abstract
> " (verified by statutory declaration if so required by that
> " Board) of the accounts of the Corporation relating to
> " Corporation Stock and the loans fund in a form pre-
> " scribed by that Board, which they shall have power from
> " time to time to alter."

[NOTE.—*This Article is amended by the Provisional Order of 1895, Art. II., page 135, by the substitution for the words " Sub-Section (1) " of the following words :*

The paragraph reading " (i) The total amount of the Corporation Stock then remaining unredeemed."]

Art. VIII.   Section 46 of the Local Act shall be altered by the omission therefrom of the words " under any of the Borough Acts " be authorised to borrow at any time after the passing of this " Act," and by the insertion in lieu thereof of the words " for the "time being be authorised to borrow, re-borrow, or continue on " loan, or, being in the nature of an annuity or rent charge, to " redeem or pay off or continue payment of."

---

* *Hull Corporation Loans Act,* 1881.
† *Provisional Order of* 1888.

BOROUGH OF KINGSTON-UPON-HULL.

PROVISIONAL ORDER,

Dated 18th May, 1893.

Confirmed by the Local Government Board's Provisional Orders Confirmation (No. 15) Act, 1893, 56 & 57 Vict., Ch. CLXXXIX.

Royal Assent, 24th August, 1893.

Art. I. Notwithstanding the following provisions of the *Local Act, of the Confirming Act of 1877, and of the Confirming Act of 1886 ; that is to say,—

Of the Local Act :—

Section 79 ;

Section 88, so far as relates to drains to new buildings ; and

Section 98 as amended by Article III. of the Provisional Order of 1877, so far as it requires that every court, alley, square, or inclosure for houses to be thereafter rebuilt shall have an open area, or be of such width as the Corporation may determine in each case, and that every court, alley, square or inclosure for houses to be thereafter built or constructed on vacant ground (not being the site of any court or square theretofore formed or built immediately previously to such construction) shall have an open area, or be of the width of twenty feet at the least, measuring from front to front of the houses therein, and that the same area and width shall extend from the street throughout such court, alley, square, or inclosure, and be open from the ground upwards ;

The following words of Section 99, viz., " and every house " to be hereafter constructed on vacant ground (not being " situate at the corner of a street or place, or not being " the site of any other house erected thereon immediately " prior to such construction) shall have a back yard, or " other vacant ground and area, open from the ground up- " wards, of not less than eight feet, extending from the " main building for the whole length of such building, pro- " vided that within that space or area the pantry, coal- " house, and privy, not exceeding nine feet in height, and " not covering more than forty-eight superficial feet of the " above area, may be there constructed " ;

* *Kingston-upon-Hull Improvement Act,* 1854.

The Confirming Acts of 1877 and 1886, so far as they confirm
the following words of Article III. of the Order of 1877,
viz., " in every case where the average height of the
" houses in any court, alley, square, or inclosure for
" houses to be hereafter built or constructed on vacant
" ground (not being the site of any court or square there-
" tofore formed or built immediately previously to such
" construction) exceeds twenty feet, such court, alley,
" square, or inclosure shall have an open area, or be of a
" width, measuring from front to front, of not less than
" the average height of such houses, unless such height is
" more than thirty feet, in which case the width of the
" open area shall be at least thirty feet, and that "
the Corporation may forthwith, under and in accordance with the
provisions of the Public Health Act, 1875, and any Act amending
or extending that Act, make byelaws in regard to any of the
matters to which those provisions relate.

Art. II.   On the expiration of one year from the commencement of this Order, or of such longer period, not exceeding two years
from the commencement of this Order, as the Local Government
Board may determine, the sections and parts of sections of the
Local Act mentioned in Article I. of this Order, and the Confirming Acts of 1877 and 1886, so far as they relate to the part of
Article III. of the Order of 1877, mentioned in Article I. of this
Order, shall, to the extent referred to in Article I. of this Order, be
repealed, except so far as the same may have been acted upon; but
if before the expiration of such period as aforesaid any byelaw
made by the Corporation under Article I. of this Order with regard
to the subject-matter of any of the said sections or parts of sections,
or the said part of Article III. of the Order of 1877, shall come into
operation, the section or part of a section of the Local Act or the
Confirming Acts of 1877 and 1886, so far as they confirm the said
part of Article III. of the Order of 1877 relating to the same subject-
matter, shall thereupon be repealed, without waiting for the expiration of the said period.   Wherever in the unrepealed provisions of
the Local Act, or of any Act or Provisional Order amending that
Act, reference is made to such repealed provisions, the same shall
be deemed to refer to the byelaws relating to matters similar to

* *Kingston-upon-Hull Improvement Act*, 1854.

those mentioned in such repealed provisions: Provided that such repeal shall not affect any right, title, obligation, or liability acquired or accrued under such repealed provisions.

Art. III. The Local Act shall be amended by the addition thereto of the following provisions :—

(1.) Every dwelling-house to be hereafter built in any street, otherwise than on the site of any other house, shall, where necessary, be provided with a secondary means of access for the purpose of removing therefrom the contents of the receptacle of any privy, or of any ashpit, or of any cesspool, without carrying such contents through any dwelling-house.

(2.) The Corporation may, from time to time, make Bye-laws with respect to the level, width, and construction of such secondary means of access, whether the same are streets within the meaning of the Public Health Acts or not.

(3.) The provisions contained in the Public Health Act, 1875, with respect to byelaws and the penalties which may be imposed thereby, and the recovery and application of penalties shall apply to all byelaws made under this Article and under subdivision (5) of Article IV. of this Order, and to all penalties imposed thereby.

Art. IV. Section 101 of the Local Act shall be amended by the addition thereto of the following provisions :—

(1.) It shall not be necessary to furnish to the Corporation any plan of a building which is exempt from the provisions of the Acts or of the byelaws for the time being in force in the Borough.

(2.) In the case of any building erected after the commencement of this Order, and exempt at the time of its erection from the provisions of the Local Acts or of any byelaws for the time being in force in the Borough, with respect to new buildings, by reason of its being intended to be used for any particular purpose, no person shall use such building, or cause or suffer the same to be used, for any purpose not within the exemption unless and until the same shall conform to such of the requirements of those Acts and byelaws as are applicable to a building used for the intended purpose.

(3.) Where any person shall have erected any building which is exempt from the operation of any byelaw by reason of such building not being within a prescribed distance from any other building, he shall not, without the consent in writing of the Corporation, erect any other building within such distance from the first-mentioned building.

(4.) The approval by the Corporation of any plan or section for a new street or new building, or the rebuilding or alteration of a building, shall be null and void if the execution of the work shown on such plan be not commenced within the following periods ; (that is to say,)—

> As to plans approved after the commencement of this Order, within three years from the date of such approval ; and

> As to plans approved before the commencement of this Order, within three years from the commencement of this Order ;

and after the expiration of those respective periods fresh notice and deposit of plans and sections shall, unless the Corporation otherwise determine, be requisite.

(5.) The Corporation may, from time to time, make byelaws to provide for the retention by them of any plan, or plan and section, furnished to them in pursuance of any Act or byelaw for the time being in force in the Borough.

Art. V. Section 101 of the Local Act shall be further amended so as to include a provision that nothing in the said section contained, or in this Order, shall be deemed to restrict or in any manner interfere with the powers of the Corporation to make byelaws under any other Act with respect to the deposit of plans of buildings.

Art. VI. Any person who deems himself aggrieved by any requirement or order of the Corporation under subdivision (1) of Article III. of this Order, or any refusal of the Corporation to give consent under subdivision (3) of Article IV. of this Order, may appeal in manner provided by the Summary Jurisdiction Acts to the next practicable Borough Court of Quarter Sessions.

BOROUGH OF KINGSTON-UPON-HULL.

PROVISIONAL ORDER,

Dated 1st May, 1895.

Confirmed by the Local Government Board's Provisional Orders Confirmation (No. 6) Act, 1895, 58 and 59 Vict., Ch. LXXXVII.

Royal Assent, 6th July, 1895.

Art. I. The Confirming Act* shall be altered by the insertion in Article I. of the Order † after the word "Incorporation" of the words "or the Hull and Goole Port Sanitary Authority."

Art. II. The Confirming Act shall be further altered so that the words "the paragraph reading '(i) The total amount of the "'Corporation Stock then remaining unredeemed'" shall be deemed as from the passing of the Confirming Act to have been substituted in Article VII. of the Order for the words "subsection (1)."

Art. III. This Order may be cited as the Kingston-upon-Hull Order, 1895.

* *Local Government Board's Provisional Order Confirmation (No. 14) Act, 1890.*

† *Provisional Order of 1890.*

BORROWING POWERS (continued), period for paying off borrowed moneys to be 60 years, 80 S 70 (3).

persons advancing money to Corporation not bound to inquire into application thereof, 32 S 16.

restriction on borrowing and re-borrowing powers of Corporation, 35 S 6.

Stock created to pay off moneys borrowed for purposes of Borough Acts to be deemed to have been created for such purposes, 35 S 5.

sums payable for principal or interest of moneys borrowed by Corporation to be payable in first instance out of district fund and general district rate, 31 S 12.

trustees or executors empowered to invest money in debentures or debenture stock of any railway, may invest the same in debentures issued by Corporation, 32 S 17.

under Borough Acts, not abridged by Loans Act, 34 S 4.

BOUNDARIES of Borough extended, 62 S 9.

BOXES, Signal, North Eastern Railway Company's, may project beyond frontage of street, 83 S 76.

BRIDGE MASTER, Drypool Bridge, Corporation to provide, 105 S 12.

exercising powers unfairly shall be liable to penalty, 106 S 14.

penalty on, for receiving bribe or reward, 106 S 15.

persons offering rewards or bribes to, 106 S 15.

BUILDINGS, any person building, rebuilding, or altering any building, messuage, &c., sewer, drain, &c., without consent of Local Board, to be liable to penalty, 23 S 11.

application of proceeds of sale of, by Corporation, 73 S 48.

Corporation, with consent of Treasury, may sell on rent charge, 76 S 57.

exempt from provisions of Acts or bye-laws, plans of, need not be furnished, 6 S 4 (1), 133 S 4 (1).

not to be used for any purpose not within the exemption unless they conform to requirements of such Acts and byelaws, 6 S 101, 133 S 4 (2).

hereafter built or re-built not to be used as dwelling-houses except there be adjoining street or open space of prescribed width, 5 S 97.

in lease, expenses in respect of, may be apportioned between lessees and reversioners, 85 S 96.

intended to be built or re-built, plans of, to be furnished to Local Board, 6 S 101.

lamps, lamp-posts, &c., not to be fixed upon, without consent of owner and occupier, 1 S 31.

Local Board may enter upon and remove, to render streets more commodious, 1 S 22.

set up lamps, lamp-posts, lamp-irons, &c., upon, 1 S 31.

not commenced within specified periods, approval of plans to be null and void, 134 S 4 (4).

required for purposes for which acquired, may be let, exchanged, or disposed of by Corporation, 114 S 31.

to be commenced until plans have been approved, 6 S 101.

converted into dwelling houses without notice and plan being deposited, and approved by Local Board, 5 S 97, 6 S 100.

BUILDINGS (continued), not to be erected within prescribed distance from building exempt from Acts and byelaws, 6 S 4 (3), 134 S 4 (3).

    used as dwelling houses without consent of Local Board, unless there be street or clear space in front at least twenty feet in width, 5 S 97.

of Cottingham Local Board and Sculcoates Rural Sanitary Authority in added part of Borough to vest in Corporation, 68 S 36 (2).

Newington School Board to be transferred to School Board for extended Borough, 72 S 45.

owners may be required to sell only parts of, 114 S 30.

shall cause water to be conveyed from, 4 S 92.

power for Corporation to sell or lease, transferred to them by Extension and Improvement Act, 73 S 48.

powers of Corporation to make byelaws with respect to deposit of plans of, not interfered with, 7 S 5, 134 S 5.

private improvement expenses to be a charge on, in priority to any incumbrance, 89 S 107.

Surveyor may enter upon, for inspection of drains, privies, &c., 3 S 87.

unoccupied or unproductive, in respect of which improvements have been executed, may be let by Local Board for re-payment of expenses, 8 S 107.

BURGESS, in extended Borough to have same rights as those of existing Borough, 64 S 14.

BURGESS ROLL, for purposes of, added part of Borough to be deemed to have always been part of Borough, 66 S 27.

BURIAL ACTS, definition of, 60.

BURIAL BOARD, Corporation to be, in extended Borough, 75 S 52.

BYE-LAWS as to open areas in front of houses, Corporation may make, 131, 132 S 1.

Corporation may alter or repeal existing, 86 S 99.

    make, alter and repeal, for licensing corn and other meters and weighers, 87 S 100.

    and alter, to regulate opening of Drypool Bridge, 105 S 12.

    with respect to deposit of plans, 7 S 5, 134 S 5.

    hackney carriages, 124 S 3 (2), 126 S 4.

order proceedings for punishment of persons offending against, 85 S 97.

Drypool Bridge, disagreements as to framing or alteration of, to be determined by Board of Trade, 105 S 12.

    to be approved by Board of Trade, 105 S 12.

existing, to apply to extended Borough, 65 S 20.

Local Board may make, as to letters, goods, &c., to be carried by porters, 10 S 115.

as to quality and measure of coals to be carried by coal carriers, 16 S 115.

for ascertaining and fixing stands for porters, porters' carts, &c., 10 S 115.

fixing distances which porters, coal carriers, &c., shall be obliged to go and come, 10 S 115.

BYE-LAWS (continued), Local Board may make, for fixing rates, fares, &c., of porters, coal carriers, &c., 10 S 115.

Local Board may make, for licensing porters, porters' carts, &c., 9 S 115.

preventing frauds in the sale of coals and water, 10 S 115.

trying and punishing misconduct of porters, coal carriers, &c., 10 S 115.

made by Corporation in relation to water supply not to extend to area of Newington Water Company, 65 S 20.

former authorities to cease within added part of Borough, 65 S 20.

not to apply to buildings erected by North-Eastern Railway for railway purposes, 83 S 76.

of former School authorities to cease in added part of Borough, 72 S 14.

penalty for breach of, 105 S 13.

provisions of Public Health Act, 1875, and other Acts, &c., with respect to, and penalties imposed thereby and recovery, &c., of penalties to apply to all byelaws made by Corporation, so far as by Order of 1889 they are rendered applicable to omnibuses, and owners, drivers, and conductors, 126 S 5 (2).

requiring confirmation by Board of Trade, exception as to, 87 S 99.

retention of plans, 134 S 4 (5).

School Board, to apply to extended Borough, 72 S 41.

secondary means of access to houses, 133 S 3 (2).

provisions of Public Health Act, 1875, to apply to, 133 S 3 (2).

sections of Public Health Act, to apply to alteration and repeal of, 86 S 99.

CABINS, signal, North Eastern Railway Company's, may project beyond frontage line of street, 83 S 76.

CANALS, occupiers of, assessment of at one-fourth of net yearly value, 12 S 135, 75 S 51,

rating of, 12 S 135, 45 S 23, 75 S 51.

CANDLE HOUSES, procedure as to nuisances arising from, 7 S 105.

CARMEN, Local Board may make byelaws for trying and punishing misconduct of, and truckmen and labourers ; for fixing rates and fares to be taken ; and distances which they shall be obliged to go and come, 10 S 115.

CARR LANE, Corporation may widen and improve, 82 S 73 (2).

owners may be required to sell parts only of lands and buildings in, 83 S 75.

CARRIAGE WAYS, Corporation may cause parts of improvements to be laid out as, 113 S 29.

Corporation may in laying out exercise powers vested in any Local Board or Urban Sanitary Authority, 113 S 29.

stop up during improvements, 107 S 21.

CARRIAGES, Local Board may make byelaws for fixing stands for, 10 S 115.

licensing and regulating, 9 S 115.

penalty for causing to stand in streets longer than necessary, 9 S 111.

DOCK COMPANY (continued), definition of, 60 S 5.

    exemption of, from liability to rates and assessments, 10 S 121, 11 S 122, 90 S 112.

    in respect of land covered with water to be assessed at one-fourth of the net yearly value, 11 S 122.

    meters and weighers appointed by, not subject to Corporation bye-laws, 87 S 100.

    saving rights of, 91 S 114, 107 S 18.

    so long as they light and cleanse legal quay and adjoining ground, &c., not to be liable to assessments for lighting and cleansing, 11 S 123.

    streets, quays, &c., lighted, repaired, maintained, cleansed, or drained by, still to be so lighted, &c., 90 S 113.

    to be assessed in respect of docks in added part of the Borough at one-fourth of the net annual value, 79 S 67.

DOCKS, in added part of borough to be assessed at one-fourth of net annual value, 79, S 67.

    Railway and Victoria, quays, basins and entrances thereof, for purposes of lighting, to be deemed public streets, and to be lighted by Local Board. 10 S 120.

    rating of, 45 S 33.

DOCUMENTS, Bankers' Books Evidence Act, 1879, to apply to all, kept by registrar of stock, 42 S 28 (b).

    issued by Corporation, authentication of, 86 S 98 (1).

    may be partly in print and partly in writing, 85 S 98 (1).

    of Newington Local Board, to remain valid and effectual, 67 S 32.

    notwithstanding dissolution to be evidence, 68 S 35.

    power of Commissioner under Extension Act, with regard to production of, 67 S 29.

    receivable as evidence notwithstanding repealed enactments, 61 S 6 (d).

DOGS or other animals suspected to be in a rabid state may be destroyed by constables, 9 S 109.

DOLPHINS, mooring posts, &c., to be erected by Corporation at Drypool Bridge, under direction of Trinity House, 104 S 8.

DRAINAGE, of Cottingham Local Board district, Corporation to be liable for part of balance of loan for, 71 S 40.

        Loan for, 71 S 40.

        may be discharged into Cottingham Road and Clough Road sewers, 70 S 39.

    Outfall, agreement to be made between Corporation and Cottingham Local Board for discharge of loan for works of, 71 S 40.

    streets, quays, &c., drained by Dock Company, still to be so drained, 90 S 113.

DRAINS, alteration and interference of by Corporation, 108 S 22.

    any person building, re-building, making, clearing out, unstopping or altering any drain, privy, cesspool, or ashpit, without consent of Local Board to be liable to penalty, 23 S 11.

    before interrupting flow of sewage in, Corporation to provide substituted, 108 S 22.

PAVING, courts or passages to be paved by owners, 3 S 83.
Nelson Street to be paved as one of the streets of the borough, 27 S 3.
of altered, diverted, or stopped up streets, to rest in Corporation, 108 S 22.
courts or passages to be kept in good repair by owners. 3 S 83.

PEACE, CLERK OF THE, jurisdiction of, to extend throughout extended borough,
63 S 12.

PEACE, JUSTICES OF, jurisdiction of, to extend throughout extended borough,
63 S 12.

PENALTIES, Corporation may make byelaws for imposing, on unlicensed meters
and weighers. 87 S 100.
Corporation may order proceedings for recovery of, 85 S 97.
for failing to deliver to Coal Inspector, pit note, account or declaration; making
false, feigned, or forged pit notes; altering or mutilating pit notes; failing
to affix coal certificates as directed; making or affixing false or forged coal
certificates; altering or mutilating certificates; making or delivering false
accounts of coal; bringing coal of one quality as coal of another; making
false declarations in respect of coal and failing to have requisite figures
painted on coal carts, 19 S 17.
offences at Drypool Bridge, recovery of, 105, S 11.
connected with coal, recovery of, 20 S 21-22.
landing places, to be recoverable in accordance with 11 and 12 Vict.,
cap. 43, 25 S 14.
on Corporation for failing to exhibit, at Drypool Bridge, such lights as Trinity
House direct, 104 S 10.
lights during construction of Drypool Bridge, 104 S 9.
to be carried to Borough Fund, 84 S 88.
under Hull Extension and Improvement Act, 1882, may be prosecuted as pro-
v ded by Summary Jurisdiction Acts, 81 S 88.
Improvement Act, &c., to be recoverable in accordance with 11 and 12
Vict. cap. 43., 20 S 22.

PENALTY, for breach of byelaws respecting Drypool Bridge, 105 S 13.
for building, rebuilding or altering buildings, dwelling-houses, sewers, drains,
privies cesspools, or ashpits, without consent of Local Board, 23 S 11.
causing carts, wagons trucks, &c., to stand in streets longer than necessary for
loading and unloading, 9 S 111.
collecting or carrying away dust, &c., 2 S 74.
delivering a less number than 16 sacks for a ton of coal, or sacks not filled to
the top, 14 S 166.
erecting walls, &c., over sewers, 2 S 69.
failing to discontinue or remedy nuisances, 8 S 106.
flag or pave and drain courts or passages, 3 S 83.
keep vaults, arches, cellars and drains under streets in repair, 4 S 90.
provide and cleanse urinals at public houses and beershops, 7 S 104.
frauds in sale of coals, 12 S 151.
nuisances, not to be inflicted until after determination of appeal, 8 S 105.

URBAN SANITARY AUTHORITY, Corporation, in laying out carriageways and footways, may exercise such powers as are vested in any, 113 S 29.

URINALS, owner or occupier of licensed victualler's house or beershop to provide and cleanse, 7 S 104.
penalty for failing to provide and cleanse, when required by Local Board, 7 S 104.

VAULTS, Corporation may construct, 113 S 29.
in or under streets to be kept in repair by owners, 4 S 90.
may be repaired by Local Board in default of owners, 4 S 90.
penalty for failing to keep in repair, 4 S 90.

VERDICTS, &c., not to be quashed for want of form, 84 S 91.

VICTORIA PIER, Corporation may repair or reconstruct, and approaches thereto, 27 S 2.
Corporation may, issue debentures for repayment of moneys borrowed for, 28 S 9.
on certain days, exclude public from free admission to roof of covered way from Nelson Street to, 28 S 7.
provide covered way, with roof available as promenade, 27 S 2.

VISITORS, COMMITTEE OF. Council may confer on committee powers of, under Lunatic Asylums Acts, 78 S 63.

WAGONS, penalty for causing to stand in streets longer than necessary, 9 S 111.

WALLS not to be erected over sewers without consent of Local Board, 2 S 69.

WARD, three Councillors at least to be returned by each, 66 S 26.

WARDS, Borough to be divided into, 65 S 21.
Commissioner, power of, to examine witnesses, 67 S 29.
to be appointed by Local Government Board to divide Borough into, 65 S 21.
prepare scheme for allocating councillors amongst new, 66 S 23.
report within limited time, 66 S 24.
Councillors to hold office in allocated, for residue of term, 66 S 25.
names numbers and boundaries of, for all purposes to be those set forth in order of Local Government Board, 66 S 25.
to be determined by order of Local Government Board, 65 S 21.
order of Local Government Board respecting, to be published, 66 S 25.

WATER, Corporation may charge cost of obtaining, for flushing and cleansing Ferry Boat Dock to General District Rate, 28 S 5.
from houses to be conveyed away by drains or tunnels below surface of pavement, 4 S 92.
Local Board may make byelaws for preventing frauds in sale of, 10 S 115.
pipes, Corporation not to remove in St. John's Wood, 68 S 36 (2).
or mains, alteration of, to be done under superintendence of owner, and to satisfaction of owner's engineer, 112 S 28.

CONTENTS.

BOROUGH OF KINGSTON-UPON-HULL.
PROVISIONAL ORDER.

Dated 24th March, 1897.

Confirmed by the Local Government Board's Provisional Orders Confirmation (No. 2) Act, 1897 60 & 61 Vict., Ch. LXVIII.

Royal Assent, 15th July, 1897.

ART. 1.   The confirming Act of 1890* shall be altered by the insertion in Article I. of the Order of 1890† as altered by the Order of 1895‡ of the words "or the Guardians of the Poor of the Sculcoates Union" before the words "or the Hull and Goole Port Sanitary Authority."

ART. 2.   The Order of 1890 may be cited as the Kingston-upon-Hull Order 1890 this Order may be cited as the Kingston-upon-Hull Order 1897 and the Orders of 1890 and 1895 and this Order may be cited together as the Kingston-upon-Hull Orders 1890 to 1897.

* *Local Government Board's Provisional Order Confirmation (No. 14) Act, 1890.*

† *Provisional Order of 1890.*

‡ *Provisional Order of 1895.*

CONTENTS.

CONTENTS.   iii.

KINGSTON-UPON-HULL CORPORATION ACT, 1897.

60 and 61 Vict., Ch. CCXLIX.

Royal Assent, 6th August, 1897.

PART I.

Preliminary.

1. This Act may be cited as The Kingston-upon-Hull Corporation Act 1897. *Short Title.*

2. For the purposes of proceedings preliminary to the municipal elections of one thousand eight hundred and ninety-seven and for the purposes of the lists of county electors and the county registers to be made for the county in pursuance of the County Electors Act 1888 or any Act amending that Act and for the purposes of the lists and registers of parochial electors and any other lists or registers to be made in pursuance of the Local Government Act 1894 this Act shall take effect on its passing but except for those purposes and except as hereinafter otherwise expressly provided this Act shall commence and take effect from and immediately after the thirtieth day of September one thousand eight hundred and ninety-seven (which last-mentioned time is in this Act referred to as the commencement of this Act) Provided that for the purposes of Sections 20 22 23 24 and 26 of the Local Government Act 1888 and for the purposes of the Local Taxation (Customs and Excise) Act 1890 the city shall be deemed not to have been extended until after the thirty-first day of March one thousand eight hundred and ninety-eight. *Commencement of Act.*

3. This Act is divided into parts as follows :— *Division of Act into parts.*

Part I.—Preliminary.
Part II.—City Extension.
Part III.—Bridge over River Hull and New Streets.
Part IV.—Crematory.
Part V.—Lands.
Part VI.—Powers of Borrowing ; Existing Debt.
Part VII.—Rates.
Part VIII.—Recreation Grounds.
Part IX.—Stock.
Part X.—Supply of Gas.
Part XI.—Water.
Part XII.—Miscellaneous and Procedure.

Incorpora-
tion of general
enactments.

4. The Lands Clauses Acts (except Section 127 of the Lands Clauses Consolidation Act 1845) the Waterworks Clauses Act 1847 (except the provisions with respect to the amount of profit to be received by the Undertakers and with respect to the yearly receipt and expenditure of the Undertakers and except the words in Section 44 " with the consent in writing of the owner or reputed owner of any such house or of the agent of such owner ") and Sections 13 to 21 of the Waterworks Clauses Act 1863 so far as the same are applicable for the purposes of and not expressly varied by or inconsistent with this Act are hereby incorporated with this Act.

In construing those Acts for the purposes of this Act, the expression " the Promoters of the Undertaking " and " the Undertakers " shall mean the Corporation.

Interpreta-
tion.

5. In this Act unless the context otherwise requires—

"The existing City" means the City and County of Kingston-upon-Hull as existing immediately before the passing of this Act ;

"The added part of the City" means the area added to the existing city by this Act ;

"The City" used without any qualification or "the extended City" means the existing City with the added part of the City ;

"The Corporation" means the Mayor Aldermen and Citizens of the existing City or of the extended City (as the case may require) ;

"The Borough Fund" and the "Borough Rate" and "the District Fund" and "the General District Rate" mean respectively the Borough Fund Borough Rate and District Fund and General District Rate of the City ;

"The Town Clerk" and "the City Engineer" mean respectively the Town Clerk and the City Engineer of the City and "the Water Engineer" means the Engineer of the Waterworks of the Corporation ;

"The Improvement Act" means the Kingston-upon-Hull Improvement Act 1854 ;

"The Act of 1882" means the Hull Extension and Improvement Act 1882 ;

" The Municipal Corporation Acts " means the Municipal Corporations Act 1882 and all Acts for the time being in force amending the same ;

" The Public Health Acts " means the Public Health Act 1875 and all Acts for the time being in force amending the same ;

Words and expressions to which meanings are assigned by the Acts incorporated herewith have in this Act the same respective meanings Provided that the expression "superior courts" or "court of competent jurisdiction" or any other like term shall have effect as if the debt or demand with respect to which it is used were a simple contract debt and not a debt or demand created by statute.

6. This Act shall be carried into execution by the Corporation acting by the Council.

Execution of Act.

PART II.

CITY EXTENSION.

(i.) Extension of Boundaries and of Powers of Corporation &c.

7. The boundaries of the existing city are hereby extended so as to comprise and the city shall accordingly comprise in addition to the existing city so much of the district of the Cottingham Urban District Council in the East Riding of the county of York as is described in the First Schedule to this Act.

Extension of boundaries of city.

8. The following sections of the Hull Extension and Improvement Act 1882 (that is to say) :—

Application of certain provisions of Act of 1882.

Section 10 (Authority of Corporation extended);

Section 12 (Jurisdiction of the sheriff recorder and other officers extended) ;

Section 14 (Added part of borough to be part of county of town of Hull);

Section 16 (Vesting property of Corporation);

Section 20 (Bye-laws &c. to apply to extended borough) ;

shall apply to the extension of the city effected by this Act as if they had been re-enacted in this Act.

The added part of the city shall be added to and form part of the parish of Cottingham Within.

Exemption from liability to county and other rates and collection of arrears.

9. The added part of the city shall as respects contributions to county expenditure be as if it had always formed part of the existing city and (subject to the provisions of the Local Government Act 1888 relating to county boroughs) lands and other property in the added part of the city shall not be liable to contribute or to be rated to any expenditure of the County Council for the East Riding of Yorkshire or of any District Council :

Provided that all arrears of rates due in the added part of the city immediately before the commencement of this Act may be collected and recovered therein as if this Act had not been passed.

Adjustment of financial relations with the East Riding.

10. In any case where the extension of the city effected by this Act shall affect the distribution of the proceeds of the local taxation licenses and probate and estate duty grant and of the local taxation (customs and excise) duties between the county of the East Riding of York and the city or any financial relations or questions between the county and the city equitable adjustments between the areas interested may be made by the Councils of the said county and city by agreement within twelve months from the commencement of this Act and in default of such agreement by the Local Government Board and for the purposes of such adjustments the provisions of the Local Government Act 1888 relating to adjustments between administrative counties and county boroughs shall apply with the necessary modifications and the Local Government Board shall be substituted in such provisions for the Commissioners appointed under the said Act of 1888:

Provided that in lieu of Sub-section (6) of Section 61 of the said Act of 1888 Sub-sections (1) and (5) of Section 87 of the said Act of 1888 shall apply to any inquiries which may be directed by the Local Government Board under this section and to the costs of such inquiries.

Deposit of plan of extended city.

11. A plan of the city as extended by this Act signed in triplicate by James William Lowther the Chairman of the Committee of the House of Commons to which the Bill for this Act was referred (in this Act called the city plan) shall within two weeks after the passing of this Act be deposited at the office of the Clerk of the Parliaments House of Lords and in the Private Bill Office of the House of Commons and with the town clerk at his office and copies thereof certified by the town clerk shall be sent as soon as may be after such deposit to the Board of Agriculture the Board of Inland Revenue and to the Local Government Board   In case of any discrepancy between the city plan and the description of the added part of the city in the First Schedule to this Act the city plan shall prevail.

12. Copies of the said plan deposited with the town clerk or any extract therefrom certified by him or by the city engineer to be true shall be received by all courts of justice and elsewhere as primâ facie evidence of the contents of such plan and such plan shall at all reasonable times be open to inspection on payment of a charge to be fixed by the Council not exceeding one shilling and any person shall be entitled to a copy of or extract from such plan certified by the town clerk or city engineer on payment of the costs of every such copy or extract All sums received under this section shall be carried to the credit of the borough fund.

Copies of city plan to be evidence.

13. Nothing in this Act shall extend alter or affect the parliamentary boundaries of the city.

Parliamentary limits not affected.

(ii) *Division into Wards.—Provisions as to Elections.*

14. From the commencement of this Act the extended city shall be divided into sixteen wards whereof the names and boundaries are set out in the Second Schedule to this Act But nothing in this Act shall take away or affect the power to alter the number or boundaries of the wards of the city under the provisions of the Municipal Corporation Acts.

Division of city into wards.

15. After the division of the city into wards the Council for the city shall consist of sixteen aldermen and forty-eight councillors and each ward shall return three councillors.

Constitution and number of the Council.

16. Before the commencement of this Act the Council shall allocate the existing councillors among fourteen of the new wards so as to provide (as far as practicable) for each councillor continuing to represent as large a number as possible of his former constituents and on the commencement of this Act the councillors shall accordingly be deemed to have been respectively elected for the wards to which they shall have been so allocated.

Provision for existing councillors representing same constituents.

17. For the purposes of the roll of citizens the citizens lists and other lists to be made after the passing of this Act under the Municipal Corporation Acts and in relation to the functions and offices of the mayor town clerk and other officers under those Acts the added part of the city shall be deemed to have always been part of the city.

As to citizens roll &c.

General
saving for
elections of
councillors
&c.

18. Subject to the provisions of this Act respecting the division of the city into wards the allocation of councillors among the new wards and other relative matters the retirement and elections of mayor aldermen and councillors shall take effect and be held in like manner as if this Act had not been passed Provided that any doubt or difficulty as to the order of retirement of any of the councillors elected in the year 1897 shall be settled by order of the mayor and such order shall be final.

(iii) Provisions as to Cottingham Urban District Council; School Board; and Burial Board.

Cesser of
jurisdiction of
Cottingham
Urban District
Council over
part of
district.

19. (1) The Cottingham Urban District Council shall cease from and after the commencement of this Act to have or exercise any power rights or jurisdiction in or in relation to the parts of its district which are by this Act added to the city But nothing in this Act shall be construed to prevent the Cottingham Urban District Council from suing for and recovering any rates or sums of money due to them immediately before the commencement of this Act and the said district council may accordingly sue for and recover all such rates and sums in the same manner as if this Act had not been passed.

(2) All buildings lamps lamp-posts mains pipes sewers and other property of the said district council in the said parts of its district shall from and after the commencement of this Act be transferred to and vest in the Corporation for all the estate and interest therein of the said district council.

(3) The Corporation shall pay to the said district council for the property by this section transferred to the Corporation the sum of one hundred and sixty-one pounds one shilling and seven-pence and the Corporation shall withdraw and shall not enforce their claim for a contribution from the said District Council of the sum of one hundred and thirty-eight pounds eighteen shillings and five pence towards the cost of certain works recently executed by the Corporation under Section 38 (Provision as to outfall sewers) of the Act of 1882.

(4) The Corporation shall also take over and discharge as from the first day of August one thousand eight hundred and ninety seven the liability of the said District Council in respect of the instalments falling due after that date of—

(A) Certain annual payments expiring in the year one thousand nine hundred and six amounting to the sum of one hundred and seventy pounds three shillings and five pence each :

(B) Certain annual payments expiring in the year one thousand nine hundred and five amounting to the sum of nineteen pounds each :

The said annual sums being respectively the portions chargeable to the Newland Ward of a main drainage loan and joint outfall sewer loan contracted by the said District Council.

(5) The said District Council shall not be liable to contribute towards any cost hereafter incurred by the Corporation in the execution of new works under Section 38 (Provision as to outfall sewers) of the Act of 1882 save so far as such new works may be necessary or desirable in consequence of the increase of the population of or additional drainage matter from the area for the time being under the jurisdiction of the said District Council.

(6) The provisions of Section 39 (As to use and maintenance of outfall and other sewers) of the Act of 1882 shall apply mutatis mutandis in the case of the existing sewers and drains in that part of the Cottingham Urban District which is by this Act added to the City.

(7) In respect of all property within the added part of the City and for the period of fifteen years from the commencement of this Act the total amount in the pound of the borough school board watch library highway and general district rates and of any other rates (except the poor rate) levied or raised therein shall not exceed the total amount in the pound of the general district school board and county rates and of any other rates (except the poor rate) levied or raised in the added part of the city during the year ending on the thirty-first day of March one thousand eight hundred and ninety-seven and for the like period the highway rate shall be assessed and levied in the added part of the city on the same assessment as a general district rate is levied under Section 211 of the Public Health Act 1875.

(8) Nothing in this Act shall affect the operation in the added part of the city of the Agricultural Rates Act 1896 so long as that Act remains in force.

(9) For the period of fifteen years from the commencement of this Act the Corporation shall pay to the said District Council the sum of ninety-two pounds per annum towards the establishment expenses of the said District Council and in consideration thereof compensation shall not be payable by the Corporation to any officers of the said District Council.

(10) The Corporation shall not charge in respect of the interment in any of their cemeteries of any person resident in that part of the Newland Ward which is to remain in the Cottingham District any higher fee or fees than are for the time being charged by the Corporation in respect of the interment of any person resident in the city.

(11) The Corporation shall pay the costs charges and expenses which have been incurred by the said District Council in respect of or incidental to their negotiations with the Corporation and the passing of this Act.

Settlement of differences by arbitration.

20. Any difference arising out of the provisions of this Act between the Corporation and the Cottingham Urban District Council shall be settled by an arbitrator appointed by the parties or in default of agreement between the parties appointed by the Local Government Board.

City to be a school district.

21.—(1) For the purposes of the Elementary Education Act 1870 and the Acts amending the same the extended city shall be a school district and the School Board for the existing city shall be the School Board for that district to the exclusion of any other school authority.

(2) The members of the School Board for the existing city who are in office at the commencement of this Act shall constitute the School Board for the school district of the extended city and shall be deemed to have been elected therefor and shall hold office subject to the provisions of the said Acts and of this Act and o any order for holding a new election or otherwise which may be made by the Education Department.

As to bye-laws of School Board.

22. From and after the commencement of this Act all byelaws and regulations made by the School Board of the existing city and then in force shall apply to and be in force within the extended city (subject to any future repeal or amendment of the same) and all bye-laws and regulations made by any other school authority shall cease to be of any force or effect in the added part of the city.

23.—(1) From and after the commencement of this Act all powers and jurisdiction of the School Board for the school district of Cottingham shall cease with respect to so much of such district as is by this Act added to the existing city and all buildings with their fittings belonging to the board within such added part shall be transferred to and vested in the School Board for the extended city for all the estate and interest of the Cottingham School Board.

(2) The Corporation shall pay compensation to any clerk master or teacher in the employment of the Cottingham School Board at the commencement of this Act who by reason of any provision in this Act loses his office or is deprived of the whole or part of his emoluments within two years after the commencement of this Act and does not receive remuneration to an equal amount in respect of some office or employment under the School Board for the extended city or under any voluntary school which may be established in the part of the district of the Cottingham School Board added to the city.

(3) Such compensation may be by way of annuity or otherwise and the amount thereof shall be determined subject to the following conditions :—

(A) That such clerk master or teacher shall have been in the actual employment of the Cottingham School Board for a continuous period of not less than two years previous to the first day of November one thousand eight hundred and ninety-six :

(B) That the amount of such compensation shall be such as would be payable on retirement to such clerk master or teacher under Section 2 of the Superannuation Act 1859 in the event of his having served in an established capacity in the permanent civil service of the State for the same time as in the service of such body or person and as if ten years were added to the number of years he may have actually served :

(c) That in estimating such compensation the amount of the salary and fees upon which the same shall be calculated shall be taken on the average of the salary and fees actually received during the two years next preceding such first day of November 1896 by such clerk master or teacher as and for his own use after deducting therefrom any payments or allowances usually made by him :

(D) That no such compensation shall exceed two-thirds of the salary and fees upon which the same shall be estimated :

(E) That such compensation shall be payable in every case by two equal half-yearly payments the first of such payments to be made at the expiration of six months from the date when such clerk master or teacher shall by reason of the passing of this Act cease to receive such salary or fees :

(F) Provided that the Corporation may at any time agree with any clerk master or teacher entitled to any annuity under this enactment for the commutation of such annuity and may pay the same out of the fund and rate or rates out of which such annuity is payable or any moneys borrowed on the security thereof.

(4) If the School Board for the extended city shall within six months after the commencement of this Act offer any such clerk master or teacher any office or employment of a value equal to or greater than and with duties similar to those of the office or employment in respect of the loss of which compensation is by this Act payable to him and such clerk master or teacher accepts such office or employment or declines or fails within one month of such offer to accept such office or employment he shall forfeit his right to any compensation under this Act.

Corporation to be Burial Board.

24. The Corporation shall be the Burial Board for the extended city and shall have and may exercise within the extended city to the exclusion of any other Burial Board or authority all the powers rights and privileges and be subject to all the liabilities of a Burial Board beyond the Metropolis under the Burial Acts.

PART III.

Bridge over River Hull and New Streets.

Power to make bridge over River Hull.

25. Subject to the provisions of this Act the Corporation may make and maintain in the lines and according to the levels in that behalf shown on the deposited plans and sections the bridge over the River Hull and approaches thereto hereinafter described with all necessary arches river walls embankments lifts capstans mooring posts dolphins buildings works machinery and conveniences (that is to say) :—

An opening bridge across the River Hull together with
approaches thereto commencing in the parish of
Sculcoates on the west side of the river at a point in
Wincolmlee immediately opposite Scott Street and
terminating in the parish of Sutton on the east side
of the river in Lime Street immediately opposite
Jennings Street.

26. The following provisions shall be in force and have
effect for the protection of the Commissioners of Sewers for the
parts of the East Riding in the county of York the Beverley and
Barmston Drainage Commissioners the Holderness Drainage
Trustees the Beverley and Skidby Drainage Trustees and the
Cottingham Drainage Trustees respectively :

For protection of Commissioners of Sewers and Drainage Commissioners.

Notwithstanding anything shown on the deposited plans and
sections the bridge over the River Hull by this Act authorised
shall be constructed in accordance with the following conditions :

(1) Each of the two piers of the bridge shall be placed
parallel to the centre line of the river at the place of
crossing and neither pier shall occupy a width of waterway of more than eighteen inches exclusive of the
walings of which there may be three on each pier projecting to an extent of not more than six inches outside
the said eighteen inches for a depth of not more than
twelve inches for each waling :

(2) The clear span of the central arch of the bridge shall be
fifty-one feet and the height of the arch at the centre
shall be four feet six inches above the level of high
water of ordinary spring tides and the height of the
arch at the piers shall be the level of high water of
ordinary spring tides :

(3) The distance between the river walls at the site of the
bridge shall not be reduced but the Corporation shall
be at liberty to bring forward the river wall at the west
side of the river to an extent not exceeding three feet
conditionally on their executing the work in such
manner that the face of the new wall shall form a
uniform line with the face of the old wall above and
below the bridge and on their setting back the river
wall on the east side to a corresponding extent :

(4) The western approach to the bridge may be constructed so as to overhang tho river wall at a level not lower than twelve inches below high water of ordinary spring tides.

27. The following sections of the Hull (Drypool) Bridge and Improvements Act 1885 namely :—

Section 9 (Lights on works during construction) ;

Section 11 (Bridge and approaches to be deemed part of the streets of the borough) ;

Section 14 (Penalty if bridge master exercise powers unfairly) ;

Section 15 (Penalty if persons offer rewards or bribes to bridge master) ;

Section 21 (Power to stop up ways during the execution of the improvements) ;

Section 33 (Power to Corporation to make agreements with owners of property &c.) ;

Section 39 (Saving rights of the Crown) ;

shall apply to the bridge authorised to be constructed under this Act in the same way as they applied or apply to Drypool Bridge constructed under the said Act of 1885 and as if they were for that purpose re-enacted in this Act.

28. Previously to commencing the bridge over the River Hull or the works connected therewith the Corporation shall deposit at the Board of Trade plans sections and working drawings of the bridge and works for the approval of the Board   The approval of the Board of Trade shall be signified in writing under the hand of the secretary or an assistant secretary of the Board and the bridge and works respectively shall be constructed only in accordance with such approval and when the bridge or works shall have been commenced or constructed the Corporation shall not at any time alter or extend the same without obtaining previously to making any such alteration or extension the like consent or approval and if the bridge or works shall be commenced or completed or be altered extended or constructed contrary to the provisions of this Act the Board of Trade may abate alter and remove the same and restore the site thereof to its former condition at the cost and charge of the Corporation and the amount thereof shall be a debt due from the Corporation to the Crown and be recoverable accordingly with costs of action or may be recovered with costs as a penalty is or may be recoverable from the Corporation.

29. If at any time or times it shall be deemed expedient by the Board of Trade to order a local survey and examination of any works of the Corporation authorised by this Act in over or affecting any tidal or navigable water or river or of the intended site thereof the Corporation shall defray the costs of every such local survey and examination and the amount thereof shall be a debt due to the Crown from the Corporation and if not paid upon demand may be recovered as a debt due to the Crown with the costs of action or may be recovered with costs as a penalty is or may be recoverable from the Corporation. *Board of Trade may order local survey.*

30. If any works by this Act authorised to be constructed by the Corporation in under over through or across any tidal water or navigable river or if any portion of any work which affects or may affect any such water or river or access thereto shall be abandoned or suffered to fall into disuse or decay the Board of Trade may abate and remove the same or such part or parts thereof as that Board may at any time or times deem fit and proper and restore the site thereof to its former condition at the cost and charge of the Corporation and the amount thereof shall be a debt due from the Corporation to the Crown and if not paid upon demand may be recovered as a debt due to the Crown with the costs of action or may be recovered with costs as a penalty is or may be recoverable from the Corporation. *If any works be abandoned &c., Board of Trade may direct removal.*

31. Nothing in this Act shall authorise the Corporation to take use or in any manner interfere with any portion of the shore or bed of the sea or of any river channel creek bay or estuary or any right in respect thereof belonging to the Queen's Most Excellent Majesty in right of Her Crown and under the management of the Board of Trade without the previous consent in writing of the Board of Trade on behalf of Her Majesty (which consent the Board of Trade may give) neither shall anything in this Act extend to take away prejudice diminish or alter any of the estates rights privileges powers or authorities vested in or enjoyed or exerciseable by Her Majesty. *Saving rights of the Crown in the foreshore.*

32. The Corporation shall provide erect and maintain for the assistance and use of vessels passing through or under the bridge such mooring posts dolphins or other works as the Board *Corporation to erect mooring posts.*

of Trade may from time to time direct Such works shall be placed so as to cause as little obstruction as may be to the flow of the water in the River Hull.

Corporation to exhibit lights.

33. The Corporation shall exhibit and keep burning from sunset to sunrise such lights (if any) on each side of the said bridge over the River Hull as the Board of Trade shall from time to time direct If the Corporation fail to comply in any respect with the provisions of this section they shall for each night in which they so fail be liable to a penalty not exceeding twenty pounds.

Bye-laws as to bridges.

34. The Corporation may make bye-laws for prescribing the times of opening and shutting the bridge authorised to be constructed under this Act and any other bridge of the Corporation which is an opening bridge and for regulating the traffic over through and under every such bridge but such bye-laws shall be of no effect unless confirmed by the Board of Trade and shall as regards the Drypool Bridge conform to the provisions of Section 12 (Regulations as to opening bridge) of the Hull (Drypool) Bridge and Improvements Act 1885.

Penalty for breach of bye-laws.

35. The Corporation may by any bye-laws made by them under the last preceding section impose on offenders against the same such reasonable penalties as they think fit not exceeding the sum of ten pounds for each offence and every such penalty shall be recoverable summarily.

Power to make new streets.

36. Subject to the provisions of this Act the Corporation may make and maintain in the lines and according to the levels in that behalf shown on the deposited plans and sections the new streets hereinafter described together with all necessary works and conveniences connected therewith or incident thereto (that is to say) :—

> A new street partly in the parish of Sculcoates and partly in the united parishes of Holy Trinity and St. Mary commencing in the parish of Sculcoates at the junction of Prospect Street and Story Street and terminating in the parish of Sculcoates at the junction of Waterworks Street and Savile Street.

> A new street wholly within the parish of Sculcoates commencing at a point on the before-mentioned new street one hundred and thirty-nine yards from the commencement of the same and terminating at the junction of Savile Street and George Street.

37. In constructing any of the works shown on the deposited **Power to deviate.** plans the Corporation may deviate laterally from the lines thereof to any extent not exceeding the limits of lateral deviation shown on the deposited plans and may also deviate from the levels shown on the deposited sections to any extent not exceeding two feet Provided that no deviation either lateral or vertical below high-water mark shall be made without the consent in writing of the Board of Trade Provided also that no such deviation shall be made so as to alter or affect the conditions contained in the section of this Act the marginal note of which is " For protection of Commissioners of Sewers and Drainage Commissioners " without the consent in writing of the said Commissioners.

38. If the bridge and new streets by this Act authorised are **Period for completion of works.** not respectively completed within five years from the passing of this Act then on the expiration of that period the powers by this Act granted to the Corporation for making and completing the same respectively or otherwise in relation thereto shall cease except as to so much thereof respectively as is then completed.

39. In connection with the new streets by this Act **Power to stop up certain streets.** authorised the Corporation may stop up and appropriate and divert all or any of the following streets and roads namely :—

> Vincent Street for a distance of seventy-one yards from its south end Medley Street for a distance of forty-three yards from its east end Edward's Court Edward's Place Union Square Richmond Square Vine Court Green's Place Admiral Place Dyer's Place Brewery Buildings the eastern and central branches of Wells Yard the western branch of Wells Yard for a distance of thirty yards from its north end Vincent Place Medley Place Providence Row the eastern branch of Blue Bell Yard the western branch of Blue Bell Yard for a distance of forty yards from its north end Fishwick's Yard for a distance of thirteen yards from its north end Mountain Square and Carlisle Square and may make junctions or communications with roads sewers and drains and if necessary alter the levels thereof and remove alter or interfere with sewers drains gas water or other mains or pipes and telegraphic telephonic or other apparatus :

From and immediately after the stopping up of any street by the Corporation all rights of way over the same shall be by virtue of this Act extinguished and the site and soil thereof shall be vested in the Corporation freed and discharged from all rights of way and other rights or easements over or affecting the same :

Provided that the Corporation shall not remove alter or interfere with any telegraphic telephonic or other apparatus belonging to or used by the Postmaster-General except in accordance with and subject to the provisions of the Telegraph Act 1878.

PART IV.

CREMATORY.

Power of Corporation to provide crematory.

40.—(1) The Corporation may if they think fit erect fit up and maintain a suitable building or buildings with all necessary and proper furnaces and appliances for the cremation of dead human bodies by the application of heat (in this Act called a crematory) within the following limits namely :—

A piece of land within the city adjoining the Hedon Road Cemetery bounded on the north by the Withernsea branch of the North Eastern Railway on the west by the said cemetery and on the east and south by the Sanatorium Grounds and other land of the Corporation.

(2) The Corporation shall prepare bye-laws as to cremation and submit them to a Secretary of State and the Secretary of State may approve of such bye-laws with or without modifications and after having approved of such bye-laws he may at any time require them to be submitted to him for revision or modification.

(3) The bye-laws shall prescribe in what cases in what mode and under what conditions cremations may take place and they may prescribe the forms of the certificates and declarations to be given or made before a cremation is permitted to take place and such declarations shall be made under and by virtue of the Statutory Declarations Act 1835 and such certificates shall be confirmed by a declaration made under and by virtue of the same Act.

(4) Every person who shall contravene any such bye-laws or shall wilfully carry out or procure or take part in the cremation of any human remains in such crematory except in accordance with

such bye-laws shall (in addition to any liability or penalty which he may otherwise incur) be liable on summary conviction to a penalty not exceeding fifty pounds.

(5) Every person who shall wilfully make any false declaration or representation or sign or utter any false certificate with a view to procuring the cremation of any human remains in such crematory shall (in addition to any penalty or liability which he may otherwise incur) be liable on summary conviction to a fine not exceeding fifty pounds.

(6) The Corporation may demand payment of any such charges or fees for such cremation as may be authorised by any table approved by a Secretary of State and such charges or fees shall be deemed to be a debt due to the Corporation from the estate of the deceased.

(7) Nothing in this section shall interefere with the jurisdiction of any coroner and jury under the Coroners Act 1887 or any Act amending the same.

(8) All expenditure incurred under this section shall be payable out of moneys borrowed under this Act or out of the borough fund and borough rate.

PART V.

LANDS.

41. Subject to the provisions of this Act the Corporation may for the purposes of the proposed bridge over the river Hull and of the approaches thereto and of the new streets by this Act authorised enter on take and use all or any of the lands in that behalf respectively shown on the deposited plans and described in the deposited book of reference.

Power to acquire lands.

42. If any omission misstatement or erroneous description is found to have been made of any lands or of any owners lessees or occupiers of any lands shown or described or intended to be shown or described on the deposited plans or in the deposited book of reference the Corporation may apply to two justices for the correction thereof after giving ten days notice to the owners lessees and occupiers of the lands affected by the proposed correction and if it appears to the justices that the omission

Correction of errors &c. in deposited plans and book of reference.

misstatement or erroneous description arose from mistake they shall certify the same accordingly stating the particulars of the omission misstatement or erroneous description and such certificate shall be deposited with the clerk of the peace for the city and shall be kept by him with the other documents to which it relates and subject and according to the same enactments and provisions as apply to those other documents and thereupon the deposited plans or book of reference (as the case requires) shall be deemed to be corrected according to the certificate and the Corporation may enter on take hold and use those lands accordingly.

43. The powers of the Corporation for the compulsory purchase of lands easements or rights for the purposes of this Act shall cease after the expiration of three years after the passing of this Act.

Period for compulsory purchase of lands.

44. Persons empowered by the Lands Clauses Consolidation Act 1845 to sell and convey or release land may if they think fit subject to the provisions of that Act and of the Lands Clauses Consolidation Acts 1860 and 1869 and of this Act grant to the Corporation any easement right or privilege (not being an easement right or privilege of water in which persons other than the grantors have an interest) required for the purposes of this Act in over or affecting any such lands and the provisions of the said Acts with respect to lands and rent charges so far as the same are applicable in this behalf shall extend and apply to such grants and to such easements rights and privileges as aforesaid respectively.

Persons empowered by Lands Clauses Acts to sell lands may grant easements &c.

45.—(1) The Corporation shall not under the powers of this Act purchase or acquire ten or more houses which on the fifteenth day of December last were or have been since that date or shall hereafter be occupied either wholly or partially by persons belonging to the labouring class as tenants or lodgers unless and until—

Restrictions on displacing persons of labouring class.

(A) They shall have obtained the approval of the Local Government Board to a scheme for providing new dwellings for such number of persons as were residing in such houses on the fifteenth day of December last or for such number of persons as the Local Government Board shall after inquiry deem necessary having regard to the number of persons on or after that date residing in such houses and working within one mile therefrom and to the amount of vacant suitable accommodation in the immediate neighbourhood of such houses or to the place of employment of such persons and to all the circumstances of the case ; and

(b) They shall have given security to the satisfaction of the Local Government Board for the carrying out of the scheme.

(2) The approval of the Local Government Board to any scheme under this section may be given either absolutely or conditionally and after the Local Government Board have approved of any such scheme they may from time to time approve either absolutely or conditionally of any modifications in the scheme.

(3) Every scheme under this section shall contain provisions prescribing the time within which it shall be carried out and shall require the new dwellings proposed to be provided under the scheme to be completed fit for occupation before the persons residing in the houses in respect of which the scheme is made are displaced :

Provided that the Local Government Board may dispense with the last-mentioned requirement subject to such conditions (if any) as they may see fit.

(4) Any provisions of any scheme under this section or any conditions subject to which the Local Government Board may have approved of any scheme or of any modifications of any scheme under this section or subject to which they may have dispensed with the above-mentioned requirement shall be enforceable by a writ of mandamus to be obtained by the Local Government Board out of the High Court.

(5) If the Corporation acquire or appropriate any house or houses for the purposes of this Act in contravention of the foregoing provisions or displace or cause to be displaced the persons residing in any house or houses in contravention of the requirements of the scheme they shall be liable to a penalty of five hundred pounds in respect of every such house which penalty shall be recoverable by the Local Government Board by action in the High Court and shall be carried to and form part of the Consolidated Fund of the United Kingdom :

Provided that the Court may if it think fit reduce such penalty.

(6) For the purpose of carrying out any scheme under this section the Corporation may appropriate any lands for the time being belonging to them or which they have power to acquire :

Provided that nothing in this section shall relieve the Corporation from the necessity of obtaining the approval of the Local Government Board for such appropriation or use of their corporate land as would require such approval under the Municipal Corporations Act 1882 (as amended by section 72 of the Local Government Act 1888) or any other general Act.

(7) Subject to the provisions of this section the Corporation and the Local Government Board and their inspectors shall have and may exercise for any purpose in connection with any scheme under this section all or any of the powers vested in them under the Public Health Act 1875 in the same manner in every respect as if the preparation and carrying into effect of such scheme were one of the general purposes of that Act :

Provided that all lands on which any buildings have been erected or provided by the Corporation in pursuance of any scheme under this section shall for a period of twenty-five years from the date of the scheme be appropriated for the purpose of dwellings and every conveyance demise or lease of such lands and buildings shall be endorsed with notice of this enactment :

Provided also that the Local Government Board may at any time dispense with all or any of the requirements of this sub-section subject to such conditions (if any) as they may see fit.

(8) The Corporation shall pay to the Local Government Board a sum to be fixed by that Board in respect of the preparation and issue of any Provisional Order in pursuance of this section and any expenses incurred by that Board in relation to any inquiries under this section including the expenses of any witnesses summoned by the inspector holding the inquiry and a sum to be fixed by that Board not exceeding three guineas a day for the services of such inspector.

(9) For the purposes of this section the expression " labouring class " includes mechanics artisans labourers and others working for wages hawkers costermongers persons not working for wages but working at some trade or handicraft without employing others except members of their own family and persons other than domestic servants whose income does not exceed an average of thirty shillings a week and the families of any of such persons who may be residing with them.

46.—(1) Every case of disputed compensation arising under this Act in respect of any hereditament not exceeding in rateable value twenty pounds per annum shall be heard and determined by a single arbitrator to be appointed unless both parties concur in making the appointment by the Judge of the County Court of Yorkshire holden at Kingston-upon-Hull on the application of either party.

Single arbitrator to determine compensation.

(2) Any such application to the Judge must state that fourteen days (at least) have elapsed since service of the notice to treat and that the parties have failed to concur in making a joint appointment.

(3) Every arbitrator appointed under this Act shall have all the powers of a single arbitrator appointed under the Lands Clauses Acts and the provisions of those Acts incorporated with this Act shall apply accordingly.

(4) In the event of the death removal resignation or incapacity refusal or neglect to act of any arbitrator before he shall have made his award the Judge may appoint another arbitrator to whom all documents relating to the matter of the arbitration which were in the possession of the former arbitrator shall be delivered.

(5) Where two or more hereditaments belong to the same owner or owners or are included in one notice to treat the provisions of this section shall apply notwithstanding that the aggregate rateable value of such hereditaments may exceed twenty pounds per annum but shall not apply if any of such hereditaments exceeds the said rateable value of twenty pounds per annum.

47. Notwithstanding Section 69 of the Lands Clauses Consolidation Act 1845 any purchase or compensation moneys payable in pursuance of this Act may be paid direct to any trustee or trustees who on a sale under the Settled Land Acts 1882 to 1890 or otherwise could give a legal discharge for such purchase money.

Provision for payment to trustees.

48. And whereas in the construction of the works by this Act authorised or otherwise in the exercise by the Corporation of the powers of this Act it may happen that portions only of certain properties shown or partly shown on the deposited plans will be sufficient for the purposes of the Corporation and that such portions or some other portions less than the whole can be severed from the remainder of the said properties without material detriment thereto Therefore the following provisions shall have effect :—

Owners may be required to sell parts only of certain properties.

(1) The owner of and persons interested in any of the properties whereof the whole or part is described in the Third Schedule to this Act and whereof a portion only is required for the purposes of the Corporation or each or any of them are hereinafter included in the term the owner and the said properties are hereinafter referred to as the scheduled properties :

(2) If for twenty-one days after the service of notice to treat in respect of a specified portion of any of the scheduled properties the owner shall fail to notify in writing to the Corporation that he alleges that such portion cannot be severed from the remainder of the property without material detriment thereto he may be required to sell and convey to the Corporation such portion only without the Corporation being obliged or compellable to purchase the whole the Corporation paying for the portion so taken and making compensation for any damage sustained by the owner by severance or otherwise :

(3) If within such twenty-one days the owner shall by notice in writing to the Corporation allege that such portion cannot be so severed the jury arbitrators or other authority to whom the question of disputed compensation shall be submitted (hereinafter referred to as the tribunal) shall in addition to the other questions required to be determined by them determine whether the portion of the scheduled property specified in the notice to treat can be severed from the remainder without material detriment thereto and if not whether any and what other portion less than the whole (but not exceeding the portion over which the Corporation have compulsory powers of purchase) can be so severed :

(4) If the tribunal determine that the portion of the scheduled property specified in the notice to treat or any such other portion as aforesaid can be severed from the remainder without material detriment thereto the owner may be required to sell and convey to the Corporation the portion which the tribunal shall have determined to be so severable without the Corporation

being obliged or compellable to purchase the whole the Corporation paying such sum for the portion taken by them including compensation for any damage sustained by the owner by severance or otherwise as shall be awarded by the tribunal :

(5) If. the tribunal determine that the portion of the scheduled property specified in the notice to treat can notwithstanding the allegation of the owner be severed from the remainder without material detriment thereto the tribunal may in their absolute discretion determine and order that the costs charges and expenses incurred by the owner incident to the arbitration or inquiry shall be born and paid by the owner :

(6) If the tribunal determine that the portion of the scheduled property specified in the notice to treat cannot be severed from the remainder without material detriment thereto (and whether or not they shall determine that any other portion can be so severed) the Corporation may withdraw their notice to treat and thereupon they shall pay to the owner all costs charges and expenses reasonably and properly incurred by him in consequence of such notice :

(7) If the tribunal determine that the portion of the scheduled property specified in the notice to treat cannot be severed from the remainder without material detriment thereto but that any such other portion as aforesaid can be so severed the Corporation in case they shall not withdraw the notice to treat shall pay to the owner all costs charges and expenses reasonably and properly incurred by him in consequence of such notice or such portion thereof as the tribunal shall having regard to the circumstances of the case and their final determination think fit.

The provisions of this section shall be in force notwithstanding anything in the Lands Clauses Consolidation Act 1845 contained and nothing contained in or done under this section shall be held as determining or as being or implying an admission that any of the scheduled properties or any part thereof is or is not or but for this section would or would not be subject to the provisions of Section 92 of the Lands Clauses Consolidation Act 1845.

The provisions of this section shall be stated in every notice given thereunder to sell and convey any premises.

49. Subject to the provisions of this Act the Corporation may from time to time appropriate and use for any of the purposes of this Act or of any other local or public Acts in force within the city and conferring powers on the Corporation any lands for the time being vested in them as part of their corporate estates or in their capacity of a sanitary authority and which are not required for the purposes for which the same were acquired or are at present generally applied.

Power to appropriate lands for purposes of Act

50. Section 57 (Power to sell lands) of the Act of 1882 shall be read and have effect as if " the Local Government Board " were therein substituted for " the Treasury."

Amendment of s. 57 of Act of 1882.

51. Section 58 (Corporation may lease lands not required for purposes of Act) ; and

Application of ss. 58 and 59 of Act of 1882.

Section 59 (Application of purchase money of land) of the Act of 1882 ;

shall extend and apply to lands acquired by the Corporation under this Act and not required for the purposes of this Act.

PART VI.

Powers of Borrowing.   Existing Debt.

(i) Borrowing Powers.

52. (1) The Corporation may from time to time independently of any other borrowing power borrow in manner provided by this Act any sum not exceeding twenty-five thousand pounds for the acquisition of land for and for the construction of the new bridge by this Act authorised and any sum not exceeding two hundred thousand pounds for the acquisition of land for and for the making of the new streets by this Act authorised and any sum not exceeding one thousand nine hundred pounds for the provision of a crematory and such sums as may be requisite for the purchase of the undertaking of the Kingston-upon-Hull Gas Light Company and for carrying out the other purposes of this Act

Power to borrow for purposes of Act.

and the Corporation may also borrrow for the payment of the costs charges and expenses of obtaining this Act the amount of such costs charges and expenses.

(2) The Corporation may raise all or any of the moneys which they are authorised to borrow by the creation and issue of Hull Corporation Redeemable Stock in accordance with the provisions of the Hull Corporation Loans Act 1881 as amended by any subsequent Act or Order confirmed by Parliament or by any of the methods provided by the Local Loans Act 1875.

(3) The contributions to the sums directed by the said Corporation Loans Act to be carried to the Corporation Loans Fund in respect of interest on and of redemption of stock shall in the case of stock created and issued under this Act for the purposes of the new streets by this Act authorised be payable out of the District Fund and General District Rate and in the case of stock created and issued under this Act for any other purpose of this Act including the payment of the costs charges and expenses of preparing and obtaining this Act shall be payable out of the Borough Fund and Borough Rate.

(4) In the case of any moneys raised under this Act by any of the methods provided by the Local Loans Act 1875 the local rate for the purposes of that Act shall be as regards moneys raised for the purposes of the new streets by this Act authorised the General District Rate and as regards moneys raised for any other purpose of this Act including the payment of the costs charges and expenses of preparing and obtaining this Act shall be the Borough Rate.

(5) The powers of borrowing money by this Act given shall not be restricted by any of the regulations contained in Section 234 of the Public Health Act 1875 and in calculating the amount which the Corporation may borrow under that Act any sums which they may borrow under this Act shall not be reckoned.

53. The Corporation shall pay off all moneys borrowed by them under this Act within fifty years from the time or respective times of borrowing the same except moneys borrowed for the payment of the costs charges and expenses of obtaining this Act which shall be paid off within ten years from the date of the borrowing of the same.

Period for payment off of money borrowed.

Protection of
lenders from
inquiry.

54. A person lending money to the Corporation under this Act shall not be bound to inquire as to the observance by them of any provisions of this Act or be bound to see to the application or be answerable for any loss misapplication or non-application of the money lent or of any part thereof.

Corporation
not to regard
trusts.

55. The Corporation shall not be bound to recognise or see to the execution of any trust whether expressed or implied or constructive to which any loan or security for loan given by them under this Act may be subject but the receipt of the person or any one of the persons or (as the case may be) of the personal representative or representatives of the person or the last survivor of the persons in whose name or names any loan or security for loan stands in the books of the Corporation shall from time to time be a sufficient discharge to the Corporation in respect thereof notwithstanding any trusts to which such loan or security may be subject and whether or not the Corporation have had express or implied notice of any such trust or of any charge or incumbrance or transfer of such loan or security.

Application
of money
borrowed.

56. Money borrowed by the Corporation under this Act shall be applied only for the purposes of this Act for which it is authorised to be borrowed and to which capital is properly applicable.

(ii.) Existing Debt.

Provision as
to existing
debt.

57. And whereas the Corporation have from time to time under statutory authority or the sanction of Government Departments borrowed large sums the particulars whereof are contained in the Fifth Schedule to this Act which sums are repayable within different periods and it is expedient to equate the periods of repayment of the sums owing in respect of each debt

Therefore the following provisions shall have effect : (namely)

All the provisions of any Act or Order confirmed by Parliament or of any sanction of a Government Department prescribing the periods within which any sums forming part of the debts referred to in the Fifth Schedule are to be repaid shall so far as regards the said sums be repealed as from the thirty-first day of March one thousand eight hundred and ninety-eight and in lieu thereof it is hereby enacted that :—

(i) All sums owing in respect of the borough fund debt and any moneys re-borrowed in lieu thereof shall be repaid within fifty-five years from the thirty-first day of March one thousand eight hundred and ninety-eight;

(ii) All moneys owing in respect of the waterworks debt and any moneys re-borrowed in lieu thereof shall be re-paid within fifty years from the thirty-first day of March one thousand eight hundred and ninety-eight ;

(iii.) All moneys owing in respect of the sanitary and general debt and any moneys re-borrowed in lieu thereof shall be repaid within thirty-five years from the thirty-first day of March one thousand eight hundred and ninety-eight ;

(iv.) The annual payments to be made to the Loans Fund or any sinking fund established for the repayment of the said sums shall be made on or before the thirty-first day of March in each year and the first payments thereto shall be made on or before the thirty-first day of March one thousand eight hundred and ninety-nine ;

(v.) The Corporation shall on or before the thirty-first day of March one thousand eight hundred and ninety-eight pay into the Loans Fund or any sinking fund existing at the commencement of this Act in respect of the said sums all sums due to those funds on that day.

PART VII.

RATES.

58. The exemptions from payment of rates which were granted or continued by Sections 121 and 123 of the Improvement Act and Sections 112 and 114 of the Act of 1882 to or in favour of the North Eastern Railway Company as the successors of the Dock Company at Kingston-upon-Hull and their tenants and to or in favour of any dwelling-houses warehouses lands or hereditaments of the said Railway Company as such successors as aforesaid whether occupied by the said Railway Company or their tenants

Discontinuance of exemption from certain rates.

and to or in favour of the owners and occupiers of properties
situate in certain streets quays and other places within the city
which prior to the passing of the North Eastern Railway (Hull
Docks) Act 1893 were lighted cleansed repaired maintained or
drained by the Dock Company at Kingston-upon-Hull shall cease
and determine from and after the commencement of this Act and
from and after the commencement of this Act the said sections
and all other enactments (if any) granting or continuing such
exemptions as aforesaid shall be repealed and the North Eastern
Railway Company and their tenants and the said owners and
occupiers shall thenceforth be liable to all rates in common with
all other owners and occupiers within the city.

Consideration
for discon-
tinuance of
exemption.

59. In consideration of such repeal—

(1) The Corporation shall pay to the said Railway Company
the sum of four thousand five hundred pounds;

(2) The Corporation shall cease to exercise the statutory
rights and powers of receiving and recovering from
such owners and occupiers as aforesaid payments or
contributions in respect of lighting which rights and
powers were transferred to the Corporation by Section
29 of the North Eastern Railway (Hull Docks)
Act 1893;

(3) For a period of ten years from the thirty-first day of
March next after the commencement of this Act the
owners and occupiers for the time being of the
properties respectively mentioned or described in a list
signed by the said Chairman of the Committee to which
the Bill for this Act was referred shall be entitled to
and shall be allowed by the Corporation an exemption
or rebate from the general district rate in each year of
the amount set opposite to the respective properties in
that list but subject as aforesaid the owners and
occupiers of such properties shall be liable to be rated
to the general district rate equally with all other
owners and occupiers within the city;

(4) Copies of the said list shall within one month from the
passing of this Act be deposited with the Town Clerk
and with the firm of Messieurs Rollit and Sons

solicitors at their offices in Kingston-upon-Hull and such copies shall be open to the inspection of any of the owners and occupiers aforesaid.

60.—(1) Section 113 (As to streets &c. repaired &c. under the Hull Dock Acts) of the Act of 1882 is hereby repealed.

Repeal of certain rating exemptions.

(2) From and after the expiration of fifteen years from the passing of this Act Section 67 (As to rating of railway and dock properties in the added part of the borough) of the Act of 1882 shall be repealed.

61. Section 51 (Exemptions under Section 211 of Public Health Act to apply to property in added part of borough) of the Act of 1882 is hereby repealed.

Repeal of Section 51 of Act of 1882.

62. The Corporation may make such rebates or allowances as they may from time to time resolve not necessarily on an uniform scale in all cases but not exceeding in any case one shilling in the pound on all or any rates which are paid at the office of the city treasurer within one month from the date of the service of the demand note for such rates.

Power to Corporation to allow rebates on personal payment of rates.

63. All rates which the Corporation are entitled to levy and raise under this Act or any other Act for the time being in force shall be recoverable and the payment thereof may be enforced by the Corporation in like manner as if they were poor rates and with the like right of appeal but without prejudice to any other mode of recovery and enforcement lawfully exerciseable by the Corporation.

Recovery of rates.

PART VIII.

RECREATION GROUNDS.

64.—(1) The Corporation may from time to time set apart portions of any park or place of public resort or recreation for the time being belonging to or held by them for cricket football archery and other games but so that the same shall be open to the public when not in use for such games and the Corporation may make bye-laws for regulating the use of and the charges (if any) for the use of the portions of the park or place so set apart.

Power to set apart land for games and regulations as to fishing and skating.

(2) The Corporation may make bye-laws for regulating the fishing in and skating upon any lake or piece of water in any such park or place of public resort or recreation.

Power to
provide
apparatus
for games.

65. The Corporation may provide swings gymnasium apparatus and apparatus for games and recreation for the use of the public frequenting the parks and places of public resort or recreation for the time being belonging to or held by the Corporation and may charge for the use thereof and they may lease or grant for any term not exceeding three years the right of providing and charging for such swings or apparatus on such terms and conditions as they think proper.

Contribution
to band of
music.

66. The Corporation may from time to time pay or contribute towards the payment of a band of music to perform in any park or place of public resort or recreation for the time being belonging to or held by the Corporation and the Corporation may enclose an area within which such band shall play and may make alter and repeal bye-laws for regulating the time and place for the playing of the band the payments to be made for admission within the said enclosure and for securing good and orderly conduct during the playing of the band Provided that the payments or contributions of the Corporation for or towards such band shall not in any year exceed the sum of five hundred pounds and shall be paid out of the borough rate.

Chairs and
seats for
public use.

67. The Corporation may from time to time place or authorise any person or persons to place seats or chairs in any street park recreation ground or other public place for the use of the public and may if they think fit charge or allow such person or persons to charge a reasonable sum for the use of chairs and may make alter and repeal bye-laws for regulating the use of seats and chairs and for preventing injury or damage thereto.

Power to Cor-
poration to
pay expenses
of keeping
animals &c.

68. The Corporation may defray out of the general district rate the expenses of providing suitable accommodation for and of keeping any animals birds reptiles or insects or any objects of interest which may be presented to the city and any other incidental expenses incurred in connection therewith.

As to Drypool
Green.

69. The open space in the city known as Drypool Green and the two triangular pieces of waste land in the said city situate respectively at the junction of Church Street with the Hedon Road and at the junction of the Hedon Road with Great Union Street shall on and after the commencement of this Act be by virtue of this Act vested in the Corporation to be by them held and managed as and for city recreation grounds but subject to the right of the overseers of the parish of Drypool to regulate the Drypool feasts and pleasure fairs thereon and to take the tolls and dues payable thereat and apply and disburse the same as heretofore and subject as to the said Drypool Green to such right of way (if any) over the same as belongs to the North Eastern Railway Company in respect of lands of the said Company abutting on the said Green and subject as to the said triangular piece of waste land situate at the junction of the Hedon Road with Great Union Street to such right of drainage and such easements in through upon and over the same as belonged to the owner or owners of the hereditaments to the east of such piece of land immediately before the passing of this Act and all the enactments and bye-laws in force for the time being with respect to the other recreation grounds or public places under the control of the Corporation shall subject as aforesaid extend and apply to Drypool Green and the two said pieces of waste land in the hands of the Corporation.

PART IX.

Stock.

Scheme for Conversion of Existing Irredeemable Stock.

70. (1) The Corporation may at any time after the commencement of this Act prepare and submit to the Local Government Board a scheme for enabling the Corporation by agreement with the holders of and persons interested in any Corporation stock which is only redeemable by agreement between the Corporation and the holder of such stock (in this Act referred to as irredeemable stock) to convert that stock into Corporation stock redeemable not later than the thirty-first day of December one thousand nine hundred and fifty and bearing interest at such rate not exceeding four pounds per centum per annum as may be specified in the scheme.

Scheme for conversion by agreement of irredeemable stock.

(2) The scheme may vary the provisions of the Hull Corporation Loans Act 1881 and of any Act or Order amending the same with respect to the contributions to the loans fund and their investment and application and with respect to any other matter for the purpose of adapting them to the case of redeemable stock and generally may make any provisions necessary or proper for carrying it into effect subject to the provisions of this Act.

(3) If and when the scheme is approved by the Local Government Board (but not otherwise) it shall be lawful for the Corporation to put it into execution and for any holder of or other person interested in any Corporation irredeemable stock including trustees executors administrators and persons under any disability to agree or consent to the conversion of that stock subject and according to the provisions of this Act and of the scheme.

(4) A scheme made under this section may on the application of the Corporation be amended by order of the Local Government Board.

PART X.

SUPPLY OF GAS.

Power for Corporation to acquire undertaking of old Gas Company.

71. The Agreement set forth in the seventh schedule to this Act between the Corporation and the Kingston-upon-Hull Gas Light Company (in this Act referred to as the old Company) for the sale and transfer of the undertaking of the said Company to the Corporation is hereby confirmed Provided that such Agreement shall not be carried into effect without the sanction of the Local Government Board The Corporation shall within one month from the passing of this Act apply to the Local Government Board for such sanction and forthwith take all necessary steps for obtaining the same.

Power to make agreements for supplying district of old Company.

72. In the event of such transfer taking place the Corporation may enter into and carry into effect an agreement or agreements with the British Gas Light Company Limited and the Sutton Southcoates and Drypool Gas Company or with either of those companies for the supply of gas by those companies or by one of them within or for or to the whole or any part or parts of the district now supplied by the old Company or for the sale of gas by both or one of those companies to the Corporation at such price and on such terms and conditions as may be agreed for the purpose of being supplied by the Corporation.

As to gas-works of old company.

73. In the event of such agreement or agreements being made it shall not be obligatory on the Corporation to carry on the Undertaking of the old Company or to supply gas within the district now supplied by the old Company if the Corporation shall have procured the British Gas Light Company Limited and the Sutton Southcoates and Drypool Gas Company or one of them to enter into an undertaking satisfactory to the Corporation binding those Companies or one of them to supply gas within the said district and in that case it shall be lawful for the Corporation to pull down and remove the gasworks of the old Company and to sell and dispose of all plant materials and other property belonging to them and either to sell or let or to utilise for any purpose of any of the public or local Acts in force within the city the site of the said gasworks and other lands (if any) transferred to the Corporation by the old Company.

74. In the event of such transfer taking place as aforesaid the British Gas Light Company Limited and the Sutton Southcoates and Drypool Gas Company and each of them are and is hereby authorised to enter into the agreements or agreement and undertaking mentioned or referred to in the last two preceding sections and notwithstanding anything in the Memorandum or Articles of Association or in the Act of Incorporation of the said Companies respectively to supply gas for consumption within the limits of the old Company in accordance with such agreement or undertaking as aforesaid.

Power to British and Sutton Companies to make agreements.

75. If the Undertaking of the old Company shall be transferred to the Corporation under the powers of this Act the committee of management of the Company then in office shall continue in office without re-election and may and shall exercise all powers and do all acts necessary or proper for winding up the affairs of the Company and when the affairs of the Company have been completely wound up the committee of management or any two members thereof acting in pursuance of a resolution of the committee shall certify under their hands to that effect and shall cause a copy of their certificate to be published in the London Gazette and on the expiration of one month from the date of that publication the Company shall be by virtue of this Act dissolved The powers by this section given to the committee of management shall continue in force notwithstanding the death resignation or incapacity of any member or members so long as the number of the committee is not less than five.

Winding-up and dissolution of old Company in certain events.

PART XI.

WATER.

Water
Undertaking
to continue
vested in
Corporation.

76. The Water Undertaking of the Corporation as it exists at the commencement of this Act including the Newington Water Undertaking transferred to them by the Newington Water Order 1893 and including all property rights powers and privileges of every description which at the commencement of this Act are vested in the Corporation in relation to the construction and maintenance of waterworks and the diversion collection storage and distribution of water or otherwise in relation to the supply of water shall continue vested in the Corporation and be held exercised and enjoyed by them subject to the provisions of this Act.

Power to
maintain
waterworks
and supply
water.

77. The Corporation may from time to time maintain renew alter and discontinue their existing waterworks and (subject to the provisions of this Act) may construct provide and maintain additional and other aqueducts mains pipes tanks meters buildings works and apparatus both within and outside of the water limits and may sell and supply water within the water limits and do all other acts and provide all other things in any way connected with waterworks or with the supply of water in such manner as they from time to time think proper.

Power to lay
mains beneath
the River Hull
at Stoneferry.

78. The Corporation may carry one or more mains conduits or pipes beneath the bed of the River Hull at or near Stoneferry for the purpose of conveying water from their waterworks to the east side of the said river and thence by mains to such parts of the city as lie on the east side of the River Hull as it may be intended to supply with water by means of such mains and may erect all necessary temporary dams and other works in the said river but so as always to leave a free passage for ships boats and vessels.

Power to lay
mains across
bridges.

79. The Corporation may carry mains conduits and pipes over across or through any bridge made or to be made over or across any stream drain or sewer already existing or made or hereafter to be made in or through the parishes of Cottingham Sculcoates Sutton Drypool Holy Trinity Saint Mary or Garrison Side or may make or enlarge any bridge across any such stream drain or sewer or erect any new bridge across the same for the purpose of carrying such mains conduits or pipes across the same or may carry such mains conduits or pipes under the bottom or bed of any such stream drain or sewer and shall have all necessary powers for the execution of such works doing as little damage as may be in the execution thereof and making good all such damage as shall be occasioned thereby.

80. The limits within which the Corporation shall be authorised to sell and supply water (in this Act referred to as the water limits) shall be those described in the Fourth Schedule to this Act.

Limits for
water supply.

81. All the provisions of this Act authorising and regulating the supply of water by the Corporation shall extend and apply and be enforceable throughout the whole of the water limits.

Application
of water
enactments
throughout
water limits.

82. A supply of water for domestic purposes shall not include a supply of water for fixed baths horses cattle or washing carriages nor for any trade or business whatsoever nor for watering gardens nor for fountains nor for any ornamental purpose.

Definition of
supply for
domestic
purposes.

83. The water to be supplied need not be constantly laid on under a greater pressure than the works of the Corporation will supply in the district to be supplied by such works.

Pressure.

84. If any water-closet urinal or private bath or the apparatus or pipes connected therewith respectively on any premises be so constructed and used as to admit of the waste or undue consumption of the water of the Corporation and the return of foul air or noisome or impure matter into the mains or pipes belonging to or connected with the mains or pipes of the Corporation the owner of the premises shall be liable to a penalty not exceeding five pounds.

Penalty for
waste or
fouling of
water.

85. The water rate which the Corporation shall be authorised to charge for the supply of water for domestic purposes shall not exceed seven pounds per centum per annum on the net annual value of the premises supplied.

Rates for
supply for
domestic
purposes.

86. When several houses or parts of houses in the occupation of several persons are supplied by one common pipe the several owners or occupiers of such houses or parts of houses shall be liable to contribute the amount of any expenses from time to time incurred by the Corporation in the maintenance and repair of such pipe and their respective proportions of contributions shall be settled by the water engineer.

Maintenance
of common
pipe.

87. With respect to the supply of water to courts alleys and other like places the following provisions shall have effect (namely) :—

(1) The Corporation or the owners of houses in those courts alleys and other places may erect standpipes therein for the use of all the persons occupying the houses therein with proper fittings and apparatus and keep the same in good repair :

(2) The supply of water so provided shall for the purposes of the levying and recovering of water rents and for all other purposes relative to the Waterworks Undertaking of the Corporation be deemed to be a separate supply for each house the occupiers whereof use the same :

(3) Where any such standpipe and apparatus are erected by the Corporation in lieu of an existing system of supply by pipes and taps or in lieu of any standpipe and apparatus used at the passing of this Act the expense of providing the same shall be borne by the Corporation :

(4) In all other cases that expense shall be borne by the owner of the house the occupiers whereof have the right of using such standpipe and apparatus :

(5) In all cases the expense of the maintenance and repair of any such standpipe and apparatus shall be borne by such owner :

(6) If any such standpipe and apparatus are at any time not kept in good repair the Corporation may cause all proper repairs to be made thereto and the expense thereof shall be recoverable by the Corporation from the owner as water rent is recoverable :

(7) In case of there being more owners than one liable to contribute to any expense under this section their respective proportion thereof shall be settled by the water engineer :

(8) Whenever any standpipe or apparatus is worn out or has become obsolete the maintenance or repair thereof shall for the purposes of this section include the provision of a new or improved standpipe or apparatus.

88. Nothing in this Act shall be construed to prevent the Corporation from entering into agreements for supplying water for domestic purposes within the water limits on such terms as may be agreed between them and the persons receiving the supply but so that the same terms shall be conceded to all persons in similar circumstances or from exercising within the water limits any other powers in relation to their Water Undertaking or the supply of water which are vested in them under the Public Health Acts.

Power to supply by agreement for domestic purposes &c.

89. The Corporation from time to time may supply any person with water for other than domestic purposes for such remuneration and on such terms and conditions as shall be agreed between the Corporation and the person desirous of having the supply provided that such supply shall not interfere with the supply of water for domestic purposes within the water limits.

Power to supply for other than domestic purposes.

90. Any supply of water which may be afforded by the Corporation for other than domestic purposes shall be supplied by measure if so required by either the intending consumer or the Corporation :

Supply by measure.

Provided that the charge for water supplied by measure to any premises not supplied for domestic purposes shall not in any case be less than the charge which would be made for supplying such premises for domestic purposes.

91. Where water is supplied by measure by the Corporation the register of the meter or other instrument for measuring water shall be primâ facie evidence of the quantity of water consumed.

Register of meter to be evidence.

92. If any person wilfully or by culpable negligence injures or suffers to be injured any meter or fittings belonging to the Corporation or fraudulently alters the index to any meter or prevents any meter from duly registering the quantity of water supplied or fraudulently abstracts or uses water of the Corporation he shall (without prejudice to any other right or remedy of the Corporation) be liable to a penalty not exceeding forty shillings and the Corporation may in addition thereto recover the amount of any damage sustained.

Penalty for injuring meters.

The existence of artificial means under the control of the consumer for causing any such alteration prevention abstraction or use shall be primâ facie evidence that the consumer has fraudulently effected the same.

Regulations
for preventing
waste &c. of
water.

93. For preventing waste misuse undue consumption or contamination of the water of the Corporation the following provisions shall so long as a constant supply of water is given by the Corporation have effect namely :—

(1) The Corporation may from time to time make bye-laws for the objects aforesaid :

(2) By any such bye-laws the Corporation may direct the use and prescribe the size nature strength and materials and the mode of arrangement alteration and repair of pipes valves cocks cisterns soil-pans water-closets and other apparatus or receptacles to be used by such persons for conveying delivering and receiving water and may regulate the supply of fittings by the Corporation and the testing and stamping of fittings and may interdict any arrangement and the use of any pipe valve cock cistern bath soil-pan water-closet or other apparatus or receptacle in their judgment likely to occasion waste misuse undue consumption or contamination of water and such bye-laws or any of them may if the Corporation think fit apply to any pipe valve cock cistern soil-pan water-closet fittings or other apparatus or receptacle existing at the time of the making of the bye-laws :

(3) The Corporation shall not be bound under any agreement or otherwise to supply or continue to supply water to any person unless such bye-laws as are for the time being in force are duly observed by him :

(4) In case of failure of any such person to observe such bye-laws as are for the time being in force the Corporation may if they think fit after twenty-four hours notice in writing enter and by or under the direction of their authorised officer repair replace or alter any pipe valve cock cistern bath soil-pan water-closet or other apparatus or receptacle belonging to or used by any person supplied by them and the power of entry given by Section 15 of the Waterworks Clauses Act 1863 and the provisions of that section relative thereto shall extend and apply to entry for the purpose of such repair replacement or alteration and the expense of

every such repair replacement or alteration shall be repaid to the Corporation by the person on whose credit the water is supplied and may be recovered as water rates or rents are recoverable.

94. The Corporation may if requested by any person supplied or about to be supplied by them with water furnish to him and from time to time repair or alter any such pipes valves meters cocks cisterns baths soil-pans water-closets apparatus and receptacles as are required or permitted by this Act or by their bye-laws and may provide all materials and do all work necessary or proper in that behalf at the expense of the person making the request to them.

Power to the Corporation to supply fittings.

95. All rates or rents payable to the Corporation for a supply of water and all sums payable to the Corporation under any agreement made under the provisions of this part of this Act shall be recoverable by the Corporation in like manner as the rates leviable by the Corporation or at the option of the Corporation as a civil debt :

Payment of water rates.

All rates or rents payable to the Corporation for the supply of water and all sums payable to the Corporation under any such agreement as aforesaid shall be deemed to be parochial or other local rates within the meaning of section 1 (1) (a) of the Preferential Payments in Bankruptcy Act 1888 :

Provided that this section shall not apply to any sums payable to the Corporation for fittings supplied and work done under the preceding section.

96. A notice to the Corporation for the discontinuance of a supply of water shall not be of any effect unless it is in writing.

Notice of discontinuance of supply.

97. The Corporation may from time to time enter into and carry into effect such agreements as they think fit with any district council or other local authority or public body for the supply of water in bulk by the Corporation to the contracting council authority or body for distribution in their district beyond the water limits Provided that this section shall not authorise any such agreement as aforesaid unless the supply can be given without prejudice to a full supply to the inhabitants within the water limits.

Power to supply local authorities in bulk.

98. —(1) The Corporation shall apply all money from time to time received by them in respect of their waterworks except borrowed money as follows :—

Application of receipts in respect of waterworks.

First   In paying the working and establishment expenses and the cost of maintenance of their waterworks ;

Secondly   In paying the annual sum of two thousand six hundred pounds to the account of the borough fund by two equal half-yearly payments ;

Thirdly   In paying the interest on moneys borrowed for the purposes of their waterworks or for the repayment of moneys borrowed for such purposes ;

Fourthly   In paying the annuity certificates if any issued for the purposes of their waterworks or for the repayment of moneys borrowed for such purposes ;

Fifthly   In providing for the repayment of moneys borrowed for the purposes of their waterworks the annual instalments appropriations and sinking funds required to be provided under the provisions hereinbefore contained for the repayment of the existing debt of the Corporation ;

Sixthly   In providing a reserve fund if they think fit by setting aside such money as they from time to time think reasonable and accumulating the same at compound interest but so that the reserve fund thus formed shall not at any time exceed ten thousand pounds.

(2) The reserve fund to be formed as hereinbefore provided shall be applicable to meet any extraordinary claim or demand at any time arising against the Corporation in respect of their waterworks or any expenses incurred by the Corporation in carrying out any extensions of such waterworks.

(3) The Corporation after applying in the manner hereinbefore provided the moneys received by them as aforesaid in respect of their waterworks may apply any balance of the moneys so received remaining in any year and when the reserve fund amounts to ten thousand pounds the annual proceeds of such fund to such purposes whether water municipal or urban sanitary purposes and in payment of such expenses as the Corporation may think fit.

Corporation to supply water to Cottingham Urban District Council.

99.—(1) The Corporation shall continue to maintain at their own expense all works necessary for connecting at or near the junction of Millhouse Woods lane and Northgate the line of pipes commencing at the engine house in the parish of Cottingham with any main laid by the Cottingham Urban District Council for supplying the Cottingham urban district with water and the Corporation shall so long as they shall use the works at Cottingham authorised by the Kingston-upon-Hull Corporation Water Act 1884 and there shall be an adequate yield therefrom supply water through such connection to the Cottingham Urban District Council gratuitously in such quantity as the said Council shall from time to time require not exceeding in any one day fifty thousand gallons.

(2) The Corporation shall supply the said water at a constant pressure sufficient to cause the water to flow into the mains and pipes of the said district Council and to supply the village of Cottingham and the houses in the neighbourhood thereof to which the said district council have already laid or shall at any time hereafter lay their mains.

(3) The water so supplied shall be supplied at as high a pressure and of as good a quality as water for the time being supplied to the city.

(4) If the said district council shall require more than the above-mentioned quantity of water the Corporation shall so long as they use the said works and there shall be an adequate yield therefrom supply such additional quantity of water to the said district council in manner aforesaid at the price of threepence per thousand gallons   Provided that the Corporation shall not be required to supply a greater quantity of water to the district council under this section than ninety thousand gallons in any one day in the whole.

100. The Corporation shall continue to supply water in the townships of Anlaby Kirk Ella and Willerby on the same terms and conditions as for the time being regulate the supply of water in the city. *Supply to Anlaby&c.*

PART XII.

MISCELLANEOUS AND PROCEDURE &c.

(i.) Miscellaneous Enactments.

Paid auditors.   **101.** The Corporation may from time to time appoint and pay one or more members of the Institute of Chartered Accountants to act as auditor or auditors of the accounts of the Corporation in such manner as the Corporation direct in addition to the auditors appointed under the Municipal Corporation Acts.

Crossings for horses or vehicles &c. over footways.   **102.** Every person desirous of forming a communication for horses or vehicles across any kerbed footpath so as to afford access to any premises from a street shall first give notice in writing of such desire to the Corporation and shall if so required by them submit to them for their reasonable approval a plan of the proposed communication showing where it will cut the footpath and what provision (if any) is made for kerbing for gullies and for a paved crossing and the dimensions and gradients of necessary works and shall execute the works at his own expense under the supervision and to the reasonable satisfaction of the City Engineer and in case such plan shall have been required then in accordance with the plan so approved and not otherwise   Any person who drives or permits or causes to be driven any horse or vehicle across any footway unless and until such communication as aforesaid has been so made shall be liable to a penalty not exceeding forty shillings.

Trees or shrubs overhanging streets.   **103.** Where any tree hedge or shrub overhangs any footpath or the footway of any public street so as to obstruct or interfere with the light from any public lamp or otherwise to interfere with the free passage or comfort of passengers the Corporation may serve a notice on the owner of the tree hedge or shrub or on the occupier of the premises on which such tree hedge or shrub is growing requiring him to lop the tree hedge or shrub so as to prevent such obstruction or interference and in default of compliance with the notice may themselves carry out its requisitions doing no unnecessary damage.

Fees for licences and registration.   **104.** The Corporation may charge a fee not exceeding a shilling for the registration of any person or premises or the granting of any licence under or in pursuance of any Act of Parliament in cases where the payment of a fee is not provided for or prohibited.

(ii.) Prosecution of Offences &c.

105. All offences penalties forfeitures damages costs and expenses by this Act or any Act incorporated herewith or any bye-law thereunder authorised or directed to be prosecuted or recovered summarily or before any justices or justice or the prosecution or recovery of which is not otherwise expressly provided for may be prosecuted and recovered in manner provided by the Summary Jurisdiction Acts and all penalties recovered summarily by the Corporation within the city under this Act or any Act incorporated herewith or any bye-law thereunder shall be paid to the Corporation and carried to the borough fund.

Prosecution and recovery of offences and penalties.

106. No information shall be laid for the recovery of any penalty under this Act or any bye-law made under this Act except by the party aggrieved or by the authority of the Corporation or a committee of the Corporation.

Restriction on informations.

107. No order verdict rate assessment judgment conviction or other proceeding touching or concerning any offence against this Act or against any bye-law made under this Act shall be quashed or vacated for want of form only.

Proceedings not to be quashed for want of form.

108. A judge of any court or a justice shall not be disqualified from acting in the execution of this Act by reason of his being a member of the Corporation or liable to any rate or other charge for water or means of lighting under this Act or being interested in any contract under this Act for a supply of water or means of lighting.

Judges not disqualified.

109. Any person deeming himself aggrieved by any order judgment determination or requirement or the making or withholding of any certificate licence or consent or approval of or by the Corporation or of or by any officer or valuer of the Corporation or by any conviction or order made by a court of summary jurisdiction under any provision of this Act may (save in any case where another mode of appeal is expressly provided by this Act) appeal to the next practicable Court of Quarter Sessions under and according to the provisions of the Summary Jurisdiction Acts and in regard to any such order of a court of summary jurisdiction the Corporation may in like manner appeal.

Appeal to Quarter Sessions.

(iii.) Bye-Laws.

Provisions as to bye-laws of the Corporation.

110. All bye-laws authorised by this Act or by any other Act and at any time in force within the city may be altered or repealed from time to time by the Corporation.

Sections 182 to 185 (both inclusive) of the Public Health Act 1875 (except so much of Section 185 as applies exclusively to bye-laws made by a rural authority) shall apply to the alteration and repeal of any existing bye-laws and to the making alteration and repeal of the bye-laws made by the Corporation under this Act or any Act incorporated with this Act (except bye-laws required by any enactment applied by this Act to be confirmed by the Board of Trade or by a Secretary of State) as if they were bye-laws made by a local authority under that Act.

Expenses of Local Government Board.

111. Where the Local Government Board cause any local inquiry to be held with reference to any of the purposes of this Act the costs incurred by that Board in relation to such inquiry (including such reasonable sum not exceeding three guineas a day as that Board may determine for the services of any inspector or officer of the Board engaged in such inquiry) shall be paid by the Corporation and the Local Government Board may certify the amount of the cost so incurred and any sum so certified and directed by that Board to be paid by the Corporation shall be a debt due to the Crown from the Corporation.

(iv.) Costs and Expenses.

Costs of Act.

112. All the costs charges and expenses preliminary to and of and incidental to the preparing applying for obtaining and passing of this Act as taxed by the taxing officer of the House of Lords or of the House of Commons shall be paid by the Corporation out of the borough fund and borough rate or out of moneys to be borrowed on the security of that fund and rate.

Expenses of executing Act

113. All expenses incurred by the Corporation in carrying into execution the provisions of this Act except such of those expenses as are payable out of borrowed moneys or out of the borough fund and borough rate under any general Act of Parliament or this Act and except so far as any such expenses may be defrayed out of revenue derived from the water undertaking or any other undertaking of the Corporation or from any other property of the Corporation or be recovered from the owners or occupiers of premises or other persons shall be paid out of the district fund and general district rate.

(v.) Repeal.

114.—(1) The Water Acts and Orders which are enumerated in the Sixth Schedule to this Act are hereby repealed as from the commencement of this Act to the extent in the second column of that Schedule specified.

Repeal of Water Acts.

(2) Nothwithstanding this repeal—

(A) All acts and things before the commencement of this Act done or commenced under the powers of any of the said Acts or Orders and which were at the commencement of this Act valid or in progress and all awards deeds instruments securities contracts agreements obligations rights and remedies at the commencement of this Act existing under the same shall subject to the provisions of this Act be and continue as valid and for all purposes and for and against all parties and may be continued and completed as if this Act had not been passed ;

(B) All actions arbitrations prosecutions or other proceedings by with or against the Corporation by reason of any matter or thing done before the commencement of this Act in execution of or in relation to any of the said Acts and Orders may be continued commenced or prosecuted by or against the Corporation as if this Act had not been passed ;

(c) All rates rents tolls and other sums at the passing of this Act due or accruing due to the Corporation may be collected and recovered by the Corporation as if this Act had not been passed ;

(D) All books and documents which under any of the said Acts or Orders or otherwise would have been receivable in evidence shall be receivable in evidence as if this Act had not been passed.

(3) Notwithstanding the repeal effected by this Act of the Hull Waterworks Acts and Orders enumerated in the Sixth Schedule to this Act and of the Newington Water Order 1893 the provisions contained in those Acts and Orders for the protection or benefit of the individual persons estates public bodies and companies therein expressly mentioned shall so far as they are respectively in force at the commencement of this Act continue in

force to the like extent as but not further or otherwise than they would have continued in force if this Act had not been passed.

For the protection of Henry Edward Thornton Wilkinson.

115. Notwithstanding anything in this Act contained the Agreement dated the twenty-sixth day of July one thousand eight hundred and eighty-nine and made between William Hall Wilkinson of the one part and the Newington Water Company Limited of the other part shall be and remain binding upon the Corporation as though the Corporation were named in such Agreement instead of the Newington Water Company Limited.

Repeal of Section 107 of Act of 1882.

116. Section 107 (Expenses to be a charge on premises) of the Act of 1882 is hereby repealed to the intent that the provisions of Section 257 of the Public Health Act 1875 may apply in lieu thereof.

Saving rights of Crown under Crown Lands Act.

117. Nothing contained in this Act or to be done under the authority thereof shall in any manner affect the title to any of the subjects or any rights powers or authorities mentioned in or reserved by Sections 21 and 22 of the Crown Lands Act 1866 and belonging to or exerciseable on behalf of Her Majesty.

The SCHEDULES referred to in the foregoing Act.

FIRST SCHEDULE.

Description of added part of the City.

(1) The area within the following boundaries namely from the angle on the existing city boundary at the centre of the line of Railway known as the North Eastern Railway Hull and Scarborough Branch south of the Walton Street Crossing on the Spring Bank and extending westward along the existing city boundary south of the Spring Bank to the centre of the line of the North Eastern Railway marked on the six-inch Ordnance maps published in 1894 as the Hessle Road and Cottingham Branch and thence along the centre of such Railway in a northerly direction until it meets the old city boundary at a point called the Cottingham Junction and thence in a southerly and easterly direction along the existing city boundary until it meets the point first described.

(2) The area within the following boundaries namely from a point on the existing city boundary at the centre of the River Hull opposite the eastern end of the Clough Road and extending westward along the existing city boundary on the north side of the Clough Road and the Cottingham Road to the north-western extremity of the said city thence in a southerly direction along the existing city boundary to the south side of the Cottingham Road thence in a westerly direction for a distance of twenty-one yards or thereabouts along the south side of the Cottingham Road thence in a northerly direction across the Cottingham Road and along the east side of a ditch for a distance of three hundred and ninety yards or thereabouts from the north side of the Cottingham Road thence in an easterly direction along a fence for a distance of two hundred and fifty-five yards or thereabouts thence in a northerly direction along a fence for a distance

of two hundred and seventy yards or thereabouts thence along the south side of the Inglemire Lane in an easterly direction for a distance of twenty-five yards or thereabouts to the centre of the Cottingham Drain thence in a north-westerly direction along the centre of such drain to the north side of the Endike Lane thence in an easterly direction along the north side of the Endike Lane to the Beverley Road at Cross Bridges thence across the Beverley Road to the north side of a ditch running from Cross Bridges in an easterly direction to the River Hull thence along the north side of the said ditch to the angle in the existing city boundary in the centre of the River Hull opposite the eastern end of such ditch and thence in a southerly and easterly direction along the existing city boundary in the centre of the said River Hull to the point first described.

SECOND SCHEDULE.

NAMES AND BOUNDARIES OF WARDS.

No. 1. NORTH NEWINGTON WARD.

The boundary of North Newington Ward shall be as follows :—

An imaginary line commencing at a point in the western boundary of the city at the centre of the Hessle Road and continued thence in a northerly and easterly direction along the city boundary to the point where it meets Spring Bank thence in an easterly direction along the city boundary to the centre of the line of the North Eastern Railway marked on the six-inch ordnance maps published in 1894 as the Hessle Road and Cottingham Branch thence in a northerly direction along the centre of such railway to the centre of Spring Bank thence in an easterly direction along the centre of Spring Bank to its junction with Walton Street thence in a southerly direction along the centre of Walton Street to its junction with Anlaby Road thence in an easterly direction along the centre of Anlaby Road to a point on the main line of the North Eastern Railway at the level crossing near Selby Street thence in a south-westerly and southerly direction along the centre of the North Eastern Railway to the centre of the Hessle Road thence in a westerly direction along the centre of the Hessle Road to the point of commencement in the western boundary of the city.

No. 2. SOUTH NEWINGTON WARD.

The boundary of South Newington Ward shall be as follows :—

An imaginary line commencing at the extreme south-west point of the boundary of the city and continued thence in a northerly direction along the western boundary of the city to the centre of Hessle Road

thence in a direction generally easterly and north-
easterly along the southern and south-eastern boundary
of North Newington Ward to the railway crossing on
the Anlaby Road near Selby Street thence in an easterly
direction along the centre of Anlaby Road to its junction with the Boulevard opposite the north-west corner
of Saint Matthew's Church thence in a southerly direction along the centre of the Boulevard to its junction
with Woodcock Street thence in a westerly direction
along the centre of Woodcock Street to its junction
with Division Road thence in a southerly direction
along the centre of Division Road and West Dock
Avenue to Goulton Street and continued in the same
direction to a point in the southern boundary of
the city thence in a westerly direction along the
southern boundary of the city to the point of
commencement at the south-western extremity of the
city.

No. 3.   COLTMAN WARD.

The boundary of Coltman Ward shall be as follows :—

An imaginary line commencing at the point of junction of
the Boulevard with the Anlaby Road opposite the
north-west corner of Saint Matthew's Church and
continued thence in an easterly direction along the
centre of Anlaby Road to its junction with Bean Street
thence in a southerly direction along the centre of
Bean Street to its junction with Hessle Road thence
in a Westerly direction along the centre of Hessle Road
to its junction with Daltry Street thence in a southerly
direction along the centre of Daltry Street to its
junction with Jackson Street and continued in the
same direction to the southern boundary of the city
thence in a westerly direction along the southern
boundary of the city to the south-eastern extremity
of South Newington Ward thence in a northerly
direction along the eastern boundary of South
Newington Ward to the junction of Division Road
and Woodcock Street thence in an easterly and

northerly direction along the southern and eastern boundaries of North Newington Ward to the point of commencement at the junction of the Boulevard and Anlaby Road.

No. 4. Albert Ward.

The boundary of Albert Ward shall be as follows :—

An imaginary line commencing at the junction of Bean Street and Anlaby Road and continued thence in an easterly direction along the centre of Anlaby Road to its junction with Walker Street thence in a southerly direction along the centre of Walker Street across Hessle Road and along the centre of Saint James' Street to its junction with Humber Bank Footpath thence in a southerly direction to a point in the southern boundary of the city opposite the junction of Saint James' Street and Humber Bank Footpath thence in a westerly direction along the southern boundary of the city to the south-eastern extremity of Coltman Ward thence in a northerly direction along the eastern boundary of Coltman Ward to the point of commencement at the junction of Bean Street and Anlaby Road.

No. 5. Myton Ward.

The boundary of Myton Ward shall be as follows :—

An imaginary line commencing at the junction of Walker Street and Anlaby Road and continued thence in an easterly direction along the centre of Anlaby Road Carr Lane and Saint John's Street to the centre of Whitefriargate Bridge thence in a southerly direction along the centre of Princes Dock and Humber Dock to the Humber Dock entrance thence in a southerly direction to a point in the southern boundary of the city opposite the entrance to Humber Dock thence in a westerly direction along the southern boundary of the city to the south-eastern extremity of Albert Ward thence in a northerly direction along the eastern boundary of Albert Ward to the point of commencement at the junction of Walker Street and Anlaby Road.

No. 6.   Whitefriars Ward.

The boundary of Whitefriars Ward shall be as follows :—

An imaginary line commencing at the centre of Whitefriargate Bridge and continued thence in a northerly and easterly direction along the centre of Queen's Dock to a point in the centre of the River Hull opposite the Queen's Dock entrance thence in a southerly direction along the centre of the River Hull to its junction with the Humber thence in a southerly direction to a point in the southern boundary of the city opposite the junction of the Rivers Hull and Humber thence in a westerly direction along the southern boundary of the city to the south-eastern extremity of Myton Ward thence in a northerly direction along the eastern boundary of Myton Ward to the point of commencement at the centre of Whitefriargate Bridge.

No. 7.   Botanic Ward.

The boundary of Botanic Ward shall be as follows :

An imaginary line commencing at the junction of Spring Bank and Walton Street and continued thence in an easterly direction along the centre of Spring Bank to its junction with Park Street thence in a southerly direction along the centre of Park Street to its junction with Anlaby Road thence in a westerly direction along the centre of Anlaby Road to its junction with Walton Street thence in a northerly direction along the centre of Walton Street to the point of commencement at its junction with Spring Bank.

No. 8. Paragon Ward.

The boundary of Paragon Ward shall be as follows :—

An imaginary line commencing at the junction of Park
Street with Spring Bank and continued thence
in a south-easterly direction along the centre
of Spring Bank and Prospect Street to its junction
with Wright Street thence in an easterly direction along the centre of Wright Street King Street
Sykes Street Charterhouse Lane and Charterhouse
Lane Staith to the centre of the River Hull
opposite Charterhouse Lane Staith thence in a southerly
direction along the centre of the River Hull to the
north-eastern extremity of Whitefriars Ward opposite
the Queen's Dock entrance thence in a westerly and
southerly direction along the northern and eastern
boundary of Whitefriars Ward to the centre of Whitefriargate Bridge thence in a westerly direction along
the northern boundary of Myton Ward to the junction
of Anlaby Road and Park Street thence in a northerly
direction along the centre of Park Street to the point
of commencement at its junction with Spring Bank.

No. 9. Newland Ward.

The boundary of Newland Ward shall be as follows :—

An imaginary line commencing at a point in the western
boundary of the city as extended at the centre
of Spring Bank and continued thence in a northerly
and easterly direction along the boundary of the
city as extended to the centre of Beverley Road
thence in a southerly direction along the centre of
Beverley Road to its junction with Queen's Road
thence in a westerly direction along the centre of
Queen's Road to its junction with Princes Avenue
thence in a south-westerly direction along the centre
of Princes Avenue to its junction with Spring Bank
thence in a westerly direction along the centre of
Spring Bank to the point of commencement at the
western boundary of the city.

No. 10.   Park Ward.

The boundary of Park Ward shall be as follows :—

An imaginary line commencing at the junction of Spring Bank and Princes Avenue and continued in a north-easterly and easterly direction along the south-eastern and southern boundaries of Newland Ward to the junction of Queen's Road and Beverley Road thence in a southerly direction along the centre of Beverley Road to its junction with Spring Bank thence in a north-westerly direction along the centre of Spring Bank to the point of commencement at the junction of Spring Bank and Princes Avenue.

No. 11.   West Central Ward.

The boundary of West Central Ward shall be as follows :—

An imaginary line commencing at the junction of Beverley Road and Fountain Road and continued thence in an easterly direction along the centre of Fountain Road to its junction with Saint Paul's Street thence in a southerly direction along the centre of Saint Paul's Street to its junction with Liddell Street and continued in the same direction to the centre of the Cottingham drain opposite Saint Paul's Street thence in a westerly direction along the centre of the Cottingham drain to the centre of Charles Street Bridge thence in a southerly direction along the centre of Charles Street to its junction with Wright Street thence in a westerly direction along the centre of Wright Street to its junction with Prospect Street thence in a north-westerly direction along the centre of Prospect Street to the junction of Prospect Street and Beverley Road thence in a northerly direction along the centre of Beverley Road to the point of commencement at the junction of Beverley Road and Fountain Road.

No. 12.   EAST CENTRAL WARD.

The boundary of the East Central Ward shall be as follows:—

An imaginary line commencing at the junction of Fountain Road and Saint Paul Street and continued in an easterly direction along the centre of Fountain Road to a point in the centre of the River Hull opposite the eastern end of Fountain Road thence in a southerly direction along the centre of the River Hull to the north-eastern extremity of Paragon Ward opposite Charterhouse Lane Staith thence in a westerly direction along the northern boundary of Paragon Ward to the junction of King Street and Charles Street thence in a direction generally northerly along the eastern boundary of West Central Ward to the point of commencement at the junction of Saint Paul Street and Fountain Road.

No. 13.   BEVERLEY WARD.

The boundary of Beverley Ward shall be as follows :—

An imaginary line commencing at a point in the centre of Beverley Road at the north-eastern extremity of Newland Ward and continued thence in an easterly direction along the boundary of the city as extended to the centre of the River Hull thence in a direction generally southerly along the centre of the River Hull to a point on the boundary of East Central Ward opposite the eastern end of Fountain Road thence in a western direction along the northern boundary of East Central Ward to the junction of Fountain Road and Saint Paul Street thence in a westerly direction along the northern boundary of West Central Ward to the junction of Fountain Road and Beverley Road thence in a northerly direction along the eastern boundary of Park Ward and Newland Ward to the point of commencement at the north-eastern extremity of Newland Ward.

No. 14. SOUTHCOATES WARD.

The boundary of Southcoates Ward shall be as follows :—

An imaginary line commencing at a point in the centre of the River Hull at the north-eastern extremity of Beverley Ward and continued thence in an easterly and south-easterly direction along the city boundary to its point of intersection by the Holderness Road thence in a south-westerly direction along the centre of Holderness Road to its junction with Wilton Street thence in a north-westerly and northerly direction along the centre of Wilton Street and Dansom Lane to the junction of Dansom Lane with Saint Mark's Street thence in a westerly direction along the centre of Saint Mark's Street to the centre of Saint Mark's Street Bridge thence in a northerly direction along the centre of Foredyke Stream to the centre of Chapman Street Bridge thence in a westerly direction along the centre of Chapman Street and the approach to Sculcoates Bridge to a point on the eastern boundary of East Central Ward at the centre of the River Hull at Sculcoates Bridge thence in a direction generally northerly along the centre of the River Hull to the point of commencement at the north-eastern extremity of Park Ward.

No. 15. DRYPOOL WARD.

The boundary of Drypool Ward shall be as follows :—

An imaginary line commencing at a point in the centre of the River Hull at Sculcoates Bridge and continued thence in an easterly direction along the centre of the approach to Sculcoates Bridge and Chapman Street to the centre of Chapman Street Bridge thence in a southerly and easterly direction along the western and southern boundary of Southcoates Ward to the junction of Wilton Street and Holderness Road thence in a south-easterly direction along the centre of Williamson Street to the Hedon Road thence in a southerly direction along the east side of the Victoria Dock and Timber Pond No. 1 to the south-eastern corner of such Timber Pond thence in a southerly direction to a point in the southern boundary of the city opposite the south-eastern corner of Timber Pond No. 1 thence in a westerly direction along the southern boundary of the city to the south-eastern extremity of Whitefriars Ward thence in a northerly direction along the eastern boundaries of Whitefriars Ward Paragon Ward and East Central Ward to the point of commencement in the centre of the River Hull at Sculcoates Bridge.

No. 16. ALEXANDRA WARD.

The boundary of Alexandra Ward shall be as follows :—

An imaginary line commencing at the point of junction of Wilton Street and Holderness Road and continued thence in a north-easterly direction along the centre of Holderness Road to the city boundary thence in an easterly and southerly direction along the city boundary to the south-eastern extremity of the city thence in a westerly direction along the southern boundary of the city to the south-eastern extremity of the boundary of Drypool Ward thence along the eastern boundary of Drypool Ward to the point of commencement at the junction of Holderness Road and Wilton Street.

THIRD SCHEDULE.

PROPERTIES OF WHICH PART ONLY IS REQUIRED TO BE TAKEN.

Parish Township or Place.	Number on Deposited Plans.
SCOTT STREET BRIDGE.	
Sutton	5, 6.
NEW STREETS.	
Sculcoates	96, 161, 280.

FOURTH SCHEDULE.

DESCRIPTION OF WATER LIMITS.

The extended city and the townships of Anlaby and Willerby and parish of Kirk Ella and so much of the parish of Hessle as is not included within the limits of the city and so much of the parish of Cottingham Without as is comprised within the following boundaries namely an imaginary line commencing at the north-west point in the city boundary on the north side of Endike Lane and extending thence along the centre of the Cottingham drain to the junction of the said drain with the drain called the " nine foot drain " from thence north by west along the centre of the said nine foot drain crossing North Carr Lane for forty-seven chains westward along the centre of the said drain for two-and-a-half chains and north by west for twenty-three chains to the junction of such drain with Moor Dike thence westward along the centre of the last mentioned dike two-and-a-half chains to its junction with Pan Bottom drain from thence extending along the centre of Pan Bottom drain for fifty-eight chains to its north end and continuing north by an undefined line to the centre of Dunswell Lane and thence extending eastward along the centre of Dunswell Lane to its junction with the Beverley Road and thence by an undefined line due east to the centre of the River Hull and thence extending southward along the centre of the River Hull to the city boundary.

FIFTH SCHEDULE.

STATEMENT AS TO KINGSTON-UPON-HULL CORPORATION DEBT 31ST MARCH, 1897.

of Debt.	Stock Issued.			Stock extinguished out of Loans Fund.			Amount raised by Bonds or otherwise.	Bond debt extinguished out of Sinking Fund or by Instalment.	Debt Outstanding.					Amounts in Loans Fund and Sinking Funds.			
	3½ per cent. Irredeemable.	3½ per cent. Redeemable.	3 per cent. Redeemable.	3½ per cent. Irredeemable.	3½ per cent. Redeemable.	3 per cent. Redeemable.			3½ per cent. Irredeemable Stock.	3½ per cent. Redeemable Stock.	3 per cent. Redeemable Stock.	Bond or other debt.	3½ per cent. Stock. (Loans Fund).	3½ per cent. Stock. (Loans Fund).	3 per cent. Stock (Loans Fund).	Bond Debt (Sinking Funds).
	£ s. d.	£	£ s. d.	£ s. d.	£	£ s. d.	£	£ s. d.	£ s. d.	£	£ s. d.	£ s. d.	£ s. d.	£ s. d.	£	£ s. d.
...pal	305,000 0 0	—	—	14,491 2 1	—	539 1 0	12,980	6,810 13 4	290,508 17 11	—	10,860 19 0	6,169 6 8	‡13,792 16 6 }3,216 12 7	—	—	‡7,456 13 1
...orks ..	123,840 3 2	100,000	—	2,973 4 2	100	—	97,300	4,200 0 0	113,867 4	0 99,900	—	93,100 0 0	‡4,727 18 0	‡1,480 12 9	—	‡7,456 13 1
...nitary	126,565 4 11	—	121,991 3 11	29,791 9 11	—	9,163 18 3	18,850	8,500 0 0	426,773 18 1	—	116,827 5 8	60,350 0 0	§49,965 9 1	—	—	†12,023 15 7
...als	843,105 13 1	100,000	126,391 3 11	54,235 13 1	100	9,702 19 3	†179,130 13 4	19,510 13 4	831,150 0	0 99,900	*126,488 4 8	†159,619 6 8	71,602 16 2	1,180 12 9	—	19,487 8 8

* Exclusive of £15,931 12s. 6d. Stock issued for the purpose of lending money to the School Board and £900 Stock unallocated.
† Exclusive of the sum of £15,882 12s. 11d., the balance of moneys taken out of the Loans Fund to pay off annuities by way of investment of the Loans Fund. The Fund is being recouped by annual instalments. (The £15,882 12s. 11d. is owing in respect of Bridge, Newland, and Newington Loans).
‡ Invested in Hull Corporation 3 per cent. Stock.
§ £33,982 16s. 3d. of this sum is invested in Hull Corporation 3 per cent. Stock. The residue (viz. £15,882 12s. 11d.) is invested as shown in note †.

SIXTH SCHEDULE.

WATER ACTS AND ORDERS REPEALED.

[Enactments which have been already repealed are in some cases included in this repeal in order to prevent the necessity for referring to previous Acts.]

An Act for better supplying with water the borough of Kingston-upon-Hull.--(6 & 7 Vict. c. lxxiii.)	The whole Act.
The Kingston - upon - Hull Water Act 1872.—35 & 36 Vict. c. cc.)	The whole Act.
The Gas and Water Orders Confirmation Act 1875.	So much of the Act as confirms the Newington Water Order 1875 and the whole of that Order.
The Local Government Board's Provisional Orders Confirmation (Aspull &c.) Act 1879 (42 & 43 Vict. c. cv.)	So much as confirms the Provisional Order for partially repealing and altering a local Act in force in the city and the whole of the said Order.
The Hull Extension and Improvement Act 1882.	Part VIII.—That is to say Sections 77 to 87 Section 95 and Sections 11 66 and 122 (relating to the Newington Waterworks).
The Local Government Board's Provisional Orders Confirmation (No. 8) Act 1883 (46 & 47 Vict. c. xcix.)	Article 1 of the Provisional Order for partially repealing and altering local Acts and confirming Acts in force in the city and so much of the confirming Act as confirms the said Article.
The Kingston-upon-Hull Corporation Water Act 1884—(47 & 48 Vict. c. lx.)	The whole Act except Section 16 (which amends Article II. of the Kingston-upon-Hull Order 1883).
The Newington Water Order 1893.—(Confirmed by 56 & 57 Vict. c. cxxv.)	The whole Order and so much of the confirming Act as confirms the said Order.

SEVENTH SCHEDULE.

AN AGREEMENT made the tenth day of April one thousand eight hundred and ninety-seven between the KINGSTON-UPON-HULL GAS LIGHT COMPANY (hereinafter called "the Company") of the one part and the MAYOR ALDERMEN AND BURGESSES OF THE BOROUGH OF KINGSTON-UPON-HULL (hereinafter called "the Corporation") of the other part whereby it is mutually agreed as follows:—

1. The Company shall sell and the Corporation shall purchase free from all charges and incumbrances the whole of the Undertaking and all the property real and personal of every description (except cash in hand or at bank the reserve fund coals and debts due) and all the rights powers and privileges of the Company at or for the sum of ninety thousand pounds for such purchase together with two thousand five hundred pounds to be applied towards the compensation of the Committee of Management and officers of the Company and expenses of this sale and the winding up of the Company The premises hereby agreed to be sold are hereinafter referred to as "the Undertaking."

2. The purchase shall be completed on the thirty-first day of March one thousand eight hundred and ninety eight and the Company and all other necessary parties (if any) shall execute and do such assurances and things as may be reasonably required for vesting the Undertaking in the Corporation and giving them the full benefit of this Agreement If through any fault of the Corporation the purchase shall not be completed on the day fixed by this Agreement for its completion the Corporation shall pay interest at four per cent. upon the said purchase money until completion.

3. The Company shall be entitled to all their revenue accruing up to the date hereby fixed for completion of the purchase and shall discharge and fulfil all their contracts obligations debts and liabilities up to that date and any current outgoings payable in respect of the property of the Company shall if necessary be apportioned for the purposes of this clause   The Corporation shall collect on behalf of the Company all gas rents and meter rents and other payments due to them in connection with the works (if any) that may be due to the Company at the time of the completion of the purchase and shall account to the Company therefor.

4. Until the completion of the purchase the Company shall maintain the Undertaking and all their works plant and appliances in proper condition and repair and upon the said completion the Company shall hand over the Undertaking in proper order as a going concern and shall transfer to the Corporation the benefit of existing Fire Insurance policies and of all contracts with the Company existing at the date of this Agreement.

5. The Company shall within three months from the date hereof deliver to the Town Clerk a statutory declaration by their clerk that the property agreed to be sold is vested in the Company in fee simple in possession free from incumbrances and at the same time an abstract of the conveyances to the Company of such properties as have been acquired by them within the last twenty years   The Corporation shall not require any other evidence of the title of the Company than the said declaration and conveyances.

6. Until the completion of the purchase the Company shall afford to the Corporation all reasonable facilities for inspecting the Undertaking and all the plant and appliances and plans and books of the Company and the manufacturing of gas at their works and shall give to the Corporation all information in their power with reference to the carrying on of the said works and the management of the Undertaking.

7. The Corporation shall take over the services of Thomas Bull manager and Thomas Johnson accountant at salaries after

the rate respectively of three hundred pounds and two hundred and fifty pounds per annum upon and subject to the following conditions (namely) :—

    (A) In the event of the Corporation at any time determining the engagement of the said Thomas Bull for any reason other than that for which a servant might be dismissed by his Master the Corporation shall pay to the said Thomas Bull an annuity of one hundred and fifty pounds per annum or the capitalised value of such annuity computed upon the Post Office Scale for Immediate Life Annuities for one hundred pounds and the Government Life Annuity Tables 10 George IV. c. 24 and 51 and 52 Vict. c. 15 for the remaining fifty pounds ;

    (B) In the event of the Corporation desiring to determine the engagement of the said Thomas Johnson at any time before the expiration of five years from the said thirty-first day of March one thousand eight hundred and ninety eight for any reason other than that for which a servant might be dismissed by his master the Corporation shall pay to the said Thomas Johnson a sum equal to the amount of his salary for the unexpired part of the said period of five years :

Provided always and it is hereby agreed and declared that in the event of the Corporation entering into any agreement with the Sutton and Southcoates Gas Company or the British Gas Light Company Limited under which either of those Companies take over the obligations of the Corporation under this clause with respect to the said Thomas Bull and Thomas Johnson or either of them the obligations of the Corporation under this clause shall to the extent so taken over thereupon cease and determine.

    8. This Agreement is subject to the sanction of Parliament or the Local Government Board.

IN WITNESS whereof the Company and the Corporation have hereunto affixed their respective Common Seals the day and year first before written.

The Common Seal of the Company was
affixed hereto in the presence of

   FREDK. A. SCOTT
    Clerk to the Company.

     Seal
     of the
     Company.

    F. PETERS SMITH
     Chairman.

The Common Seal of the Corporation was
affixed hereto in the presence of

   GEO. ANSELL
    Town Clerk's Office
      Hull.

     Seal
     of the
     Corporation.

INDEX.

KINGSTON UPON HULL CORPORATION ACT, 1897.

INTERPRETATION, 2 S 5.

JUDGES AND JUSTICES not disqualified from acting in execution of this Act, 43 S 108.

LABOURING CLASS, Corporation not to acquire ten or more houses of, until Local Government Board shall have approved Scheme for providing new dwellings, and Corporation have given security to Local Government Board for carrying out of Scheme, 18 S 45 (1) (a).

Definition of expression of, 20 S 45 (9).

Scheme as to, Corporation and Local Government Board and their Inspectors may exercise powers vested in them under Public Health Act, 1875, provided that all lands on which dwellings for labouring class have been erected shall, for 25 years from date of Scheme, be appropriated for purpose of dwellings ; and every Conveyance, &c., to be endorsed to that effect, Local Government Board having power to dispense with such requirements, 20 S 45 (7).

Corporation may appropriate any lands belonging to them, or which they have power to acquire, subject to approval of Local Government Board where necessary, 19 S 45 (6).

Corporation to pay Local Government Board sum for preparation, &c., of Provisional Order, and expenses of witnesses and inspector, 20 S 45 (8).

Local Government Board's approval of, may be absolute or conditional, and they may from time to time approve of any modifications, 19 S 45 (2).

Provisions of, to be enforceable by a Writ of Mandamus obtained by the Local Government Board out of the High Court, 19 S 45 (4).

to contain provisions prescribing time within which it shall be carried out, and to require new dwellings proposed to be provided to be completed fit for occupation before persons are displaced, Local Government Board having power to dispense with last-mentioned requirement, 19 S 45 (3).

Restrictions on displacing persons of, 18 S 45.

LAND, Application of purchase money of, S 59 of Act of 1882 to apply, 24 S 51.

Two pieces of waste, near Drypool Green, enactments and bye-laws with respect to other recreation grounds in City to apply to, subject to certain conditions, 31 S 69.

LANDS and any other property in added part of City not to be liable to contribute or be rated to any expenditure of the East Riding County Council, 4 S 9.

Corporation may appropriate any, belonging to them, or which they have power to acquire, subject to approval of Local Government Board where necessary, 19 S 45 (6).

appropriate, vested in them, for purposes of this Act, or of any other local or public Acts in force within the City, 24 S 49.

RATE for supply of water for domestic purposes not to exceed £7 per cent. per annum on net annual value of premises supplied, 35 S 85.

RATES, All arrears of, due in added part of City immediately before commencement of Act, may be collected and recovered therein as if Act had not been passed, 4 S 9.

> Borough, Watch, &c., and any other rates (except Poor Rate), in added part of City : for 15 years from commencement of Act, total amount in the pound of not to exceed total amount in the pound of General District, School Board, and County rates and of any other rates (except Poor Rate) levied in added part of City during year ending 31st March, 1897, and for like period Highway Rate to be assessed and levied in added part of City on same assessment as a General District Rate under Section 211 of the Public Health Act, 1875, 7 S 19 (7).

> Corporation may enforce payment of, in like manner as if they were Poor Rates, and with like right of appeal, but without prejudice to any other mode exerciseable by Corporation, 29 S 63.

> Discontinuance of exemption from, enjoyed by the North Eastern Railway Company and certain owners and occupiers, 27 S 57.

> Nothing in Act to affect operation of Agricultural Rates Act, 1896, so long as latter Act remains in force, 7 S 19 (8).

> Power to Corporation to allow rebates not exceeding one shilling in the pound on personal payment of, at the City Treasurer's office, within one month from demand therefor, 29 S 62.

> Water, payment of, 39 S 95.

RATING EXEMPTIONS, Repeal of, 29 S 60 (1) (2).

RECEIPTS in respect of Waterworks, Application of, 39 S 98.

RECREATION GROUNDS, Power to Corporation to set apart portions of any park or place of public resort or recreation for games, and power to make bye-laws regulating same, 29 S 64 (1).

REPEAL from and after 15 years from passing of this Act, of S 67 (as to rating of railway and dock properties in the added part of the borough) of the Act of 1882, 29 S 60 (2).

> of Acts or Provisional Orders relating to repayment of sums forming part of debts referred to in the Fifth Schedule, 26 S 57.

> Section 51 (exemptions under S 211 of Public Health Act to apply to property in added part of borough) of the Act of 1882, 29 S 61.

> Section 107 of Act of 1882 (expenses to be a charge on premises) and Section 257 of Public Health Act, 1875, to apply in lieu thereof, 46 S 116.

> Section 113 (as to streets, &c., repaired, &c., under the Hull Dock Acts) of the Act of 1882, 29 S 60 (1).

> Sections 121 and 123 of the Improvement Act of 1854, and 112 and 114 of the Act of 1882, consideration for, 28 S 59.

REPEAL (continued) of Sections 121 and 123 of the Improvement Act of 1854, and 112 and 114 of the Act of 1882, granting exemptions from certain rates in favour of the North Eastern Railway Company, as successors of the Dock Company, and owners and occupiers of properties in certain streets, 27 S 58.
of Water Acts and Orders set out in Sixth Schedule, 45 S 114.

RESERVE FUND, Waterworks, Application of, 40 S 98 (2) (3).

RESTRICTION on informations, 43 S 106.

SANITARY DEBT and General Debt, and any moneys re-borrowed in lieu thereof, to be repaid within 35 years from 31st March, 1898, 27 S 57 (iii.).

SAVING CLAUSE for Henry Edward Thornton Wilkinson, 46 S 115.
RIGHTS of the Crown in the foreshore, 13 S 31.
under Crown Lands Act, 46 S 117.

SCHEDULES—
First Schedule.   Description of added part of City, 47.
Second Schedule.   Names and boundaries of Wards, 49.
Third Schedule.   Particulars of property of which part only is required to be taken, 58.
Fourth Schedule.   Description of water limits, 59.
Fifth Schedule.   Statement as to Corporation debt, 60.
Sixth Schedule.   Water Acts and Orders repealed, 61.
Seventh Schedule.   Agreement between Kingston upon Hull Gas Light Co. and Corporation, 62.

SCHOOL BOARD, Bye-laws of, for existing City to apply to extended City, 8 S 22.
for City to be School Board for extended City, 8 S 21.
DISTRICT, City to be a, 8 S 21.

SCOTT STREET BRIDGE, Power to make, 10 S 25.

SESSIONS, Quarter, any person deeming himself aggrieved by any order, &c., or withholding of any licence, &c., may appeal to, and Corporation may do same in regard to any order of a Court of Summary Jurisdiction, 43 S 109.

SHORT TITLE, 1 S 1.

STAND PIPES and Apparatus, Expenses of providing and maintaining, 36 S 87 (3) to (8).
Corporation or owners of houses in courts, alleys, and other places may erect therein, 36 S 87 (1).

STOCK, Corporation may prepare and submit to Local Government Board a scheme for conversion by agreement of irredeemable stock into stock redeemable not later than 31st December, 1950, bearing interest at not exceeding 4 per centum per annum, 31 S 70 (1).
Corporation may raise moneys by creation and issue of, in accordance with Hull Corporation Loans Act, 1881, as amended by any subsequent Act or Order, or by any of methods provided by Local Loans Act, 1875, 25 S 52 (2).

CONTENTS.

PROVISIONAL ORDER, 1890.

PRELIMINARY.

ii.   CONTENTS.

BOROUGH OF KINGSTON-UPON-HULL.
PROVISIONAL ORDER,

*Confirmed by the Electric Lighting Orders Confirmation (No. 6)
Act, 1890, 53 and 54 Vict., Ch. CXCI.*

Royal Assent, 4th August, 1890.

Preliminary.

1. This Order may be cited as the Kingston-upon-Hull Short title. Electric Lighting Order 1890.

2. This Order is to be read and construed subject in all Interpretation. respects to the provisions of the Electric Lighting Acts 1882 and 1888 and of any other Acts or parts of Acts incorporated therewith which said Acts and parts of Acts are in this Order collectively referred to as " the principal Act " and the several words terms and expressions to which by the principal Act meanings are assigned shall have in this Order the same respective meanings provided that in this Order—

The expression "energy" shall mean electrical energy and for the purposes of applying the provisions of the principal Act to this Order electrical energy shall be deemed to be an agency within the meaning of electricity as defined in the Electric Lighting Act 1882:

The expression "power" shall mean electrical power or the rate per unit of time at which energy is supplied :

The expression "main" shall mean any electric line which may be laid down by the Undertakers in any street or public place and through which energy may be supplied or intended to be supplied by the Undertakers for the purposes of general supply :

The expression "service line" shall mean any electric line through which energy may be supplied or intended to be supplied by the Undertakers to a consumer either from any main or directly from the premises of the · Undertakers :

The expression "distributing main" shall mean the portion of any main which is used for the purpose of giving origin to surface lines for the purposes of general supply :

The expression "general supply" shall mean the general supply of energy to ordinary consumers but shall not include the supply of energy to any one or more particular consumers under special agreement :

The expression "area of supply" shall mean the area within which the Undertakers are for the time being authorised to supply energy under the provisions of this Order :

The expression "consumer" shall mean any body or person supplied or entitled to be supplied with energy by the Undertakers :

The expression "consumer's terminals" shall mean the ends of the electric lines situate upon any consumer's premises and belonging to him at which the supply of energy is delivered from the service lines :

The expression "telegraphic line" when used with respect to any telegraphic line of the Postmaster General shall have the same meaning as in the Telegraphic Act 1878 and any such telegraphic line shall be deemed to be injuriously affected where telegraphic communication by means of such line is whether through induction or otherwise in any manner affected :

The expression "railway" shall include any tramroad that is to say any tramway other than a tramway as hereinafter defined :

The expression "tramway" shall mean any tramway laid along any street :

The expression "daily penalty" shall mean a penalty for each day on which any offence is continued after conviction thereof :

The expressions "First Schedule" "Second Schedule" "Third Schedule" and "Fourth Schedule" shall mean the First Second Third and Fourth Schedules to this Order annexed respectively :

The expression "deposited map" shall mean the map of the area of supply deposited at the Board of Trade by the Undertakers together with this Order and signed by an Assistant Secretary to the Board of Trade :

The expression "plan" shall mean a plan drawn to a horizontal scale of at least one inch to eighty-eight feet and where possible a section drawn to the same horizontal scale as the plan and to a vertical scale of at least one inch to eleven feet with such detail plan and sections as may be necessary.

3. This Order shall come into force and have effect upon the day when the Act confirming this Order is passed which date is in this Order referred to as "the commencement of this Order." *Commencement of Order.*

Description of the Undertakers.

4. Subject to the provisions of this Order the Undertakers for the purposes of this Order shall be the Mayor Aldermen and Burgesses of the Borough of Kingston-upon-Hull. *Description of Undertakers.*

Area of Supply.

5. Subject to the provisions of this Order the area of supply shall be the whole of the area included in the First Schedule which said area is more particularly delineated upon the deposited map and thereon verged blue. *Area of supply.*

Nature and Mode of Supply.

6. Subject to the provisions of this Order and the principal Act the Undertakers may supply energy within the area of supply for all public and private purposes as defined by the said Act provided as follows:— *Systems and mode of supply.*

(1) Such energy shall be supplied only by means of some system which shall be approved in writing by the Board of Trade and subject to such regulations and conditions for securing the safety of the public and for insuring a proper and sufficient supply of energy as the Board of Trade may from time to time impose; and

(2) The Undertakers shall not permit any part of any circuit to be connected with earth except so far as may be necessary for carrying out the provisions of any such regulations and conditions as aforesaid unless such connexion is for the time being approved of by the Board of Trade with the concurrence of the Postmaster General and is made in accordance with the conditions (if any) of such approval; and

(3) The Undertakers shall construct their mains and other works of all descriptions and shall work their undertaking in all respects so as not injuriously to affect the working of any existing electric circuits from time to time used or intended to be used for the purpose of telegraphic telephonic or electric signalling communication or the currents in such circuits and shall use every reasonable means in the construction of their mains and other works of all descriptions and the working of their undertaking to prevent injurious affection whether by induction or otherwise to any electric circuits used or intended to be used for the purposes aforesaid whether existing at the time of the construction of such mains or other works or not or the currents in such circuits If any question arises as to whether the Undertakers have constructed their mains or other works or worked their undertaking in contravention of this sub-section such question shall be determined by arbitration and the Undertakers shall be bound to make any alterations in or additions to their system which may be directed by the arbitrator : Provided that nothing in this sub-section contained shall be held to deprive the owners of such electric circuits of any existing rights to proceed against the Undertakers by indictment action or otherwise in relation to any of the matters aforesaid.

Lands.

Purchase and use of lands.

7. Subject to the provisions of this Order and the principal Act the Undertakers may from time to time acquire by purchase or on lease and use any lands for the purposes of this Order and may also for such purposes use any other lands for the time being vested in or leased by them but subject as to such last mentioned lands to the approval of the Local Government Board and may from time to time dispose of any lands acquired by them under the provisions of this section which may not for the time being be required for the purposes of this Order : Provided that the amount of land so used by them shall not at any one time exceed in the whole ten acres except with the consent of the Board of Trade.

Provided also that the Undertakers shall not except with the consent of the Local Government Board take for the purposes of this Order ten or more houses which after the passing of the Act confirming this Order have been or on the fifteenth day of December last were occupied either wholly or partially by persons belonging to the labouring class as tenants or lodgers.

For the purposes of this section the expression "labouring class" means and includes mechanics artizans labourers and others working for wages hawkers costermongers persons not working for wages but working at some trade or handicraft without employing others except members of their own family and persons other than domestic servants whose income does not exceed an average of thirty shillings a week and the families of any of such persons who may be residing with them.

Works.

8. Subject to the provisions of this Order and the principal Act the Undertakers may from time to time exercise all or any of the powers conferred on them by this Order and the principal Act and may break up such streets not repairable by the local authority and such railways and tramways (if any) as are specified in the Third Schedule so far as such streets railways and tramways may for the time being be included in the area of supply and be or be upon land dedicated to public use : Provided however as respects any such railway that the powers hereby granted shall extend only to such parts thereof as pass across or along any highway on the level.

(margin: Powers for execution of works.)

Nothing in this Order shall authorise or empower the Undertakers to break up or interfere with any street or part of a street not repairable by the local authority or any railway or tramway except such streets railways or tramways (if any) or such parts thereof as are specified in the said schedule without the consent of the authority company or person by whom such street railway or tramway is repairable or of the Board of Trade under section thirteen of the Electric Lighting Act 1882 and where the Board of Trade give such consent the provisions of this Order shall apply to the street railway or tramway to which the consent relates as if it had been specified in the said schedule.

Street boxes.

9. Subject to the provisions of this Order and the principal Act and any regulations made under this Order the Undertakers may also from time to time construct in any street such boxes as may be necessary for purposes in connexion with the supply of energy including apparatus for the proper ventilation of such boxes.

Every such box shall be for the exclusive use of the Undertakers and under their sole control except so far as the Board of Trade may otherwise order and shall be used by the Undertakers only for the purpose of leading off service lines and other distributing conductors or for examining testing regulating measuring directing or controlling the supply of energy or for examining or testing the condition of the mains or other portions of the works or for other like purposes connected with the undertaking and the Undertakers may place therein meters switches and any other suitable and proper apparatus for any of the above purposes.

Every such box including the upper surface or covering thereof shall be constructed of such materials and shall be constructed and maintained by the Undertakers in such manner as not to be a source of danger whether by reason of inequality of surface or otherwise.

Notice of works with plan to be served on the Post-master General.

10. Where the exercise of any of the powers of the Undertakers in relation to the execution of any works (including the construction of boxes) will involve the placing of any works in under along or across any street or public bridge the following provisions shall have effect :—

> (a) One month before commencing the execution of such works (not being the repairs renewals or amendments of existing works of which the character and position are not altered) the Undertakers shall serve a notice upon the Postmaster-General describing the proposed works together with a plan of the works showing the mode and position in which such works are intended to be executed and the manner in which it is intended that such street or bridge is to be interfered with and shall upon being required to do so by the Postmaster-General from time to time give him any such further information in relation thereto as he may desire.

(b) The Postmaster-General may in his discretion approve of any such works or plan subject to such amendments or conditions as may seem fit or may disapprove the same and may give notice of such approval or disapproval to the Undertakers.

(c) Where the Postmaster-General approves any such works or plan subject to any amendments or conditions with which the Undertakers are dissatisfied or disapproves of any such works or plan the Undertakers may appeal to the Board of Trade and the Board of Trade may inquire into the matter and allow or disallow such appeal and approve any such works or plan subject to such amendments or conditions as may seem fit or may disapprove the same.

(d) If the Postmaster-General fail to give any such notice of approval or disapproval to the Undertakers within one month after the service of the notice upon him he shall be deemed to have approved such works and plan.

(e) Notwithstanding anything in this Order or the principal Act the Undertakers shall not be entitled to execute any such works as above specified except so far as the same may be of a description and in accordance with a plan which has been approved or is to be deemed to have been approved by the Postmaster-General or by the Board of Trade as above mentioned but where any such works description and plan are so approved or to be deemed to be approved the Undertakers may cause such works to be executed in accordance with such description and plan subject in all respects to the provisions of this Order and of the principal Act.

(f) If the Undertakers make default in complying with any of the requirements or restrictions of this section they shall (in addition to any other compensation which they may be liable to make under the provisions of this Order or the principal Act) make full compensation to the Postmaster-General for any loss or damage which he may incur by reason thereof and in addition thereto they shall be liable to a penalty not exceeding ten pounds for every such default and to a daily penalty

not exceeding five pounds : Provided that the Undertakers shall not be subject to any such penalties as aforesaid if the court having cognizance of the case shall be of opinion that the case was one of emergency and that the Undertakers complied with the requirements of this section so far as was reasonable under the circumstances.

Nothing in this section shall exempt the Undertakers from any penalty or obligation to which they may be liable under this Order or otherwise by law in the event of any telegraphic line of the Postmaster-General being at any time injuriously affected by the Undertakers works or their supply of energy.

11. Where the exercise of the powers of the Undertakers in relation to the execution of any works will involve the placing of any works in under along or across any street or part of a street not repairable by the local authority or over or under any railway tramway or canal the following provisions shall have effect unless otherwise agreed between the parties interested :—

As to streets not repairable by local authority railways and tramways.

(a) One month before commencing the execution of any such works (not being the repairs renewals or amendments of existing works of which the character and position are not altered) the Undertakers shall in addition to any other notices which they may be required to give under this Order or the principal Act serve a notice upon the body or person for the time being liable to repair such street or part of a street or the body or person for the time being entitled to work such railway or tramway or the owners of such canal as the case may be (in this section referred to as the "owners") describing the proposed works together with a plan (as defined in the last preceding section) of the works showing the mode and position in which such works are intended to be executed and placed and shall upon being required to do so by any such owners from time to time give them any such further information in relation thereto as they may desire.

(b) Every such notice shall contain a reference to this section and direct the attention of the owners to whom it is given to the provisions thereof.

(c) Within three weeks after the service of any such notice
and plan upon any owners such owners may if they
think fit serve a requisition upon the Undertakers
requiring that any question in relation to such works
or to compensation in respect thereof and any other
question arising upon such notice or plan as aforesaid
shall be settled by arbitration and thereupon such
question unless settled by agreement shall be settled
by arbitration accordingly.

(d) In settling any question under this section an arbitrator
shall have regard to any duties or obligations which
the owners may be under in respect of such street
railway tramway or canal and may if he thinks fit
require the Undertakers to execute any temporary or
other works so as to avoid any interference with any
traffic so far as may be possible.

(e) Where no such requisition as in this section mentioned
is served upon the Undertakers or where after any
such requisition has been served upon them any
question required to be settled by arbitration has been
so settled the Undertakers may upon paying or
securing any compensation which they may be required
to pay or secure cause to be executed the works
specified in such notice and plan as aforesaid and may
from time to time repair renew and amend the same
(provided that their character and position are not
altered) but subject in all respects to the provisions of
this Order and the principal Act and only in accordance
with the notice and plan so served by them as aforesaid
or such modifications thereof respectively as may have
been settled by arbitration as herein-before mentioned
or as may be agreed upon between the parties.

(f) All works to be executed by the Undertakers under
this section shall be carried out to the reasonable
satisfaction of the owners who shall have the right to
be present during the execution of such works.

(g) Where the repair renewal or amendment of any
existing works of which the character or position are
not altered will involve any interference with any
railway level crossing or with any tramway over or

under which such works have been placed the
Undertakers shall unless otherwise agreed between the
parties or in cases of emergency give to the owners not
less than 24 hours' notice before commencing to effect
such repair renewal or amendment and the owners
shall be entitled by their officer to superintend the
work and the Undertakers shall conform to such
reasonable requirements as may from time to time be
made by the owners or such officer. The said notice
shall be in addition to any other notices which the
Undertakers may be required to give under this Order
or the principal Act.

(*h*) If the Undertakers make default in complying
with any of the requirements or restrictions of this
section they shall (in addition to any other compensation which they may be liable to make under the
provisions of this Order or the principal Act) make
full compensation to the owners affected thereby for
any loss or damage which they may incur by reason
thereof and in addition thereto they shall be liable to
a penalty not exceeding ten pounds for every such
default and to a daily penalty not exceeding five
pounds: Provided that the Undertakers shall not be
subject to any such penalties as aforesaid if the court
having cognizance of the case shall be of opinion that
the case was one of emergency and that the Undertakers complied with the requirements of this section
so far as was reasonable under the circumstances.

Street
authority &c.
may give
notice of
desire to
break up
streets &c.
on behalf of
Undertakers

12. Any body or person for the time being liable to repair
any street or part of a street or entitled to work any railway or
tramway which the Undertakers may be empowered to break up
for the purposes of this Order may if they think fit from time to
time serve a notice upon the Undertakers stating that they desire
to exercise or discharge all or any part of any of the powers or
duties of the Undertakers as therein specified in relation to the
breaking up filling in reinstating or making good any streets bridges
sewers drains tunnels or other works vested in or under the control
or management of such body or person and may from time to time
amend or revoke any such notice by another notice similarly served.

Where such body or person as aforesaid (in this section referred to as "the givers of the notice") have given notice that they desire to exercise or discharge any such specified powers and duties of the Undertakers then so long as such notice remains in force the following provisions shall have effect unless otherwise agreed between the parties interested

(a) The Undertakers shall not be entitled to proceed themselves to exercise or discharge any such specified powers or duties as aforesaid except where they have required the givers of the notice to exercise or discharge such powers or duties and the givers of the notice have refused or neglected to comply with such requisition as herein-after provided or in cases of emergency.

(b) In addition to any other notices which they may be required to give under the provisions of this Order or the principal Act the Undertakers shall not more than four days and not less than two days before the exercise or discharge of any such powers or duties so specified as aforesaid is required to be commenced serve a requisition upon the givers of the notice stating the time when such exercise or discharge is required to be commenced and the manner in which any such powers or duties are required to be exercised or discharged.

(c) Upon receipt of any such requisition as last aforesaid the givers of the notice may proceed to exercise or discharge any such powers or duties as required by the Undertakers subject to the like restrictions and conditions as the Undertakers would themselves be subject to in such exercise or discharge so far as the same may be applicable.

(d) If the givers of the notice decline or for twenty-four hours after the time when any such exercise or discharge of any powers or duties is by any requisition required to be commenced neglect to comply with such requisition the Undertakers may themselves proceed to exercise or discharge the powers or duties therein specified in like manner as they might have done if such notice as aforesaid had not been given to them by the givers of the notice.

(*e*) In any case of emergency the Undertakers may themselves proceed to at once exercise or discharge so much of any such specified powers or duties as aforesaid as may be necessary for the actual remedying of any defect from which the emergency arises without serving any requisition on the givers of the notice but in such case the Undertakers shall within twelve hours after they begin to exercise or discharge such powers or duties as aforesaid give information thereof in writing to the givers of the notice.

(*f*) If the Undertakers exercise or discharge any such specified powers or duties as aforesaid otherwise than in accordance with the provisions of this section they shall be liable to a penalty not exceeding ten pounds for every such offence and to a daily penalty not exceeding five pounds : Provided that the Undertakers shall not be subject to any such penalties as aforesaid if the court having cognizance of the case shall be of opinion that the case was one of emergency and that the Undertakers complied with the requirements of this section so far as was reasonable under the circumstances.

(*g*) All expenses properly incurred by the givers of the notice in complying with any requisition of the Undertakers under this section shall be repaid to them by the Undertakers and may be recovered summarily before a court of summary jurisdiction.

Provided that nothing in this section shall in any way affect the rights of the Undertakers to exercise or discharge any powers or duties conferred or imposed upon them by this Order or the principal Act in relation to the execution of any works beyond the actual breaking up filling in reinstating or making good any such street or part of a street or any such bridges sewers drains tunnels or other works or railway or tramway as in this section mentioned.

As to alteration of pipes wires &c. under streets.

13.   The Undertakers may from time to time alter the position of any pipes or wires being under any street or place authorised to be broken up by them which may interfere with the exercise of their powers under the principal Act or this Order and any body or person may in like manner alter the position of any electric lines or works of the Undertakers being under any such street or place as aforesaid which may interfere with the lawful exercise of any powers vested in such body or person in relation to such street or place subject to the following provisions unless otherwise agreed between the parties interested :.

(a) One month before commencing any such alteration the Undertakers or such body or person (as the case may be) in this section referred to as "the operators" shall serve a notice upon the body or persons for the time being entitled to such pipes wires electric lines or works (as the case may be) in this section referred to as "the owners" describing the proposed alteration together with a plan showing the manner in which it is intended that such alterations shall be made and shall upon being required to do so by any such owners from time to time give them any such further information in relation thereto as they may desire.

(b) Within three weeks after the service of any such notice and plan upon any owners such owners may if they think fit serve a requisition upon the operators requiring that any question in relation to such works or to compensation in respect thereof or any other question arising upon such notice or plan as aforesaid shall be settled by arbitration and thereupon such question unless settled by agreement shall be settled by arbitration accordingly.

(c) In settling any question under this section an arbitrator shall have regard to any duties or obligations which the owners may be under in respect of such pipes wires electric lines or works and may if he thinks fit require the operators to execute any temporary or other works so as to avoid interference with any purpose for which such pipes wires electric lines or works are used so far as may be possible.

(d) Where no such requisition as in this section mentioned is served upon the operators the owners shall be held to have agreed to the notice or plan served on them as aforesaid and in such case or where after any such requisition has been served upon them any question required to be settled by arbitration has been so settled the operators upon paying or securing any compensation which they may be required to pay or secure may cause the alterations specified in such notice and plan as aforesaid to be made but subject in all respects to the provisions of this Order and the principal Act and only in accordance with the notice and plan so served by them as aforesaid or such modifications thereof respectively as may have been settled by arbitration as hereinbefore mentioned or as may be agreed upon between the parties.

(e) At any time before any operators are entitled to commence any such alterations as aforesaid the owners may serve a statement upon the operators stating that they desire to execute such alterations themselves and where any such statement has been served upon the operators they shall not be entitled to proceed themselves to execute such alterations except where they have notified to such owners that they require them to execute such alterations and such owners have refused or neglected to comply with such notification as herein-after provided.

(f) Where any such statement as last aforesaid has been served upon the operators they shall not more than forty-eight hours and not less than twenty-four hours before the execution of such alterations is required to be commenced serve a notification upon the owners stating the time when such alterations are required to be commenced and the manner in which such alterations are required to be made.

(g) Upon receipt of any such notification as last aforesaid the owners may proceed to execute such alterations as required by the operators subject to the like restrictions and conditions as the operators would themselves be subject to in executing such alterations so far as the same may be applicable.

(h) If the owners decline or for twenty-four hours after the time when any such alterations are required to be commenced neglect to comply with such notification the operators may themselves proceed to execute such

alterations in like manner as they might have done if
no such statement as aforesaid had been served upon
them.

(*i*) All expenses properly incurred by any owners in complying with any notification of any operators under
this section shall be repaid to them by such operators
and may be recovered summarily before a court of
summary jurisdiction.

(*j*) Any owners may if they think fit by any statement
served by them under this section upon any operators
not being a local authority require the said operators
to give them such security for the repayment to them
of any expenses to be incurred by them in executing
any alterations as above mentioned as may be
determined in manner provided by this Order and
where the said operators have been so required to give
security they shall not be entitled to serve a notification
upon the owners requiring them to execute such
alterations until such security has been duly given.

(*k*) If the operators make default in complying with any of
the requirements or restrictions of this section they
shall (in addition to any other compensation which
they may be liable to make under the provisions of
this Order or the principal Act) make full compensation
to the owners affected thereby for any loss damage or
penalty which they may incur by reason thereof and
in addition thereto they shall be liable to a penalty not
exceeding ten pounds for every such default and to a
daily penalty not exceeding five pounds : Provided
that the operators shall not be subject to any such
additional penalties as aforesaid if the court having
cognizance of the case shall be of opinion that the
case was one of emergency and that the operators
complied with the requirements of this section so far
as was reasonable under the circumstances.

14. Whenever the Undertakers require to dig or sink any
trench for laying down or constructing any new electric lines (other
than service lines) or other works near to which any main pipe
syphon electric line or other work belonging to any gas electric

Laying of
electric lines
&c. near gas
or water
pipes or other
electric lines.

supply or water company has been lawfully placed or where any
gas or water company require to dig or sink any trench for laying
down or constructing any new mains or pipes (other than service
pipes) or other works near to which any lines or works of the
Undertakers have been lawfully placed the Undertakers or such gas
or water company (as the case may be) in this section referred to
as the "operators" shall unless otherwise agreed between the
parties interested or in case of sudden emergency give to such gas
electric supply or water company or to the Undertakers (as the
case may be) in this case referred to as the "owners" not less
than three days notice before commencing to dig or sink such
trench as aforesaid and such owners shall be entitled by their
officer to superintend the work and the operators shall conform
with such reasonable requirements as may from time to time be
made by the owners or such officer for protecting from injury
every such main pipe syphon electric line or work and for securing
access thereto and they shall also if required to do so by the owner
thereof repair any damage that may be done thereto.

Where the operators find it necessary to undermine but not
alter the position of any pipe electric line or work they shall
temporarily support the same in position during the execution of
their works and before completion provide a suitable and proper
foundation for the same where so undermined.

Where the operators (being the Undertakers) lay any electric
line crossing or liable to touch any mains pipes lines or services
belonging to any gas electric supply or water company the conduct-
ing portion of such electric line shall be effectively insulated in a
manner approved by the Board of Trade ; and the Undertakers
shall not except with the consent of the gas electric supply or water
company as the case may be and of the Board of Trade lay their
electric lines so as to come into contact with any such mains pipes
lines or services or except with the like consent employ any such
mains pipes lines or services as conductors for the purposes of their
supply of energy.

Any question or difference which may arise under this section
shall be determined by arbitration.

If the operators make default in complying with any of the
requirements or restrictions of this section they shall make full
compensation to all owners affected thereby for any loss damage

penalty or costs which they may incur by reason thereof and in addition thereto they shall be liable to a penalty not exceeding ten pounds for every such default and to a daily penalty not exceeding five pounds : Provided that the operators shall not be subject to any such penalty if the court having cognizance of the case shall be of opinion that the case was one of emergency and that the operators complied with the requirements and restrictions of this section so far as was reasonable under the circumstances or that the default in question was due to the fact that the operators were ignorant of the position of the main pipe syphon electric line or work affected thereby and that such ignorance was not owing to any negligence on the part of the operators.

For the purposes of this section the expression "gas company" shall mean any body or person lawfully supplying gas; the expression "water company" shall mean any body or person lawfully supplying water or water power; and the expression "electric supply company" shall mean any body or person supplying energy under the principal Act but not under this Order.

15. In the exercise of any of the powers of this Order relating to the execution of works the Undertakers shall not in any way injure the railways tunnels arches works or conveniences belonging to any railway or canal company nor obstruct or interfere with the working of the traffic passing along any railway or canal.

16. Seven days before commencing to lay down any electric line or to supply energy through any electric line in any manner whereby the work of telegraphic or telephonic or electric signalling communication through any wires or lines lawfully laid down or placed in any position may be injuriously affected the Undertakers shall unless otherwise agreed between the parties interested give to the body or person for the time being entitled to such wires or lines notice in writing specifying the course nature and gauge of such electric lines and the amount and nature of the currents intended to be sent along the same and the extent to and manner in which if at all earth returns are proposed to be used and the Undertakers shall conform with such reasonable requirements as may from time to time be made by such body or person as aforesaid for the purpose of preventing the communication through such wires or lines from being injuriously affected as aforesaid.

If any difference arises between any such body or person and the Undertakers with respect to the reasonableness of any requirements so made such difference shall be determined by arbitration.

Provided that nothing in this section shall apply to repairs or renewals of any electric line so long as the course nature and gauge of such electric line and the amount and nature of the current sent along the same are not altered.

If the Undertakers make default in complying with any of the requirements or restrictions of this section they shall make full compensation to the body or person entitled to any such wire or line for any loss or damage which they may incur by reason thereof and in addition thereto they shall be liable to a penalty not exceeding five pounds for every such default and to a daily penalty not exceeding forty shillings : Provided that the Undertakers shall not be subject to any such penalties as aforesaid if the court having cognizance of the case shall be of opinion that the case was one of emergency and that the Undertakers complied with the requirements and restrictions of this section so far as was reasonable under the circumstances or that the default in question was due to the fact that the Undertakers were ignorant of the position of the wires or lines affected thereby and that such ignorance was not owing to any negligence on the part of the Undertakers.

Compulsory Works.

Mains &c. to be laid down in streets specified in Second Schedule and in remainder of area of supply.

17. (1) The Undertakers shall within a period of two years after the commencement of this Order lay down suitable and sufficient distributing mains for the purposes of general supply throughout every street or part of a street specified in that behalf in the Second Schedule and shall thereafter maintain the same.

(2) In addition to the mains hereinbefore specified the Undertakers shall at any time after the expiration of eighteen months after the commencement of this Order lay down suitable and sufficient distributing mains for the purposes of general supply throughout every other street or part of a street within the area of supply upon being required to do so in manner by this Order provided.

All such mains as last above mentioned (unless already laid down) shall be laid down by the Undertakers within six months after any requisition in that behalf served upon them in accordance with the provisions of this Order has become binding upon them or such further time as may in any case be approved of by the Board of Trade.

(3) When any such requisition is made in respect of any street not repairable by the local authority which is not mentioned in the Third Schedule the Undertakers shall (unless the authority company or person by whom such street is repairable consent to the breaking up thereof) forthwith apply to the Board of Trade under section 13 of the Electric Lighting Act 1882 for the written consent of the Board authorising and empowering the Undertakers to break up such street and the requisition shall not be binding upon them if the Board of Trade refuse their consent in that behalf.

18. If the Undertakers make default in laying down any distributing mains in accordance with the provisions of this Order within the periods prescribed in that behalf respectively the Board of Trade may revoke this Order as to the whole or (with the consent of the Undertakers) any part of the area of supply or if the Undertakers so desire may suffer the same to remain in force as to such area or part thereof subject to such conditions as they may think fit to impose and any conditions so imposed shall be binding on and observed by the Undertakers and shall be of the like force and effect in every respect as though they were contained in this Order. _{removed}

If Undertakers fail to lay down mains &c. Order may be revoked.

19. Any requisition requiring the Undertakers to lay down distributing mains for the purposes of general supply throughout any street or part of a street may be made by six or more owners or occupiers of premises along such street or part of a street.

Manner in which requisition is to be made.

Every such requisition shall be signed by the persons making the same and shall be served upon the Undertakers.

Forms of requisitions shall be kept by the Undertakers at their office and a copy shall be supplied free of charge to any owner or occupier of premises within the area of supply on application for the same and any requisition so supplied shall be deemed valid in point of form.

20. Where any such requisition is made by any such owners or occupiers as aforesaid the Undertakers (if they think fit) may within fourteen days after the service of the requisition upon them serve a notice on all the persons by whom the requisition is signed stating that they decline to be bound by such requisition unless such persons or some of them will bind themselves to take

Provisions on requisition by owners or occupiers.

or will guarantee that there shall be taken a supply of energy for
three years of such amount in the aggregate (to be specified by the
Undertakers in such notice) as will at the rates of charge for the
time being charged by the Undertakers for a supply of energy from
distributing mains to ordinary consumers within the area of supply
produce annually such reasonable sum as shall be specified by the
Undertakers in such notice : Provided that in such notice the
Undertakers shall not without the authority of the Board of Trade
specify any sum exceeding twenty per centum upon the expense of
providing and laying down the required distributing mains and any
other mains or additions to existing mains which may be necessary
for the purpose of connecting such distributing mains with the
nearest available source of supply.

Where such notice is served the requisition shall not be
binding on the Undertakers unless within fourteen days after the
service of such notice on all the persons signing the requisition has
been effected or in the case of difference the delivery of the
arbitrator's award there be tendered to the Undertakers an
agreement severally executed by such persons or some of them
binding them to take or guaranteeing that there shall be taken for
a period of three years at the least such specified amounts of
energy respectively as will in the aggregate at the rates of charge
above specified produce an annual sum amounting to the sum
specified in the notice or determined by arbitration under this
section nor unless sufficient security for the payment to the
Undertakers of all moneys which may become due to them from
such persons under such agreement is offered to the Undertakers
(if required by them by such notice as aforesaid) within the period
limited for the tender of the agreement as aforesaid.

If the Undertakers consider that the requisition is unreasonable
or that under the circumstances of the case the provisions of this
section ought to be varied they may within fourteen days after the
service of the requisition upon them appeal to the Board of Trade
who after such inquiry (if any) as they shall think fit may by order
either determine that the requisition is unreasonable and shall not
be binding upon the Undertakers or may authorise the Undertakers
by their notice to require a supply of energy to be taken for such
longer period than three years and to specify such sum or percentage
whether calculated as hereinbefore provided or otherwise as shall
be fixed or directed by the Order and the terms of the above

mentioned agreement shall be varied accordingly. In case of any such appeal to the Board of Trade any notice by the Undertakers under this section may be served by them within fourteen days after the decision of the Board of Trade.

If any difference arises between the Undertakers and any persons signing any such requisition as to any such notice agreement or security such difference shall subject to the provisions of this section and to the decision of the Board of Trade upon any such appeal as aforesaid be determined by arbitration.

Supply.

21. The Undertakers shall upon being required to do so by the owner or occupier of any premises situate within fifty yards from any distributing main of the Undertakers in which they are for the time being required to maintain or are maintaining a supply of energy for the purposes of general supply to private consumers under this Order or any regulations and conditions subject to which they are authorised to supply energy under this Order give and continue to give a supply of energy for such premises in accordance with the provisions of this Order and of all such regulations and conditions as aforesaid and they shall furnish and lay any electric lines that may be necessary for the purpose of supplying the maximum power with which any such owner or occupier may be entitled to be supplied under this Order subject to the conditions following (that is to say),

Undertakers to furnish sufficient supply of energy to owners and occupiers within the area of supply.

> The cost of so much of any electric line for the supply of energy to any owner or occupier as may be laid upon the property of such owner or in the possession of such occupier and of so much of any such electric lines as it may be necessary to lay for a greater distance than sixty feet from any distributing main of the Undertakers although not on such property shall if the Undertakers so require be defrayed by such owner or occupier.

Every owner or occupier of premises requiring a supply of energy shall—

> Serve a notice upon the Undertakers specifying the premises in respect of which such supply is required and the maximum power required to be supplied and the day (not being an earlier day than a reasonable time after the date of the service of such notice) upon which such supply is required to commence ; and

Enter into a written contract with the Undertakers if required by them so to do to continue to receive and pay for a supply of energy for a period of at least two years of such an amount that the payment to be made for the same at the rate of charge for the time being charged by the Undertakers for a supply of energy to ordinary consumers within the area of supply shall not be less than twenty pounds per centum per annum on the outlay incurred by the undertakers in providing any electric lines required under this section to be provided by them for the purpose of such supply and give to the Undertakers (if required by them so to do) security for the payment to them of all moneys which may from time to time become due to them by such owner or occupier in respect of any electric lines to be furnished by the Undertakers and in respect of energy to be supplied by them.

Provided always that the Undertakers may after they have given a supply of energy for any premises by notice in writing require the owner or occupier of such premises within seven days after the date of the service of such notice to give to them security for the payment of all moneys which may from time to time become due to them in respect of such supply in case such owner or occupier has not already given such security or in case any security given has become invalid or is insufficient and in case any such owner or occupier fail to comply with the terms of such notice the Undertakers may if they think fit discontinue to supply energy for such premises so long as such failure continues.

Provided also that if the owner or occupier of any such premises as aforesaid uses any form of lamp or burner or uses the energy supplied to him by the Undertakers for any purposes or deals with it in any manner so as to unduly or improperly interfere with the efficient supply of energy to any other body or person by the Undertakers the Undertakers may if they think fit discontinue to supply energy to such premises so long as such user continues.

Provided also that the Undertakers shall not be compelled to give a supply of energy to any premises unless they are reasonably satisfied that the electric lines fittings and apparatus therein are in good order and condition and not calculated to affect injuriously the use of energy by the Undertakers or by other persons.

If any difference arises under this section as to any improper use of energy or as to any alleged defect in any electric lines fittings or apparatus such difference shall be determined by arbitration.

22. The maximum power with which any such consumer shall be entitled to be supplied shall be of such amount as he may from time to time require to be supplied with not exceeding what may be reasonably anticipated as the maximum consumption on his premises: Provided that where any consumer has required the Undertakers to supply him with a maximum power of any specified amount he shall not be entitled to alter that maximum except upon one month's notice to the Undertakers and any expenses reasonably incurred by the Undertakers in respect of the service lines by which energy is supplied to the premises of such consumer or any fittings or apparatus of the Undertakers upon such premises consequent upon such alteration shall be paid by him to the Undertakers and may be recovered summarily as a civil debt. *Maximum power.*

If any difference arises between any such owner or occupier and the Undertakers as to what may be reasonably anticipated as the consumption on his premises or as to the reasonableness of any expenses under this section such difference shall be determined by arbitration.

23. Whenever the Undertakers make default in supplying energy to any owner or occupier of premises to whom they may be and are required to supply energy under this Order they shall be liable to a penalty not exceeding forty shillings in respect of every such default for each day on which any such default occurs. *Penalty for failure to supply.*

Whenever the Undertakers make default in supplying energy in accordance with the terms of any regulations and conditions subject to which they are authorised to supply energy under this Order they shall be liable to such penalties as may by such regulations and conditions be prescribed in that behalf.

Provided that the penalties to be inflicted on the Undertakers under this section shall in no case exceed in the aggregate the sum of fifty pounds in respect of any defaults not being wilful defaults on the part of the Undertakers for any one day and provided also that in no case shall any penalty be inflicted in respect of any default if the Court having cognizance of the case should be of opinion that such default was caused by inevitable accident or force majeure or was of so slight or unimportant a character as not materially to affect the value of the supply

Price.

Methods of charging.

24. The Undertakers may charge for energy supplied by them to any ordinary consumer (otherwise than by agreement)—

(1) By the actual amount of energy so supplied; or

(2) By the electrical quantity contained in such supply; or

(3) By such other method as may for the time being be approved by the Board of Trade.

Provided that where the Undertakers charge by any method so approved by the Board of Trade any consumer who objects to that method of charge may by one month's notice in writing require the Undertakers to charge him at their option by the actual amount of energy supplied to him or by the electrical quantity contained in such supply and thereafter the Undertakers shall not except with the consumer's consent charge him by any other method.

Provided also that before commencing to supply energy through any distributing main for the purposes of general supply the Undertakers shall by public advertisement give notice by what method they propose to charge for energy supplied through such main and where the Undertakers have given any such notice they shall not be entitled to change such method of charging except after one month's notice of such change has been given by them to every consumer who is supplied by them from such main.

Maximum prices.

25. The prices to be charged by the Undertakers for energy supplied by them shall not exceed those stated in that behalf in the Fourth Schedule in the first and second sections thereof respectively or in the case of a method of charge approved of by the Board of Trade such price as the Board shall on approving such method determine.

Other charges by agreement.

26. Subject to the provisions of this Order and of the principal Act and to the right of the consumer to require that he shall be charged according to some one or other of the methods above mentioned the Undertakers may make any agreement with a consumer as to the price to be charged for energy and the mode in which such charges are to be ascertained and may charge accordingly.

Electric Inspectors.

27. The Board of Trade on the application of any consumer or of the Undertakers may from time to time appoint and keep appointed one or more competent and impartial person or persons to be electric inspectors under this Order and from time to time remove any person so appointed.

Appointment of electric inspectors.

The duties of an electric inspector under this Order shall be be as follows :—

(*a*) The inspection and testing periodically and in special cases of the Undertakers electric lines and works and the supply of energy given by them ;

(*b*) The certifying and examination of meters ; and

(*c*) Such other duties in relation to the undertaking as may be required of him under the provisions of this Order or of any regulations under this Order.

The Board of Trade may from time to time prescribe the fees to be taken by an electric inspector and the manner in which and the times at which his duties are to be performed.

28. The Undertakers shall pay to every electric inspector appointed under this Order such reasonable remuneration (if any) as may from time to time be determined by the Board of Trade and such remuneration may be in addition to or in substitution for any fees which are directed to be paid to electric inspectors for services rendered by them under this Order or any regulations of the Board of Trade made in pursuance of this Order as may be settled by such Board and where any such remuneration is settled to be in substitution for fees any fees payable by any party other than the Undertakers shall in lieu of being paid to such electric inspector for his own use be due and paid to him on behalf and for the use of the Undertakers and shall be carried by them to the credit of the local rate.

Remuneration of electric inspector.

29. The Board of Trade may if they deem it necessary appoint any electric inspector or other fit person or persons to inquire and report as to the cause of any accident affecting the safety of the public which may have been occasioned by or in connexion with the Undertakers works or as to the manner and extent in and to which the provisions of this Order and the principal Act and of any regulations under this Order so far as such

Inquiry by Board of Trade.

provisions affect the safety of the public have been complied with by the Undertakers and any person appointed under this section not being an electric inspector shall for the purposes of his appointment have all the powers of an electric inspector under this Order.

Testing and Inspection.

Testing of mains.

30. On the occasion of the testing of any main of the Undertakers reasonable notice thereof shall be given to the Undertakers by the electric inspector and such testing shall be carried out at such suitable hours as in the opinion of the inspector will least interfere with the supply of energy by the Undertakers and in such manner as the inspector may think expedient but except under the provisions of a special order in that behalf made by the Board of Trade he shall not be entitled to have access to or interfere with the mains of the Undertakers at any points other than those at which the Undertakers have reserved for themselves access to the said mains : Provided that the Undertakers shall not be held responsible for any interruption in the supply of energy which may be occasioned by or required by such inspector for the purpose of any such testing as aforesaid   Provided also that such testings shall not be made in regard to any particular portion of a main oftener than once in any three months unless in pursuance of a special order in that behalf made by the Board of Trade.

Testing of works and supply on consumer's premises.

31. An electric inspector if and when required to do so by any consumer shall from time to time on payment by such consumer of the prescribed fee test the variation of electric pressure at the consumer's terminals or make such other inspection and testing of the service lines apparatus and works of the Undertakers upon the consumer's premises as may be necessary for the purpose of determining whether the Undertakers have complied with the provisions of this Order and the regulations and conditions subject to which they are for the time being authorised to supply energy.

Undertakers to establish testing stations.

32. A court of summary jurisdiction may from time to time upon the application of any ten consumers direct the Undertakers at their own cost to establish at such places within a reasonable distance from a distributing main and keep in proper condition such reasonable number of testing stations as the court shall deem sufficient for testing the supply of energy by the Undertakers through such main and thereupon the Undertakers shall establish such testing places and provide thereat such proper and suitable instruments of a pattern to be approved by the Board of Trade as the Court may direct and they shall connect such stations by means of proper and sufficient electric lines with such mains and supply energy thereto for the purpose of such testing.

33. The Undertakers shall set up and keep upon all premises from which they supply energy by any distributing mains such suitable and proper instruments of such pattern and construction as may be from time to time approved of or prescribed by the Board of Trade and shall from time to time take and record and keep recorded such observations as the Board of Trade may from time to time prescribe and any observations so recorded shall be receivable in evidence. Undertakers to keep instruments on their premises.

34. The Undertakers shall keep in efficient working order all instruments which they are required by or under this Order to place set up or keep at any testing station or on their own premises and any electric inspector appointed under this Order may from time to time examine and record the readings of such instruments and any readings so recorded shall be receivable in evidence. Readings of instruments to be taken.

35. Any electric inspector appointed under this Order shall have the right to have access at all reasonable hours to the testing stations and premises of the Undertakers for the purpose of testing the electric lines and instruments of the Undertakers and ascertaining if the same are in order and in case the same are not in order he may require the Undertakers forthwith to have the same put in order. Electric inspector may test Undertakers instruments.

36. The Undertakers may if they think fit on each occasion of the testing of any main or service line or the testing or inspection of any instruments of the Undertakers by any electric inspector be represented by some officer or other agent but such officer or agent shall not interfere with the testing or inspection. Representation of Undertakers at testings.

37. The Undertakers shall afford all facilities for the proper execution of this Order with respect to inspection and testing and the readings and inspection of instruments and shall comply with all the requirements of or under this Order in that behalf and in case the Undertakers make default in complying with any of the provisions of this section they shall be liable in respect of each default to a penalty not exceeding five pounds and to a daily penalty not exceeding one pound. Undertakers to give facilities for testing.

**Report of
results of
testing.**

38. Every electric inspector shall on the day immediately
following that on which any testing has been completed by him
under this Order make and deliver a report of the results of his
testing to the Board of Trade or consumer (as the case may be) by
whom he was required to make such testing and also to the
Undertakers and such report shall be receivable in evidence.

If the Undertakers or any consumer are or is dissatisfied with
any report of any electric inspector they or he may appeal to the
Board of Trade against such report and thereupon the Board of
Trade shall inquire into and decide upon the matter of any such
appeal and their decision shall be final and binding on all parties.

**Expenses
of electric
inspector.**

39. Save as otherwise provided by this Order or by any
regulations under this Order all fees and reasonable expenses of an
electric inspector shall unless agreed be ascertained by the Board
of Trade and shall be paid by the Undertakers and may be
recovered summarily as a civil debt.

Provided that where the report of an electric inspector or the
decision of the Board of Trade shows that any consumer was
guilty of any default or negligence such fees and expenses shall on
being ascertained as above mentioned be paid by such consumer or
consumers as the Board of Trade having regard to such report
or decision shall direct and may be recovered summarily as a
civil debt.

Provided also that in any proceedings for penalties under
this Order any such fees and expenses incurred in connexion with
such proceedings shall be payable by the complainant or defendant
as the court may direct.

Meters.

**Meters to be
used except
by agreement.**

40. The amount of energy supplied by the Undertakers to
any ordinary consumer under this Order or the electrical quantity
contained in such supply (according to the method by which the
Undertakers elect to charge) in this Order referred to as " the value
of the supply" shall except as otherwise agreed between such
consumer and the Undertakers be ascertained by means of an
appropriate meter duly certified under the provisions of this Order.

41. A Meter shall be considered to be duly certified under the provisions of this Order if it be certified by an electric inspector appointed under this Order to be a correct meter and to be of some construction and pattern and to have been fixed and to have been connected with the service lines in some manner approved of by the Board of Trade and every such meter is in this Order referred to as a "certified meter" : Provided that where any alteration is made in any certified meter or where any such meter is unfixed or disconnected from the service lines such meter shall cease to be a certified meter unless and until it be again certified as a certified meter under the provisions of this Order. *Meter to be certified.*

42. Every electric inspector on being required to do so by the Undertakers or by any consumer and on payment of the prescribed fee by the party so requiring him shall examine any meter intended for ascertaining the value of the supply and shall certify the same as a certified meter if he considers it entitled to be so certified. *Inspector to certify meters.*

43. Where the value of the supply is under this Order required to be ascertained by means of an appropriate meter the Undertakers shall if required so to do by any consumer supply him with an appropriate meter and shall if required so to do fix the same upon the premises of the consumer and connect the service lines therewith and procure such meter to be duly certified under the provisions of this Order and for such purposes may authorise and empower any officer or person to enter upon such premises and execute all necessary works and do all necessary acts : Provided that previously to supplying any such meter the Undertakers may require such consumer to pay to them a reasonable sum in respect of the price of such meter or to give security therefor or (if he desires to hire such meter) may require him to enter into an agreement for the hire of such meter as herein-after provided. *Undertakers to supply meters if required to do so.*

44. No consumer shall connect any meter used or to be used under this Order for ascertaining the value of the supply with any electric line through which energy is supplied by the Undertakers or disconnect any such meter from any such electric lines unless he has given to the Undertakers not less than forty-eight hours notice in writing of his intention so to do and if any person acts in contravention of this section he shall be liable for each offence to a penalty not exceeding forty shillings. *Meters not to be connected or disconnected without notice.*

45. Every consumer shall at all times at his own expense keep all meters belonging to him whereby the value of the supply is to be ascertained in proper order for correctly registering such value and in default of his so doing the Undertakers may cease to supply energy through such meter.

The Undertakers shall have access to and be at liberty to take off remove test inspect and replace any such meter at all reasonable times proved that all reasonable expenses of and incident to any such taking off removing testing inspecting and replacing and the procuring such meter to be again duly certified where such re-certifying is thereby rendered necessary shall if the meter be found to be not in proper order be paid by the consumer but if the same be in proper order all expenses connected therewith shall be paid by the Undertakers.

46. The Undertakers may let for hire any meter for ascertaining the value of the supply and any fittings thereto for such remuneration in money and on such terms with respect to the repair of such meter or apparatus and fittings and for securing the safety and return to the Undertakers of such meter or apparatus and fittings as may be agreed upon between the hirer and the Undertakers or in case of difference decided by the Board of Trade and such remuneration shall be recoverable by the Undertakers summarily as a civil debt.

47. The Undertakers shall unless the agreement of hire otherwise provides at all times at their own expense keep all meters let for hire by them to any consumer whereby the value of the supply is ascertained in proper order for correctly registering such value and in default of their so doing the consumer shall not be liable to pay rent for the same during such time as such default continues. The Undertakers shall for the purposes aforesaid have access to and be at liberty to remove test inspect and replace any such meter at all reasonable times : Provided that the expenses of procuring any such meter to be again duly certified where such re-certifying is thereby rendered necessary shall be paid by the Undertakers.

48. If any difference arises between any consumer and the Undertakers as to whether any meter whereby the value of the supply is ascertained (whether belonging to such consumer or the Undertakers) is or is not in proper order for correctly registering such value or as to whether such value has been correctly registered in any case by any meter such difference shall be determined upon the application of either party by an electric inspector who shall order by which of the parties the costs of the proceedings before him shall be paid and the decision of such inspector shall be final and binding on all parties Subject as aforesaid the register of the meter shall be conclusive evidence in the absence of fraud of the value of the supply.

49. Where any consumer who is supplied with energy by the Undertakers from any distributing main is provided with a certified meter for the purpose of ascertaining the value of the supply and the Undertakers change the method of charging for energy supplied by them from such main the Undertakers shall pay to such consumer the reasonable expenses to which he may be put in providing a new meter for the purpose of ascertaining the value of the supply according to such new method of charging and such expenses may be recovered by the consumer from the Undertakers summarily as a civil debt.

Undertakers to pay expenses of providing new meters where method of charge altered.

50. In addition to any meter which may be placed upon the premises of any consumer to ascertain the value of the supply the Undertakers may from time to time place upon his premises such meter or other apparatus as they may desire for the purpose of ascertaining or regulating either the amount of energy supplied to such consumer or the number of hours during which such supply is given or the maximum power taken by such consumer or any other quantity or time connected with the supply : Provided that such meter or apparatus shall be of some construction and pattern and shall be fixed and connected with the services lines in some manner approved by the Board of Trade and shall be supplied and maintained entirely at the cost of the Undertakers and shall not except by agreement be placed otherwise than between the mains of the Undertakers and the consumer's terminals.

Undertakers may place meters to measure supply or to check measurement thereof.

Maps.

51. The Undertakers shall forthwith after commencement to supply energy under this Order cause a map to be made of the area of supply and shall cause to be marked thereon the line and the depth below the surface of all their then existing mains service lines and other underground works and street boxes and shall once

Map of area of supply to be made and deposited.

in every year cause such map to be duly corrected so as to show the then existing lines. The Undertakers shall also if so required by the Board of Trade or the Postmaster General cause to be made sections showing the level of all their existing mains and underground works other than service lines. The said map and sections shall be on such scale or scales as the Board of Trade shall prescribe.

Every map and section so made or corrected or a copy thereof with the date expressed thereon of the last time when it was so corrected shall be kept by the Undertakers at their principal office within the area of supply and shall at all reasonable times be open to tho inspection of all applicants and such applicants may take copies of the same or any part thereof. The Undertakers may demand and take from every such applicant as aforesaid such fee not exceeding one shilling for each inspection of such map section or copy and such further fee not exceeding five shillings for each copy of the same or any part thereof taken by such applicant as they may from time to time prescribe.

The Undertakers shall if so required by the Board of Trade or the Postmaster General supply to them or him a copy of any such map or section and from time to time cause such copy to be duly corrected so as to agree with the original or originals thereof as kept for the time being at the office of the Undertakers.

If the Undertakers fail to comply with any of the requirements of this section with respect to maps and sections they shall for every such offence be liable to a penalty not exceeding ten pounds and to a daily penalty not exceeding two pounds.

Application of Moneys Received.

Application of r venue.

52. All moneys from time to time received by the Undertakers in respect of the undertaking except (*a*) borrowed money (*b*) money arising from the disposal of lands acquired for the purposes of this Order and (*c*) money not of the nature of rent received by them in respect of any transfer under the provisions of this Order shall be applied by them as follows :—

> (1) In payment of the working and establishment expenses and cost of maintenance of the undertaking including all costs expenses penalties and damages incurred or payable by the Undertakers consequent upon any proceedings by or against the Undertakers their officers or servants in relation to the undertaking.

(2) In payment of the interest or dividend on any mortgages stock or other securities granted and issued by the Undertakers in respect of money borrowed for electricity purposes.

(3) In providing any instalments or sinking fund required to be provided in respect of moneys borrowed for electricity purposes.

(4) In payment of all other their expenses of executing this Order not being expenses properly chargeable to capital.

(5) In providing a reserve fund if they think fit by setting aside such money as they may from time to time think reasonable and investing the same and the resulting income thereof in Government securities or in any other securities in which trustees are by law for the time being authorised to invest other than stock or securities of the Undertakers and accumulating the same at compound interest until the fund so formed amounts to one tenth of the aggregate capital expenditure on the undertaking which fund shall be applicable from time to time to answer any deficiency at any time happening in the income of the Undertakers from the undertaking or to meet any extraordinary claim or demand at any time arising against the Undertakers in respect of the undertaking and so that if that fund is at any time reduced it may thereafter be again restored to the prescribed limit and so from time to time as often as such reduction happens.

The Undertakers shall carry the net surplus remaining in any year and the annual proceeds of the reserve fund when amounting to the prescribed limit to the credit of the local rate as defined by the principal Act or at their option shall apply such surplus or some part thereof to the improvement of the district for which they are the local authority or in reduction of the capital moneys borrowed for electricity purposes.

Provided always that if the surplus in any year exceed five pounds per centum per annum upon the aggregated capital expenditure on the undertaking the Undertakers shall make such a rateable reduction in the charge for the supply of energy as in their judgment will reduce the surplus to the said maximum rate of profit but this proviso shall only apply to so much of the undertaking as shall for the time being remain in the hands of the Undertakers.

Any deficiency of income in any year shall be charged upon and payable out of the local rate.

Application of capital moneys.

53. All moneys arising from the disposal of lands acquired by the Undertakers for the purposes of this Order and all moneys not of the nature of rent received by them in respect of any transfer of the undertaking under the provisions of this Order and all other capital moneys received by them in respect of the undertaking shall be applied by them as follows:—

(1) In the reduction of the capital moneys borrowed by them for electricity purposes.

(2) In the reduction of the capital moneys borrowed by them for other than electricity purposes.

Notices, &c.

Notices &c. may be printed or written.

54. Notices orders and other documents under this Order may be in writing or in print or partly in writing and partly in print and where any notice order or document requires authentication by the Undertakers the signature thereof by their clerk shall be sufficient authentication.

Service of notices &c.

55. Any notice order or document required or authorised to be served upon any body or person under this Order or the principal Act may be served by the same being addressed to such body or person and being left at or transmitted through the post to the following addresses respectively :

(a) In the case of the Board of Trade the office of the Board of Trade ;

(b) In the case of the Postmaster-General the General Post Office ;

(c) In the case of any County Council the Office of such Council ;

(d) In the case of any Local Authority the Office of such Local Authority :

(e) In the case of a company having an office or offices but no registered office the principal office of such Company ;

(f) In the case of any other person the usual or last known place of abode of such person.

Where any notice is served by post it shall be deemed to have been served at the time when the letter containing the notice would be delivered in the ordinary course of post and in proving such service it shall be sufficient to prove that the letter containing the notice was properly addressed and put into the post.

A notice order or document by this Order required or authorised to be served on the owner or occupier of any premises shall be deemed to be properly addressed if addressed by the description of the "owner" or "occupier" of the premises (naming the premises) without further name or description.

A notice order or document by this Order required or authorised to be served on the owner or occupier of premises may be served by delivering the same or a true copy thereof to some person on the premises or if there is no person on the premises to whom the same can with reasonable diligence be delivered by fixing the notice on some conspicuous part of the premises.

Subject to the provisions of this Order as to cases of emergency where the interval of time between the service of any notice or document under the provisions of this Order and the execution of any works or the performance of any duty or act is less than seven days the following days shall not be reckoned in the computation of such time that is to say Sunday Christmas Day Good Friday any bank holiday under and within the meaning of the Bank Holiday Act 1871 and any Act amending that Act and any day appointed for public fast humiliation or thanksgiving.

Revocation of Order.

56. If at any time after the commencement of this Order the Board of Trade have reason to believe that the Undertakers have made default in executing works or supplying energy in accordance with the provisions of this Order the Board of Trade may after such inquiry as they may think necessary revoke this Order as to the whole or with the consent of the Undertakers any part of the said area upon such terms and from such date as to the Board of Trade may seem just. *Revocation where works not executed.*

57. In addition to any powers which the Board of Trade may have in that behalf they may revoke this Order at any time with the consent and concurrence of the Undertakers upon such terms as the Board of Trade may think fit. *Revocation of Order with consent.*

Provisions where Order revoked.

58. If the Board of Trade at any time revoke this Order as to the whole or any part of the area affected thereby any persons who may be liable to repair any street or part of a street within such area or part thereof in which any works of the Undertakers may have been placed may after the expiration of one month from the date of such revocation remove such works with all reasonable care and the Undertakers shall pay to such persons such reasonable costs of such removal as may be specified in a notice to be served on the Undertakers by such persons or if so required by the Undertakers within one week after the service of such notice upon them as may be settled by arbitration.

If the Undertakers fail to pay such reasonable costs as aforesaid within one month after the service upon them of such notice or the delivery of the award of the arbitrator as the case may be such persons as aforesaid may without any previous notice to the Undertakers (but without prejudice to any other remedy which they may have for the recovery of the amount) sell and dispose of any such works as aforesaid either by public auction or private sale and for such sum or sums and to such person or persons as they may think fit and may out of the proceeds of such sale pay and reimburse themselves the amount of the costs so specified or settled as aforesaid and of the costs of sale and the balance (if any) of the proceeds of the sale shall be paid over by them to the Undertakers.

Transfer of Powers, &c.

Transfer of powers &c.

59. (1) At any time after the commencement of this Order the Undertakers may with the consent of the Board of Trade from time to time by deed to be approved by the Board of Trade transfer their powers duties liabilities and works to any company or person subject to such exceptions and modifications (if any) and for such period and upon such terms as may be specified therein and either as to the whole or any part or parts of the area of supply and during the said period but subject to the provisions of this Order such company or person shall to the extent of the powers duties and liabilities so transferred be the Undertakers for the purposes of this Order.

(2) One month at least before any draft deed is submitted to the Board of Trade for their approval under this section notice of the intention to make such transfer shall be published by the

Undertakers by advertisement and a copy of the said draft deed shall be deposited for public inspection during office hours at the principal office of the Undertakers within the area of supply and printed copies thereof shall be supplied to every person demanding the same at a price not exceeding sixpence for each copy.

(3) Every such advertisement shall contain the following particulars :—

(*a*) the area in respect of which the transfer is proposed to be made ;

(*b*) the period for which the transfer is proposed to be made ;

(*c*) the rent or other pecuniary consideration in respect of the transfer ;

(*d*) a general description of the powers duties or liabilities of the Undertakers proposed to be excepted or modified and of the terms upon which the transfer is proposed to be made ; and

(*e*) the address of the office at which the copy of the said draft deed is deposited for public inspection and at which printed copies of the same are on sale ;

and such advertisement shall be inserted once at least in each of two successive weeks in one and the same newspaper circulating within the area of supply and once at least in the London Gazette.

(4) The Undertakers may from time to time with the consent of the Board of Trade by deed to be approved in like manner renew or continue any such transfer for such period and subject to such variations or modifications (if any) as may be specified therein and the above provisions as to advertisements and particulars shall apply to such matters as are hereby required to be specified in such last-mentioned deed.

(5) Where in relation to any powers duties or liabilities so transferred such company or person have in the opinion of the Board of Trade been guilty of any act or default in respect of which the Board of Trade are empowered to revoke this Order the Board of Trade if they think fit in lieu of revoking this Order may by order permit the Undertakers to resume the undertaking as from such day as may be fixed by the Order and from and after the

said day the powers duties and liabilities of the said company or person as Undertakers shall cease and determine but without prejudice to anything done or suffered during the period of transfer.

(6) Any questions arising between the Undertakers and the said company or persons respecting the resumption of the undertaking by the Undertakers shall be determined on the application of either party by the Board of Trade regard being had to the deed of transfer so far as applicable and the decision of the Board of Trade shall be final and conclusive.

(7) As soon as practicable after any such deed is approved by the Board of Trade printed copies thereof shall be kept by the Undertakers for public inspection at their principal office within the area of supply and supplied to any person demanding the same at a price not exceeding sixpence for each copy and in case of any default herein the Undertakers shall be liable to a penalty not exceeding five pounds and to a daily penalty not exceeding five pounds.

(8) Nothing in this section shall affect any powers duties or liabilties of the Undertakers which shall not be transferred by any such deed and the Undertakers shall continue to have and be subject to such powers duties and liabilities if any.

General.

Remedying of system and works.

60. If at any time it is represented to the Board of Trade (a) that the Undertakers are supplying energy otherwise than by means of a system which has been approved by the Board of Trade or have permitted any part of their circuits to be connected with earth without such approval as is required by this Order or (b) that any electric lines or works of the Undertakers are defective so as not to be in accordance with the provisions of this Order or the regulations and conditions subject to which the Undertakers are for the time being authorised to supply energy under this Order or (c) that any work of the Undertakers or their supply of energy is attended with danger to the public safety or injuriously affects any telegraphic line of the Postmaster General the Board of Trade may by order in writing make such requirements as to them may seem meet in the circumstances and direct the Undertakers to take such measures as may be necessary so as to comply with the Order within such period as may be therein limited in that behalf and if the Undertakers make default in complying with such order within the time so limited they shall be liable to a penalty not exceeding twenty pounds for every day during which such default continues.

Provided that in any case affecting the public safety or any telegraphic line of the Postmaster General the Board of Trade may if they think fit by the same or any other order forbid the use of any such electric line or work as from such date as may be specified in that behalf until the order is complied with or for such time as may be so specified and if the Undertakers make use of any such electric line or work while the use thereof is so forbidden they shall be liable to a penalty not exceeding one hundred pounds for every day during which such user continues.

Provided also that where the Undertakers are supplying energy otherwise than by means of a system which has been approved by the Board of Trade and fail to comply with any such order in respect thereof with the time therein limited in that behalf the Board of Trade may if they think fit revoke this order on such terms as they may think just.

61. All regulations and conditions made by the Board of Trade under this Order or the principal Act affecting the undertaking and for the time being in force shall within one month after the same as made or last altered have come into force be printed at the expense of the Undertakers and true copies thereof certified by or on behalf of the Undertakers shall be kept by them at their principal office within the area of supply and supplied to any person demanding the same at a price not exceeding sixpence for each copy. *Publication of regulations.*

If the Undertakers make default in complying with the provisions of this section they shall be liable to a penalty not exceeding five pounds and to a daily penalty not exceeding five pounds.

62. Where any security is required under this Order to be given to or by the Undertakers such security may be by way of deposit or otherwise and of such amount as may be agreed upon between the parties or as in default of agreement may be determined on the application of either party by a court of summary jurisdiction who may also order by which of the parties the costs of the proceedings before them shall be paid and the decision of the said court shall be final and binding on all parties : Provided that where any such security is given by way of deposit the party to whom *Nature and amount of security.*

such security is given shall pay interest at the rate of four pounds per centum per annum on every sum of ten shillings so deposited for every six months during which the same remains in their hands.

Proceedings of Board of Trade.

63. All things required or authorised under this Order to be done by to or before the Board of Trade may be done by to or before the President or a secretary or assistant-secretary of the Board.

All documents purporting to be orders made by the Board of Trade and to be sealed with the seal of the Board or to be signed by a secretary or assistant secretary of the Board or by any person authorised in that behalf by the President of the Board shall be received in evidence and shall be deemed to be such orders without further proof unless the contrary is shown.

A certificate signed by the President of the Board of Trade that any order made or act done is the order or act of the Board shall be conclusive evidence of the Act so certified.

Costs of applications for approval or consent of the Board of Trade.

64. All costs and expenses of or incident to any application for any approval consent or order of the Board of Trade including the costs of any tests (if any) which may be required to be made by the Board of Trade for the purpose of determining whether the same should be given or made to such an amount as the Board of Trade shall certify to be due shall be borne and paid by the applicant or applicants therefor provided always that where any approval is given by the Board of Trade to any plan pattern or specification they may require such copies of the same as they may think fit to be prepared and deposited at their office at the expense of the said applicant or applicants and may from time to time as they think fit revoke any approval so given or permit such approval to be continued subject to such modifications as they may think necessary.

Notice of approval of Board of Trade &c. to be given by advertisement.

65. Where the Board of Trade upon the application of the Undertakers give any approval or grant any extension of any time limited for the performance of any duties by the Undertakers or revoke this Order as to the whole or any part of the area of supply notice that such approval has been given or such extension of time granted or such revocation made shall be published by public advertisement once at least in each of two successive weeks in some one and the same local newspaper by the Undertakers.

66. All penalties under this Order or under any regulations made under this Order or the principal Act the recovery of which is not otherwise specially provided for may be recovered in a summary manner before a court of summary jurisdiction. Recovery and application of penalties.

Any such penalty recovered on prosecution by any body or person or any part thereof may if the Court shall so direct be paid to such body or person.

67. The Undertakers shall be answerable for all accidents damages and injuries happening through the act or default of the Undertakers or of any person in their employment by reason of or in consequence of any of the Undertakers works and shall save harmless all authorities bodies and persons by whom any street is repairable and all other authorities companies and bodies collectively and individually and their officers and servants from all damages and costs in respect of such accidents damages and injuries. Undertakers to be responsible for all damages.

68. The provisions of sections two hundred and sixty-four and two hundred and sixty-five of the Public Health Act 1875 shall be incorporated with this Order and for the purposes of this Order in the construction of the said provisions "this Act" means this Order and the principal Act and the "local authority" means the Undertakers. Incorporation of Sections 264 and 265 of Public Health Act 1875.

69. Nothing in this Order shall affect any right or remedy of the Postmaster General under the principal Act or the Telegraph Acts 1863 to 1885 and all provisions contained in this Order in favour of the Postmaster General shall be construed to be in addition to and not in modification of the provisions of those Acts. Saving clause for Postmaster General.

70. Nothing in this Order shall authorise the Undertakers to take use or in any manner interfere with any portion of the shore or bed of the sea or of any river channel creek bay or estuary or any right in respect thereof belonging to the Queen's most Excellent Majesty in right of Her crown and under the management of the Board of Trade without the previous consent in writing of the Board of Trade on behalf of Her Majesty (which consent the Board of Trade may give) neither shall anything in this Order contained extend to take away prejudice diminish or alter any of the estates rights privileges powers or authorities vested in or enjoyed or exerciseable by the Queen's Majesty. Saving rights of the Crown in the foreshore.

Undertakers
not exempted
from proceed-
ings for
nuisance.

71. Nothing in this order shall exonerate the Undertakers from any indictment action or other proceedings for nuisance in the event of any nuisance being caused by them.

Provision as
to General
Acts.

72. Nothing in this order shall exempt the Undertakers or their undertaking from the provisions of or deprive the Undertakers of the benefits of any general Act relating to electricity or to the supply of or price to be charged for energy which may be passed after the commencement of this Order.

SCHEDULES.

FIRST SCHEDULE.

Area of Supply :—

The whole of the County Borough of Kingston-upon-Hull as the same is constituted at the commencement of this Order.

SECOND SCHEDULE.

List of streets and parts of streets throughout which the Undertakers are to lay distributing mains within a period of two years after the commencement of this Order :—

Nelson Street	Scale Lane
Queen Street	High Street (part north of Scale Lane)
Market Place	Land-of-Green-Ginger
Lowgate	Bowlalley Lane
Whitefriargate	Parliament Street
Silver Street	Quay Street

THIRD SCHEDULE.

List of streets not repairable by the local authority railways and tramways which may be broken up by the Undertakers in pursuance of the special powers granted by this Order.

(a) *Streets:*

Bridge Street   South Bridge Road
Charlotte Street   Clifford Street
Dock Office Row   Castle Street
Dock Street   Smeaton Street
George Street   West Parade (Anlaby Road)
Grimston Street   Bank Side
Humber Dock Side   Park Street Bridge
Humber Place   Argyle Street Bridge
Junction Street   Manor House Street Bridge
North Walls   Approaches to Humber Dock Bridge
Prince's Dock Side   Approaches to Mytongate Bridge
Paradise Row   Approaches to Whitefriargate Bridge
Savile Street   Approaches to Queen's Dock Bridge
Trippett Street   Approaches to Bridge over Lock
Wellington Street   between Drypool Basin and
Tower Street   Victoria Dock
Conduit Street

(b) *Railways:*

The following level crossings :—

North-eastern Railway Company

Hessle Road   Spring Bank (two crossings)
Chalk Lane   Park Road
St. George's Road   Beverley Road
Haltemprice Street   Church Street Sculcoates
Anlaby Road (two crossings) Stoneferry Road
Dansom Lane   Marfleet Lane ; and the
Holderness Road   Crossing near the South East end
Hedon Road   of Craven Street
Southcoates Lane

(c) *Railways and tramways passing along or across streets:*

(1) *North-eastern Railway Company*

Wellington Street
Kingston Street
Railway Street

(2) *Hull Dock Company*
    Approaches to Humber Dock Bridge
    Wellington Street
    Railway Street
    Castle Street
    Mytongate (West end) or approach to Mytongate Bridge
    Whitefriargate (West end) or approach to Whitefriargate
        Bridge
    South Bridge Road
    Tower Street
    Citadel Street
    Gore Street
    Approaches to Bridge over Lock between Drypool Basin
        and Victoria Dock

(3) *The Tramways of the Hull Street Tramways Company*

(4) *The Tramways of the Drypool and Marfleet Steam
    Tramways Company*

FOURTH SCHEDULE.

In this schedule—

The expression " unit " shall mean the energy contained in
a current of one thousand ampères flowing under an
electro-motive force of one volt during one hour.

Section I.

Where the Undertakers charge any consumer by the actual
amount of energy supplied to him they shall be entitled to charge
him at the following rates per quarter :—For any amount up to
twenty units thirteen shillings and fourpence and for each unit
over twenty units eightpence.

Section 2.

Where the Undertakers charge any consumer by the electrical
quantity contained in the supply given to him they shall be entitled
to charge him according to the rates set forth in section 1 of this
schedule the amount of energy supplied to him being taken to be
the product of such electrical quantity and the declared pressure at
the consumer's terminals that is to say such a constant pressure at
those terminals as may be declared by the Undertakers under any
regulations made under this Order.

INDEX.

ELECTRIC LIGHTING PROVISIONAL ORDER, 1890.

CONTENTS.

PROVISIONAL ORDER, 1896.

TRAMWAYS ORDERS CONFIRMATION (No. 1) ACT, 1896.

59 AND 60 VICT., CH. CXX.

Royal Assent, 20th July, 1896.

3. The Promoters mentioned in the said Orders* shall not in the exercise of the powers of this Act or of the said Orders purchase or acquire in any city borough or other urban district or in any parish or part of a parish not being within an urban district ten or more houses which on the fifteenth day of December last were occupied either wholly or partially by persons belonging to the labouring class as tenants or lodgers or except with the consent of the Local Government Board ten or more houses which were not so occupied on the said fifteenth day of December but have been or shall be subsequently so occupied.

For the purposes of this section the expression " labouring class" includes mechanics artisans labourers and others working for wages hawkers costermongers persons not working for wages but working at some trade or handicraft without employing others except members of their own family and persons other than domestic servants whose income does not exceed an average of thirty shillings a week and the families of any such persons who may be residing with them.

* *Hull Corporation Tramways, etc.*

BOROUGH OF KINGSTON-UPON-HULL.
PROVISIONAL ORDER.

Confirmed by the Tramways Orders Confirmation (No. 1) Act, 1896,
59 and 60 Vict., Ch. CXX.

Royal Assent, 20th July, 1896.

1. This Order may be cited as "The Hull Corporation *Short Title.*
Tramways Order 1896."

2. The provisions of the Lands Clauses Acts (except with *Incorporation of Acts.* ᵀ
respect to the purchase and taking of lands otherwise than by
agreement and with respect to the entry upon lands by the
Promoters of the undertaking) and of the Tramways Act 1870 are
hereby incorporated with this Order except where the same are
inconsistent with or expressly varied by this Order.

3. The several words terms and expressions to which by the *Interpretation.*
Acts in whole or in part incorporated with this Order meanings
are assigned have in this Order the same respective meanings.

Provided that in this Order—

The expression "the Order of 1872" means the Hull
Tramways Order 1872;

The expression "the Act of 1875" means the Hull Street
Tramways Act 1875;

The expression "the Order of 1877" means the Hull Street
Tramways (Extension) Order, 1877;

The expression "the existing Tramways" means all the
Tramways now in existence which were constructed
under the authority of the Order of 1872 the Act of
1875 and the Order of 1877 or any of such Orders and
Act;

The expression "the Tramways" means the Tramways and
works by this Order authorised and such parts of the
existing Tramways as are proposed to be re-laid;

The expression "the Undertaking" means the undertaking
authorised by the Order of 1872 the Act of 1875 the
Order of 1877 and this Order;

The expression "Mechanical Power" includes steam power
(other than steam locomotives) and gas or oil or haulage
by wires ropes cables chains or other appliances placed

under ground in connection with stationary engines or otherwise but does not include electrical power ;

The expression "the Borough" means the County Borough and the Town and County of the Town of Kingston-upon-Hull ;

The expression "the Company" means the Hull Street Tramways Company.

Promoters.

4. The Mayor Aldermen and Burgesses of the Borough shall be the Promoters for the purposes of this Order and are in this Order referred to as "the Promoters."

Lands.

5. The Promoters may appropriate and use for the purposes of the undertaking any lands not dedicated to public use now vested in them and forming part of their corporate estates and they may also by agreement from time to time purchase take on lease and acquire for the purposes of the Undertaking such lands as they may require and may from time to time sell let and dispose of any such lands which may not be necessary for such purposes and may erect or construct on any such lands any offices stables sheds workshops stores waiting-rooms or other buildings yards works and conveniences for the purposes of the Undertaking Provided that they shall not at any time hold for those purposes more than five acres of land but nothing in this Order shall exonerate the Promoters from any indictment action or other proceeding for nuisance in the event of any nuisance being caused by them upon lands taken or appropriated under the powers of this Section.

Construction of Tramways.

6. Subject to the provisions of this Order the Promoters may make form lay down use and maintain wholly within the Borough the Tramways hereinafter described in the lines and according to the levels shown on the plans and sections deposited for the purposes of this Order at the office of the Board of Trade as the same have been amended previous to the passing of the Act confirming this Order (in this Order referred to respectively as " the deposited plans " and " the deposited sections ") and in all respects in accordance with those plans and sections with all such rails junctions crossing-places turnouts plates tubes channels offices weigh-bridges turn-tables power stations engine-sheds stables carriage-houses works mechanical appliances plant and conveniences connected therewith as may be necessary or proper therefor and for connecting and using the same with the existing Tramways.

Provided that in any street or road where the carriageway is less than 28 feet in width the Promoters shall not lay a double line of Tramway with the distance between the centre lines shown upon the deposited plans unless and until the carriageway shall be made not less than 28 feet in width but in place of such double line the Promoters may lay a single line or may lay an interlacing line or double line with such reduced distance between the centre lines that for a distance of 30 feet or upwards a space of less than 7 feet 6 inches shall not at any point intervene between the outside of the footpath on either side of the street or road and the nearest rail of the Tramway.

The Tramways authorised by this Order are :—

TRAMWAY No. 1.—1 mile 1 furlong 8·77 chains in length which will be a double line throughout and in substitution for a portion of the existing Tramways and commencing in the Parish of Newington at a point 2·40 chains or thereabouts westward from the intersection of the centre lines of Carlton Street and Hessle Road passing thence in an easterly direction along Hessle Road and terminating therein in the United Parishes of Holy Trinity and Saint Mary by a junction with the existing Tramways at a point 1·60 chains or thereabouts eastward from the intersection of the centre lines of Alfred Street and Hessle Road.

TRAMWAY No. 2.—2 furlongs 9·30 chains in length which will be a double line throughout and in substitution for a portion of the existing Tramways and wholly situated in the United Parishes of Holy Trinity and Saint Mary commencing in Hessle Road by a junction with the existing Tramways at a point 0·60 chain or thereabouts westward from the intersection of the centre lines of Walker Street and Hessle Road passing thence in an easterly direction along Hessle Road and north easterly into and along Porter Street and

northerly into and along Midland Street and
terminating in the last named street by a junction
with the existing Tramways at a point 2·50 chains or
thereabouts northward from the intersection of the
centre lines of Osborne Street and Midland Street
The part of this Tramway in Midland Street shall not
be laid so that for a distance of 30 feet or upwards a
less space than 9 feet 6 inches shall intervene between
the outside of the footpath on either side of the street
or road and the nearest rail of the Tramway.

TRAMWAY No. 3.—1 mile 7 furlongs 0·71 chain in length
which will be a double line throughout and in
substitution for a portion of the existing Tramways
and commencing in the Parish of Newington at a
point 1·80 chains or thereabouts westward from the
intersection of the centre lines of Wheeler Street and
Anlaby Road passing thence in an easterly direction
along Anlaby Road and into and along Carr Lane and
Saint John Street and terminating in the last-named
street in the United Parishes of Holy Trinity and Saint
Mary by a junction with the existing Tramways at a
point 1·30 chains or thereabouts eastward from the
intersection of the centre lines of Engine Street and
Saint John Street.

TRAMWAY No. 4.—1 mile 1 furlong 7·68 chains in length
which will be a double line throughout and for a part
of its length in substitution for a portion of the existing
Tramways and commencing in the Parish of Cottingham
at a point 0·20 chain or thereabouts southward from
the intersection of the centre lines of Queen's Road
and Prince's Avenue passing thence in a southerly
direction along Prince's Avenue and easterly into and
along Spring Bank on or near the boundary between
the Parish of Sculcoates and the United Parishes of
Holy Trinity and Saint Mary and part in the said United
Parishes and south-easterly into and along Prospect
Street and terminating in the last-named street in the
Parish of Sculcoates by a junction with the existing
Tramways at the intersection of the centre lines of
Pearson Street and Prospect Street.

TRAMWAY No. 5.—1 mile 3 furlongs 3·37 chains in length which will be a double line throughout and in substitution for a portion of the existing Tramways and commencing in the Parish of Cottingham at a point 0·35 chain or thereabouts southward from the intersection of the centre lines of Cottingham Road and Beverley Road passing thence in a southerly direction along Beverley Road and terminating therein in the Parish of Sculcoates by a junction with the existing Tramways at the intersection of the centre lines of Marlborough Terrace and Beverley Road.

TRAMWAY No. 6.—1 furlong 6·09 chains in length which will be a double line throughout and in substitution for a portion of the existing Tramways and wholly situate in the Parish of Sculcoates commencing in Prospect Street by a junction with the existing Tramways at a point 0·80 chain or thereabouts north-westward from the intersection of the centre lines of Pryme Street and Prospect Street passing thence in a south-easterly direction along Prospect Street and easterly into and along Albion Street and terminating in the last-named street by a junction with the existing Tramways at a point 1·80 chains or thereabouts eastward from the intersection of the centre lines of Prospect Street and Albion Street.

TRAMWAY No. 7.--2 furlongs 1·67 chains in length which will be a double line throughout and in substitution for a portion of the existing Tramways and commencing in the Parish of Sculcoates by a junction with the existing Tramways in Albion Street at a point 1·40 chains or thereabouts westward from the intersection of the centre lines of Union Street and Albion Street passing thence in an easterly direction along Albion Street in a southerly and easterly direction into and along Bond Street in a southerly direction into and along Savile Street and in a south-easterly direction into and along Junction Street and terminating in the last-named street in the United Parishes of Holy Trinity and Saint Mary by a junction with the existing

Tramways at a point 1·60 chains or thereabouts westward from the intersection of the centre lines of Whitefriargate Bridge and the Lock-pit connecting Queen's Dock and Prince's Dock.

Tramway No. 8.—6·50 chains in length which will be a double line throughout and in substitution for a portion of the existing Tramways and wholly situate in the United Parishes of Holy Trinity and Saint Mary commencing by a junction with the existing Tramways at a point 0·50 chain or thereabouts southward from the intersection of the centre lines of Silver Street and Market Place passing thence in a southerly direction along Market Place and terminating in the last-named street by a junction with the existing Tramways at a point 0·40 chain or thereabouts northward from the intersection of the centre lines of South Church Side and Market Place.

Tramway No. 9.—1 furlong 8·39 chains in length which will be a double line throughout and in substitution for a portion of the existing Tramways and wholly situate in the United Parishes of Holy Trinity and Saint Mary commencing in Market Place by a junction with the existing Tramways at a point 0·70 chain or thereabouts northward from the intersection of the centre lines of Mytongate and Market Place passing thence in a southerly direction along Market Place and into and along Queen Street and westerly into and along Nelson Street and terminating in the last-named street at a point 0·50 chain or thereabouts eastward from the intersection of the centre lines of Pier Street and Nelson Street.

Tramway No. 10.—3 furlongs 2·17 chains in length which will be a double line throughout and in substitution for a portion of the existing Tramways and commencing in the Parish of Sculcoates by a junction with Tramway No. 7 at a point 0·50 chain or thereabouts southward of the intersection of the centre lines of George Street and Savile Street passing thence in a north-easterly direction along Savile Street and easterly

into and along George Street and Charlotte Street
and terminating in the last-named street in the United
Parishes of Holy Trinity and Saint Mary by a junction
with the existing Tramways at a point 0·86 chain or
thereabouts eastward from the intersection of the
centre lines of Wincolmlee and Charlotte Street   The
part of this Tramway in Charlotte Street east of Dock
Office Row shall not be laid so that for a distance of
30 feet or upwards a less space than 9 feet 6 inches shall
intervene between the outside of the footpath on the
south side of the street or road and the nearest rail of
the Tramway.

TRAMWAY No. 11.—1 mile 4 furlongs 0·95 chain in length
which will be a double line throughout and for a part
of its length in substitution for a portion of the
existing Tramways and commencing in the Parish of
Sutton by a junction with the existing Tramways at a
point 1·80 chains or thereabouts north-eastward from
the intersection of the centre lines of Great Union
Street and Witham passing thence in an easterly
direction along Witham and north-easterly into and
along Holderness Road and running for a part of its
length through the Parish of Drypool and terminating
in Holderness Road in the Parish of Southcoates at a
point opposite to the centre of the main entrance to
the East Park   This Tramway near its termination
shall not be laid so that for a distance of 30 feet or
upwards a less space than 9 feet 6 inches shall
intervene between the outside of the footpath on the
north-west side of the street or road and the nearest
rail of the Tramway.

The intended Tramways will be made and pass through in
from and into the following townships and parishes or some of them
namely :—

Newington Holy Trinity and Saint Mary Sculcoates
Cottingham Sutton Drypool and Southcoates.

Such Tramways will be wholly in the Borough.

7. Notwithstanding anything in this Order contained the
following provisions shall apply to the Tramways in Whitefriargate
and Silver Street.

1) The position of the Tramway in Whitefriargate and Silver Street as at present existing shall not be altered to a greater extent than 18 inches.

(2) In no case shall more than one Tramcar be between the West end of Whitefriargate and the East end of Silver Street at one and the same time.

8. The Promoters may take up renew and relay the existing Tramways wherever Tramways are not authorised to be constructed by this Order and the existing Tramways to be relaid as aforesaid shall be deemed to be part of the Tramways authorised by and constructed under the authority of this Order.

9. The Tramways shall be constructed on a gauge of four feet eight and a half inches or such lesser gauge as the Board of Trade may prescribe.

10. In addition to the requirements of section twenty-six of the Tramways Act 1870 the Promoters shall before they proceed to open or break up any road for the purpose of constructing laying down maintaining or renewing any of the Tramways lay before the Board of Trade a plan showing the proposed mode of constructing laying down maintaining and renewing such Tramways and a statement of the materials intended to be used therein and the Promoters shall not commence the construction laying down maintenance or renewal of any of the Tramways or part of any of the Tramways respectively except for the purpose of necessary repairs until such plan and statement have been approved by the Board of Trade and after such approval the works shall be executed in accordance in all respects with such plan and statement.

11. The Promoters in any street or road in which by virtue of the Provisions of this Order or any other Order or any Act a double line of Tramway has been laid down or authorised may with the consent of the Board of Trade in writing in lieu thereof lay down a single or an interlacing line of Tramway.

The Promoters may also with such consent as aforesaid alter the position of the Tramways in any street or road provided that if the space authorised between the outside of the footpath and the nearest rail be in any case less than 9 feet 6 inches the space between such footpath and the altered rail shall not be less than the space authorised.

12. The rails of the Tramways shall be such as the Board of Trade may approve.

13. For the protection of the North Eastern Railway Company (in this section called "the Railway Company") the following provisions shall apply and have effect (that is to say) :—

(1) In the relaying or construction as the case may be of the Tramways across the rails of the Railway Company now laid upon the level of the roads known or called respectively the Anlaby the Beverley and the Holderness Roads and the Spring Bank and in the execution and maintenance of works in connection therewith authorised by this Order the same shall be relaid constructed executed and maintained as the case may be in accordance with a plan to be agreed upon by the engineers for the time being of the Railway Company and of the Promoters and under the superintendence and to the reasonable satisfaction of the engineer for the time being of the Railway Company at the cost of the Promoters unless after seven days notice given by the Promoters of their intention to commence such works such superintendence is refused or withheld and the said Tramways at the said level crossings and the said works in connection therewith including the roadway between the rails of the Tramways and so much of the road as extends 18 inches beyond the rails of and on each side of the Tramways shall be maintained and kept in constant and efficient repair to the reasonable satisfaction of the Railway Company's engineer for the time being and in default thereof the Railway Company may effect the necessary repairs and recover from the Promoters the cost thereof and any damages losses costs and expenses sustained by them by reason of such default.

(2) The Promoters shall not stop their carriages on or otherwise interfere with or obstruct the traffic of the Railway Company on the level crossings of the railway of the Railway Company over the Anlaby the Beverley and the Holderness Roads and the Spring Bank and

the traffic of the Railway Company shall at all times have precedence of the traffic of the Promoters who shall be subject to such rules bye-laws and regulations relating thereto as shall be agreed upon between the Promoters and the Railway Company.

to injury
Railway
rks

(3) If by reason of the execution of any of the works or any proceedings of the Promoters or the failure of any such works or any act or omission of the Promoters or of their servants the said railway or any of the works of the Railway Company shall be injured or damaged such injury or damage shall be forthwith made good by the Promoters at their own expense or in the event of their failure so to do then the Railway Company may make good the same and recover the expense thereof against the Promoters in any court of competent jurisdiction.

to Pipes

(4) The North Eastern Railway (Hull Docks) Act 1893 Section 30 Sub-section 14 shall apply to any pipes wires cables or culverts which the Promoters may require to lay or construct under the docks or locks of the Railway Company for the purposes of the Tramways.

to crossing
Whitefriar-
te Bridge.

(5) In the relaying or construction and use of the Tramways over the Whitefriargate Bridge belonging to the Railway Company the Promoters shall observe and be bound by the following conditions :—

(a) The promoters as Owners of the Tramways shall have no ownership or other interest in the said bridge other than an easement of laying and maintaining the Tramways ;

(b) The laying down of the Tramways and all alterations or repairs thereof shall be done under the superintendence and to the reasonable satisfaction of the engineer to the Railway Company and at the cost of the Promoters unless after seven days' notice given by the Promoters of their intention to commence such works such superintendence is refused or withheld ;

(o) The Railway Company shall be at liberty to stop the traffic and the passing of the Promoters carriages over the said bridge at such times as shall be necessary for the opening and passage of vessels through the said bridge and for all repairs thereto or to the approaches or machinery thereof :

(d) The passing of vessels through the said bridge shall at all times have precedence of the traffic of the Promoters ;

(e) If at any time the said ·bridge is not sufficiently strong for the safe passage thereon of the traffic of the Tramways the Promoters shall forthwith upon notice from the Railway Company cease to run their carriages over such bridge and if required by the Railway Company shall take up and remove the rails of the Tramways from the bridge and restore the roadway to a good state and condition   Provided always that in the event of such notice being given by the Railway Company it shall be lawful for the Promoters to require the Railway Company to reconstruct the said bridge of such dimensions and construction as shall be agreed between the Promoters and the Railway Company or in case of difference as shall be settled by an engineer to be appointed by the Board of Trade and the Promoters shall contribute to the cost of such reconstruction such proportion (not being less than one fourth or more than one half of such cost) as shall be agreed between the Promoters and the Railway Company or in case of difference as shall be settled by an engineer to be appointed by the Board of Trade.

(6) In the event of any difference between the Railway Company or their engineer and the Promoters or their engineer the same shall be settled by a referee to be appointed by the Board of Trade in the manner provided by Section 33 of the Tramways Act 1870.

14.   The Promoters shall at all times maintain and keep in good condition and repair and so as not to be a danger or annoyance to the ordinary traffic the rails of the Tramways and the sub-

structure upon which the same rest and if the Promoters at any
time make default in complying with this provision they shall for
every such offence be subject on information laid or complaint
made to a penalty not exceeding five pounds and in case of a
continuing offence to a further penalty not exceeding five pounds
for every day after the first on which such default continues and
such penalties may be recovered as by Section 56 of the Tramways
Act 1870 is provided   In any case in which it is represented in
writing to the Board of Trade by twenty inhabitant ratepayers of
the Borough that the Promoters have made any such default as
aforesaid the Board of Trade may if they think fit direct an
inspection by an officer to be appointed by the said Board and if
such officer report that the default mentioned in such representation
has been proved to his satisfaction then and in every such case a
copy of such report certified by a secretary or an assistant secretary
of the Board of Trade may be adduced as evidence of such default
and of the liability of the Promoters to such penalty or penalties
in respect thereof as is or are by this section imposed.

oters
lay down
maintain
s neces-
for using
a cable
rical or
anical
r.
15. The Promoters may construct lay down execute and
maintain in on or under the surface of any road bridge railway or
place in or on which the Tramways are authorised all such rails
grooves channels tubes passages mains plates wires ropes cables
chains engines machinery or apparatus and also all such openings
or ways in or under any such surface as may be necessary or
expedient either for the working of the Tramways by steam cable
electrical or mechanical power or for working any such wires ropes
cables chains or apparatus and such manholes or other means for
providing access to or in connection with any engines or machinery
used for the purposes aforesaid provided that all powers restrictions
and provisions relating to the construction and maintenance of the
Tramways under or by virtue of this Order shall apply and have
effect with regard to the construction execution and maintenance
of such works and things as aforesaid.

oval of
ing
ways.
16. The Promoters may for the purpose of constructing or
relaying the Tramways or any of them take up and remove the
existing Tramways or so much thereof as may be necessary   On
the granting by the Board of Trade of its Certificate under the
Tramways Act 1870 that any of the Tramways is or are fit for
public traffic all rights powers authorities obligations and liabilities

in relation to any portion of the existing Tramways for which the Tramways shall be substituted shall as from the date of such Certificate cease and determine so far as regards such portion of the existing Tramways.

17. The Promoters may from time to time make maintain alter or remove all such crossings passing places sidings junctions and other works in addition to those particularly specified in and authorised by this Order as may be necessary or convenient for the efficient working of the Tramways or any of them or for affording access to any stables engine-houses carriage-houses sheds or works of the Promoters   Provided that in the construction of any such works no rail shall for a distance of thirty feet or upwards be so laid that a less space than nine feet six inches shall intervene between the said rail and the outside of the footpath on either side of the road if any owner or occupier of any house shop or warehouse abutting on the place where such rail is proposed to be so laid by writing under his hand addressed to the Promoters express his objection thereto.

Additional crossings & may be ma where necessary.

18. Where by reason of the execution of any work in or the alteration widening or improvement of any street road or highway in which any of the Tramways is laid it is in the opinion of the Promoters necessary or expedient so to do the Promoters may temporarily alter such Tramway or temporarily remove or discontinue the use of such Tramway or any part thereof and may from time to time construct in the same or any adjacent road and maintain so long as occasion may require a temporary Tramway or temporary Tramways in lieu of the Tramway or part of a Tramway so removed or discontinued.

Temporary Tramways may be made whei necessary.

19. Any paving metalling or material excavated by the Promoters in the construction of any works under the authority of this Order from any road under their jurisdiction or control shall absolutely vest in and belong to the Promoters and may be dealt with removed and disposed of by them in such manner as they may think fit.

Applicatio road mater: excavated constructic of works.

20. The Tramways shall not be opened for public traffic until the same have been inspected and certified to be fit for such traffic by the Board of Trade.

Tramways to be open until certif by Board c Trade.

Motive Power.

21. The carriages used upon the Tramways may subject to the provisions of this Order be moved by animal power and with the consent in writing of the Board of Trade by any form of mechanical or electrical power specially approved by the Board of Trade in writing.

Provided always that the exercise of the powers hereby conferred with respect to the use of any mechanical or electrical power shall be subject to the regulations set forth in the First Schedule to this Order annexed and to any regulations which may be added thereto or substituted therefor respectively by any order which the Board of Trade may and which they are hereby empowered to make from time to time as and when they may think fit for securing to the public all reasonable protection against danger in the exercise of the powers by this Order conferred with respect to the use of any mechanical or electrical power on the Tramways.

Provided also that the lessees under any lease made by the Promoters shall not use electrical steam or any mechanical power on the Tramways or any part thereof unless they are authorised to do so by special permission in such lease and the Promoters may with the consent of the Board of Trade and subject to the provisions of this Order attach to such special permission such conditions and restrictions (not being inconsistent with the provisions of this Order) as they may think fit.

22. Subject to the provisions of this Order the Promoters may place and maintain in on or over any street road bridge or railway in on or over which any of the Tramways may be laid such poles and overhead electric wires as may be necessary and proper for working such Tramways by electric power.

Provided that before placing such poles or wires the Promoters shall lay before the Board of Trade a plan showing the position of every such pole and wire and shall not commence the erection thereof until such plan shall have been approved by the said Board and all such poles and wires shall be placed and erected in accordance with the plan so approved.

23. If the Promoters or any Company or person shall use electrical or mechanical power on any of the Tramways contrary to the provisions of this Order or to any of the regulations set forth in the first Schedule to this Order annexed or to any regulation added thereto or substituted therefor by any Order made by the Board of Trade under the authority of this Order they shall for every such offence be subject to a penalty not exceeding Ten Pounds and also in case of a continuing offence to a further penalty not exceeding Five Pounds for every day after the first during which such offence continues after conviction thereof Provided always that whether any such penalty has been recovered or not the Board of Trade in case in their opinion the Promoters or any Company or person using electrical or mechanical power on the Tramways under the authority of this Order have or has made default in complying with the provisions of this Order or with any of the regulations set forth in the first Schedule to this Order annexed or with any regulation which may have been added thereto or substituted therefor as aforesaid or in case the said Board is satisfied that the use of such power cannot be continued without danger may by Order direct the Promoters or such Company or person to cease to exercise the powers aforesaid and thereupon the Promoters or such Company or person shall cease to exercise the powers aforesaid and shall not again exercise the same or any of the same unless with the authority of the Board of Trade and in every such case the Board of Trade shall make a special report to Parliament notifying the making of such Order.

Penalty for using steam cable electrical or mechanical power contrary to Order or Regulations.

24. Subject to the provisions of this Order the Board of Trade may from time to time in the event of electrical or mechanical power being used under the authority of this Order upon the Tramways make and when made may rescind annul or add to bye-laws with regard to the Tramways for all or any of the following purposes (that is to say) :—

Bye-laws.

> For regulating the use of the bell whistle or other warning apparatus fitted to the carriage ;
>
> For providing that carriages shall be brought to a stand at the intersection of cross streets and at such places and in such cases of horses being frightened or of impending danger as the Board of Trade may deem proper for securing safety ;

For regulating the entrance to exit from and accommodation in the carriages used on such Tramways and the protection of passengers from the machinery of any engine used for drawing or propelling such carriages ;

For providing for the due publicity of all regulations and bye-laws in force for the time being in relation to such Tramways by exhibition of the same in conspicuous places on the carriages and elsewhere.

Any person offending against or committing a breach of any of the bye-laws made by the Board of Trade under the authority of this Order shall be liable to a penalty not exceeding Forty Shillings.

As to recovery of penalties.

25. The provisions of the Tramways Act 1870 with respect to the recovery of penalties shall apply to any penalty under this Order and to any penalty for non-observance of any bye-law made by the Board of Trade under the authority of this Order.

Amendment of the Tramways Act 1870 as to Bye-laws by Local Authority.

26. The provisions of the Tramways Act 1870 relating to the making of bye-laws by the Local Authority with respect to the rate of speed to be observed in travelling on the Tramways shall not authorise the Local Authority to make any bye-law sanctioning a higher rate of speed than that authorised by this Order or by any regulation made by the Board of Trade under the authority of this Order at which engines and carriages are to be driven or propelled on the Tramways under the authority of this Order but the Local Authority may if they think fit make bye-laws under the provisions of the said Act for restricting the rate of speed to a lower rate than that so prescribed.

Orders and Bye-laws to be signed &c.

27. All orders and bye-laws made and consents approvals and certificates given by the Board of Trade under the authority of this Order shall be signed by a Secretary or an Assistant Secretary of the Board of Trade and when purporting to be so signed the same shall be deemed to have been duly made or given in accordance with the provisions of this Order and may be proved in manner provided by the Documentary Evidence Act 1868 with respect to orders and regulations.

Provisions as to use of electric power.

28. The following provisions shall apply to the use by the Promoters of electric power upon any of the Tramways unless such power is entirely contained in and carried along with the carriages :—

(1) The Promoters shall employ either insulated returns or uninsulated metallic returns of low resistance.

(2) The Promoters shall take all reasonable precautions in constructing placing and maintaining their electric lines and circuits and other works of all descriptions and also in working their undertaking so as not injuriously to affect by fusion or electrolytic action any gas or water pipes or other metallic pipes structures or substances.

(3) The powers by this Order conferred with respect to the use of electric power shall be exercised only in accordance with the regulations to be prescribed by the Board of Trade (hereinafter referred to as "the prescribed regulations") and to any regulations which may be added thereto or substituted therefor respectively by any Order which the Board of Trade may and which they are hereby empowered to make from time to time as or when they may think fit for regulating the employment of insulated returns or of uninsulated metallic returns of low resistance for preventing fusion or injurious electrolytic action of or on gas or water pipes or other metallic pipes structures or substances and for minimising as far as is reasonably practicable injurious interference with the electric wires lines and apparatus of other parties and the currents therein whether such lines do or do not use the earth as a return.

(4) If the Promoters use electric power contrary to the provisions of this Order or to any of the prescribed regulations or to any regulation added thereto or substituted therefor by any order made by the Board of Trade under the authority of this Order they shall for every such offence be subject to a penalty not exceeding ten pounds and also in the case of a continuing offence to a further penalty not exceeding five pounds for every day during which such offence continues after conviction thereof Provided always that whether any such penalty has been recovered or not the Board of Trade if in their opinion the Pro-

moters in the use of electric power under the authority
of this Order have made default in complying with the
provisions of this Order or with any of the prescribed
regulations or with any regulations which may have
been added thereto or substituted therefor as aforesaid
may by order direct the Promoters to cease to use
electric power and thereupon the Promoters shall cease
to use electric power and shall not again use the same
unless with the authority of the Board of Trade and
in every such case the Board of Trade shall make a
special report to Parliament notifying the making of
such Order.

(5) The Promoters shall take all reasonable and proper
precautions in constructing placing and maintaining
their electric lines circuits and other works of any
description and in using their electric lines circuits and
other works so as not injuriously to interfere with the
working of any wire line or apparatus from time to time
used for the purpose of transmitting electric power or
of telegraphic telephonic or electric signalling communication or the currents in such wire line or apparatus.
Provided always that the Promoters shall be deemed
to take all such reasonable and proper precautions as
aforesaid if and so long as they adopt and employ at
the option of the Promoters either such insulated
returns or such uninsulated metallic returns of low
resistance and such other means of preventing injurious
interference with the electric wires lines and apparatus
of other parties and the currents therein as the Board
of Trade shall direct and in giving such directions the
Board shall have regard to the expense involved and
to the effect thereof upon the commercial prospects of
the undertaking   Provided also that at the expiration
of a period of two years from the passing of the Act
confirming this Order nothing in this subsection shall
operate to give any right of action in respect of or to
protect any electric wires lines or apparatus or the
currents therein unless in the construction erection
maintaining and working of such wires lines and
apparatus all reasonable and proper precautions

including the use of an insulated return have been taken to prevent injurious interference therewith and with the currents therein by or from other electric currents If any difference arises between the Promoters and any other party with respect to anything in this subsection contained such difference shall unless the parties otherwise agree be determined by the Board of Trade or at the option of the Board by an arbitrator to be appointed by the Board and the costs of such determination shall be in the discretion of the Board or of the arbitrator as the case may be.

(6) Nothing in this section shall apply to the use of any electric line circuit or work of any company corporation or person authorised by Act of Parliament or Provisional Order confirmed by Parliament to supply energy for electric lighting purposes so far as such use is limited to such purposes.

(7) The expression "the Promoters" in this section shall include their lessees and the licensees and any company or person owning or using any Tramway of the Promoters.

29. In the event of any of the tramways being worked by electricity the following provisions shall have effect :—

(1) The Promoters shall construct their electric lines and other works of all descriptions and shall work their undertaking in all respects with due regard to the telegraphic lines from time to time used or intended to be used by Her Majesty's Postmaster-General and the currents in such telegraphic lines and shall use every reasonable means in the construction of their electric lines and other works of all descriptions and the working of their undertaking to prevent injurious affection whether by induction or otherwise to such telegraphic lines or the currents therein If any question arises as to whether the Promoters have constructed their electric lines or other works or worked their undertaking in contravention of this subsection such question shall be determined by arbitration and the Promoters shall be bound to make any alteration

in or addition to their system which may be directed by the arbitrator.

(2) If any telegraphic line of the Postmaster-General is injuriously affected by the construction by the Promoters of their electric lines and works or by the working of the undertaking of the Promoters the Promoters shall pay the expense of all such alterations in the telegraphic lines of the Postmaster-General as may be necessary to remedy such injurious affection.

(3) (a) Before any electric line is laid down or any act or work for working the Tramways by electricity is done within ten yards of any part of a telegraphic line of the Postmaster-General (other than repairs or the laying of lines crossing the line of the Postmaster-General at right angles at the point of shortest distance and so continuing for a distance of six feet on each side of such point) the Promoters or their agents not more than twenty-eight nor less than fourteen days before commencing the work shall give written notice to the Postmaster-General specifying the course of the line and nature of the work including the gauge of any wire and the Promoters and their agents shall conform with such reasonable requirements (either general or special) as may from time to time be made by the Postmaster-General for the purpose of preventing any telegraphic line of the Postmaster-General from being injuriously affected by the said act or work.

(b) Any difference which arises between the Postmaster-General and the Promoters or their agents with respect to any requirements so made shall be determined by arbitration.

(4) In the event of any contravention of or wilful non-compliance with this section by the Promoters or their Agents the Promoters shall be liable to a fine not exceeding ten pounds for every day during which such contravention or non-compliance continues or if the telegraphic communication is wilfully interrupted not exceeding fifty pounds for every day on which such interruption continues.

(5) Provided that nothing in this section shall subject the Promoters or their agents to a fine under this section if they satisfy the court having cognizance of the case that the immediate doing of the act or execution of the work was required to avoid an accident or otherwise was a work of emergency and that they forthwith served on the postmaster or sub-postmaster of the postal telegraph office nearest to the place where the act or work was done a notice of the execution thereof stating the reasons for doing or executing the same without previous notice.

(6) For the purposes of this section a telegraphic line of the Postmaster-General shall be deemed to be injuriously affected by an act or work if telegraphic communication by means of such line is whether through induction or otherwise in any manner affected by such act or work or by any use made of such work.

(7) For the purposes of this section and subject as therein provided sections two eight nine ten eleven and twelve of the Telegraph Act 1878 shall be deemed to be incorporated with this Order as if the Promoters were undertakers within the meaning of those sections without prejudice nevertheless to any operation which the other sections of the said Act would have had if this section had not been enacted and in particular nothing in this section shall be deemed to exclude the provisions of section seven of the Telegraph Act 1878 in relation to the matters mentioned in that section.

(8) The expression "electric line" has the same meaning in this section as in the Electric Lighting Act 1882.

(9) Any question or difference arising under this section which is directed to be determined by arbitration shall be determined by an arbitrator appointed by the Board of Trade on the application of either party whose decision shall be final and sections thirty to thirty-two both inclusive of the Regulation of Railways Act 1868 shall apply in like manner as if the Promoters or their agents were a company within the meaning of that Act.

(10) Nothing in this section contained shall be held to deprive the Postmaster-General of any existing right to proceed against the Promoters by indictment action or otherwise in relation to any matters aforesaid.

(11) In this section the expression "the Promoters" includes their lessees and any person owning working or running carriages on any of the Tramways of the Promoters.

Traffic.

Promoters not to carry goods.
30. The Tramways shall be used exclusively for passenger traffic and for the conveyance of parcels.

Interchange of traffic.
31. The Promoters or their Lessees on the one hand and any company or person owning or lawfully working or using any Tramways on the other hand may enter into and fulfil contracts and agreements for and in relation to the interchange accommodation and forwarding of carriages passengers and traffic on from or to any of such Tramways on to or from the Tramways or any of them and for and in relation to the user by the contracting parties or any or either of them of the whole or any part of their respective Tramway undertakings or of any or either of them respectively.

Tolls.

Tolls for passengers
32. The Promoters if licensed to work the Tramways or their Lessees may demand and take for every passenger travelling upon any of the Tramways or any part or parts thereof respectively including tolls for the use of the Tramways and of carriages and for motive power and every other expense incidental to such conveyance any tolls or charges not exceeding the following (that is to say)—For every person conveyed for any distance not exceeding two miles twopence and for any distance beyond two miles for every mile or portion of a mile one penny.

As to fares on Sundays and holidays.
33. It shall not be lawful for the Promoters or their Lessees to take or demand on Sunday or on any Bank or other Public Holiday any higher rates or charges than those levied by them on ordinary week days.

Passenger luggage.
34. Every passenger travelling upon the Tramways may take with him his personal luggage not exceeding twenty-eight pounds in weight without any charge being made for the carriage thereof.

35. The Promoters at all times after the opening of the Tramways or any part or parts thereof for public traffic shall and they are hereby required to run at least one carriage or more if required each way every morning in the week and every evening in the week (Sundays Christmas Day and Good Friday always excepted) at such hours not being later than seven in the morning or earlier than half-past five in the evening respectively as the Promoters think convenient for artizans mechanics and daily labourers at fares not exceeding one penny for the journey from any point on one Tramway to any point either on the same or any other Tramway Provided that in case of any complaint made to the Board of Trade of the hours appointed by the Promoters for the running of such carriages or the number of passengers carried the said Board shall have power to fix and regulate the same from time to time.

Cheap fare for labouring classes.

36. The Promoters may demand and take in respect of any articles or things in small parcels conveyed by them upon the Tramways or any of them including tolls for the use of the Tramways and for carriages and motive power and every other expense incidental to such conveyance any tolls or charges not exceeding the rates specified in the second schedule to this Order annexed and the word "journey" wherever used in this Order or the said second schedule shall mean the distance traversed in the same direction upon the Tramways or any of them or any part thereof at any time.

Tolls for parcels &c.

37. The tolls and charges by this Order authorised shall be paid to such persons and at such places upon or near to the Tramways and in such manner and under such regulations as the Promoters may by notice to be annexed to the list of tolls from time to time appoint.

As to paym of tolls.

Miscellaneous.

38. Notwithstanding anything contained in the Tramways Act 1870 or this Order the Promoters may place and run carriages on and work and use any Tramways for the time being belonging to them and may provide such plant materials and things as may be requisite or convenient therefor and in such case the provisions of this Order relating to the working of the said Tramways and the taking of tolls rates and charges therefor shall so far as they are applicable extend and apply mutatis mutandis to and in relation to the Promoters.

Power to Corporation to work Tramways.

39. The Promoters may under and according to the provisions contained in section twenty of the Tramways Act 1870 borrow for the purposes of this Order any sum or sums of money not exceeding in the whole the sum of three hundred thousand pounds and the time for which the said sum of three hundred thousand pounds may be borrowed shall be thirty years.

40. Where under the provisions of the Tramways Act 1870 and this Order any matter in difference is referred to the arbitration of any person nominated by the Board of Trade the provisions of the Arbitration Act 1889 shall except where otherwise specially provided apply to every such arbitration and the decision of the arbitrator shall be final and conclusive and binding on all parties and the costs of and incidental to the arbitration and award shall if either party so require be taxed and settled as between the parties by any one of the taxing masters of the High Court and such fees may be taken in respect of the taxation as may be fixed in pursuance of the enactments relating to the fees to be demanded and taken in the offices of such masters and all those enactments including the enactments relating to the taking of fees by means of stamps shall extend to the fees in respect of the said taxation.

41. With respect to notices and to the delivery thereof by or to the Promoters the following provisions shall have effect (that is to say) :—

> (1) Every notice shall be in writing or print or partly in writing and partly in print and if given by the Promoters shall be signed by the Town Clerk and if given by any Company or by any Local Authority or Road Authority by their Secretary or Clerk.

> (2) Any notice to be delivered by or to the Promoters to or by any Local Authority or any Road Authority or other body or any company may be delivered by being left at the principal office of such Authority body or Company or at the Town Hall in the Borough as the case may be or by being sent by post in a registered letter addressed to their respective clerk or secretary at their principal office or to the Town Clerk at the Town Hall.

42. Section 265 (Protection of Local Authority and their officers from personal liability) of the Public Health Act 1875 is hereby incorporated with this Order and in construing that section for the purposes of this Order the expression "this Act" when used in that section shall mean this Order.

Section 26 of the Pul Health Ac 1875 incor porated.

43. The Order of 1872 the Act of 1875 and the Order of 1877 shall be applicable in all respects to the existing Tramways until they are relaid or superseded by the Tramways by this Order authorised as the case may be and on and from the opening of the Tramways for public traffic the same shall be subject only to the provisions of this Order and the Order of 1872 the Act of 1875 and the Order of 1877 shall be and they are hereby repealed.

Repeal of previous enactment

44. The agreement between the Company and the Promoters set out in the third Schedule hereto annexed shall be and the same is hereby confirmed and full effect may and shall be given thereto.

Confirmat of Agreem

45. Notwithstanding anything in this Order contained the Promoters Lessees and any person using the said Tramways shall be subject and liable to the provisions of any general Act now in force or which may hereafter be passed during this or any future session of Parliament relating to Tramways or by which any tax or duty may be granted or imposed for or in respect of Tramways or the passengers or traffic conveyed thereon and to any future revision or alteration under the authority of Parliament of the maximum rates of tolls or charges authorised to be charged in respect of the use of the said Tramways or any of them and to any condition regulation or restriction which may be imposed upon the use of Tramways or upon the use on Tramways of animal power steam power or any mechanical power by any such general Act as aforesaid.

Saving fo general A

46. The costs charges and expenses of applying for and obtaining this Order shall be paid by the Promoters.

Costs of Order.

SCHEDULES.

FIRST SCHEDULE.

ake power
en lines.

Every engine used on the Tramways shall be fitted with such mechanical appliances for preventing the motive power of such engine from operating and for bringing such engine and any carriage drawn or propelled by such engine to a stand as the Board of Trade may from time to time think sufficient.

to fittings
engines &c.

Every engine used on the Tramways shall have its number shown in some conspicuous part thereof and shall be fitted:—

With an indicator by means of which the speed shall be shown.

With a suitable fender to push aside obstructions.

With a special bell whistle or other apparatus to be sounded as a warning when necessary and

With a seat for the driver of such engine so placed in front of such engine as to command the fullest possible view of the road before him.

Every such engine shall be free from noise produced by blast or clatter of machinery and the machinery shall be concealed from view at all points above four inches from the level of the rails and all fire used on such engine shall be concealed from view.

to
riages.

Every carriage used on the Tramways shall be so constructed as to provide for the safety of passengers and for their safe entrance to exit from and accommodation in such carriage and their protection from the machinery of any engine used for drawing or propelling such carriage.

ga tion of
fines and
riages.

The Board of Trade shall on the application of the Promoters and may on complaint made by any person from time to time inspect any engine or carriage used on the Tramways and the machinery therein and may whenever they think fit prohibit the use on the Tramways of any such engine or carriage which in their opinion may not be safe for use on the Tramways.

to speed

The speed at which engines and carriages may be driven or propelled along the Tramways shall not exceed the rate of eight miles an hour.

The speed at which engines and carriages may pass through movable facing points shall not exceed the rate of four miles an hour.

SECOND SCHEDULE.

RATES FOR CONVEYANCE OF PARCELS.

Small Parcels.

For any parcel not exceeding seven pounds in weight threepence per journey.

For any parcel exceeding seven pounds and not exceeding fourteen pounds in weight fivepence per journey.

For any parcel exceeding fourteen pounds and not exceeding twenty-eight pounds in weight sevenpence per journey.

For any parcel exceeding twenty-eight pounds and not exceeding fifty-six pounds in weight ninepence per journey.

THIRD SCHEDULE.

AN AGREEMENT made the FIRST day of AUGUST 1895 BETWEEN THE HULL STREET TRAMWAYS COMPANY (hereinafter called "the Company") acting by WILLIAM PARKER BURKINSHAW of the Borough of Kingston-upon-Hull the Official Liquidator and Manager and Receiver thereof of the one part and THE MAYOR ALDERMEN AND BURGESSES of the said Borough of Kingston-upon-Hull (hereinafter called "the Corporation") of the other part WHEREAS the Company were incorporated by the Hull Street Tramways Act 1875 for the purposes and with the powers and subject to the provisoes and stipulations therein contained and such purposes powers provisoes and stipulations have from time to time been extended or varied by various Acts of Parliament and Orders of the Board of Trade AND WHEREAS by an Order of the Chancery Division of the High Court of Justice dated the 30th day of November 1889 it was ordered that the Company should be wound up by the Court and by an Order of the said Chancery Division dated the 16th day of January 1890 the said

William Parker Burkinshaw was appointed the Official Liquidator of the Company AND WHEREAS by an Order of the said Chancery Division dated the 28th day of January 1890 the said William Parker Burkinshaw was appointed Manager and Receiver of the undertaking of the Company NOW IT IS HEREBY AGREED as follows :—

1. The Company shall sell and the Corporation shall purchase for the sum of £12,500 the whole of the tramways and undertaking of the Company and all the rights powers and authorities of the Company in respect thereof together with the inheritance in fee simple in possession free from incumbrances of and in the freehold pieces of land situate respectively on the Beverley Road the Hessle Road and the Holderness Road in the said Borough of Kingston-upon-Hull with the stables depots offices workshops granaries and buildings respectively erected thereon and all easements rights of way and other rights appurtenant or necessary thereto or hitherto exercised or enjoyed therewith and which said pieces of land contain respectively on the Beverley Road 1430 square yards on the Hessle Road 1805 square yards and on the Holderness Road 680 square yards or thereabouts but not including the horses cars and harness of the Company and not including the articles mentioned in the Schedule hereto all of which are expressly excepted from this Agreement. The premises hereby agreed to be sold are hereinafter referred to as "the undertaking" and are sold subject to all easements (if any) subsisting thereon.

2. If the Corporation shall on or before the 15th day of October 1895 give to the Company notice of their desire to complete the purchase on the 15th day of November 1895 the purchase money shall be paid into Court and the purchase shall be completed on the said 15th day of November 1895 but if not the purchase money shall be paid into Court and the purchase shall be completed on the 15th day of October 1896 and the Company and all other necessary parties (if any) shall execute and do such assurances and things as may be reasonably required for vesting the undertaking in the Corporation and giving them the full benefit of this Agreement. The Company shall obtain without expense to the Corporation the necessary order or direction for the payment of the said money into Court.

3. On the payment of the said purchase money the Corporation shall be let into possession of the whole of the undertaking except the said stables and depots on the Beverley Hessle and Holderness Roads and possession of the said stables and depots shall be given to the Corporation within one calendar month from the date of such payment as aforesaid.

4. The Company shall be entitled to the receipts and profits of the undertaking and shall continue to exercise the rights powers and authorities of and to be subject to all obligations and liabilities as owners and promoters of the undertaking up to the date of the payment of the said purchase money.

5. Subject to the provisions contained in the next clause the Company shall up to the date of the payment of the said purchase money run upon the said tramways a similar service of cars to that heretofore run by them and the Corporation shall maintain the roadway and rails of the said tramways in such a fair and reasonable condition as will enable the Company to comply with this clause. Provided always that the Corporation shall not be liable for any accidents or damage which may occur either to the Company or to any body or persons by or by reason or in consequence of the non-repair or defective state of the said roadway or rails.

6. The Corporation may exercise all the powers and authorities of the Company with reference to the maintenance and repair of the said Tramways the re-construction thereof and the construction of crossings passing places sidings and junctions. The Corporation may also construct any tramways authorised or to be authorised before the date of the payment of the said purchase money. For the purposes of exercising the powers authorities and rights referred to in this clause the Corporation may so far as may be reasonably necessary interfere with and wholly or partially suspend the traffic on the said tramways without paying to the Company any compensation in respect of the same. Provided always that the Corporation shall not wholly suspend the traffic on any of the said tramways for more than three days in every or any month except in the case of the Hessle Road and Holderness Road Tramways where they shall be at liberty to wholly suspend the traffic for such time as they may think requisite on giving to the Company fourteen days previous notice of their intention so to do.

Provided further that such respective suspensions of traffic as aforesaid shall not take place on more than one of the Anlaby Road Spring Bank and Beverley Road Tramways at the same time nor on both the Hessle Road and Holderness Road Tramways at the same time.

7. The Company will transfer to the Corporation the benefit of existing Fire Insurance Policies and will repair the buildings which have been damaged by the recent fire.

8. If the Corporation shall on or before the 15th day of August 1896 give to the Company notice of their desire to purchase all or any of the articles mentioned in the said schedule the Corporation shall be at liberty to purchase such as shall be in the possession of the Company at the time of giving such notice at such a price as may be mutually agreed upon between the Company and the Corporation or failing agreement as shall be determined by a Valuer to be agreed upon or to be appointed by the Board of Trade.

9. The Company shall within one calendar month from the date hereof deliver to the Town Clerk an abstract of their title to the undertaking.

10. This Agreement is conditional on the sanction of the Judge being obtained thereto on or before the expiration of three calendar months from the date hereof and the Official Liquidator shall without expense to the Corporation forthwith apply for such sanction and the Corporation shall if required by the Official Liquidator appear and consent to an Order accordingly. And if such sanction is not obtained within the time hereinbefore limited for such purpose this Agreement shall be void.

11. This Agreement is also subject to the consent of the Board of Trade.

In Witness whereof the Company and the Corporation have hereunto affixed their respective Common Seals the day and year first before written.

THE SCHEDULE.

Gas engine
Shafting and Belting
Sand spreader

Rullies
Carts
Whitechapel carts
Wheelbarrows
Corn crushers
Hay cutter
Hoisting machine
Grindstone
Drilling machine
Shop stove in harness maker's room
Benches
Tar Boilers
Portable boiler
Hot water apparatus and pipes at Hessle Road depot
Bales
Water troughs and feed tubs
Corn bins
Gas fittings
Bellows and anvils
Loose tools
Loose stable utensils
Fodder
Materials for repairs
Stores

THE COMMON SEAL of
 the Company was affixed
 hereto in the presence of

Seal of
Company.

WM. HODGSON,
Solicitor, Hull.

W. P. BURKINSHAW,
Official Liquidator.

THE COMMON SEAL of
 the Corporation was affixed
 hereto in the presence of

Seal of
Corporation

R. HILL DAWE,
Town Clerk.

INDEX.

TRAMWAYS ORDER 1896.

www.ingramcontent.com/pod-product-compliance
Lightning Source LLC
Chambersburg PA
CBHW032338280326
41935CB00008B/376